ELEANOR SHIPLEY DUCKETT has won high acclaim for her valuable and interesting studies in early medieval history and literature. She was trained for this work in England, where she holds the degree of Doctor of Letters from the Universities of both Cambridge and London; and in the United States where she is Doctor of Philosophy of Bryn Mawr College and Doctor of Humane Letters of Smith College. For many years she was Professor of Classics at Smith College.

The
WANDERING SAINTS
of the
EARLY MIDDLE AGES

BY

ELEANOR DUCKETT

The Norton Library

W · W · NORTON & COMPANY · INC ·

NEW YORK

FIRST PUBLISHED IN THE NORTON LIBRARY 1964

Books That Live
The Norton imprint on a book means that in the publisher's
estimation it is a book not for a single season but for the years.
W. W. Norton & Company, Inc.

PRINTED IN THE UNITED STATES OF AMERICA

CONTENTS

Contents

MAPS AND TABLES

ACKNOWLEDGMENTS

The Author and Publishers are grateful for permission to include passages from the following books :— *A Celtic Miscellany* by Kenneth Hurlstone Jackson : Routledge and Kegan Paul, and Harvard University Press, on pages 17, 18 25; *Selections from Ancient Irish Poetry* translated by Kuno Meyer : Constable and Co., and E. P. Dutton and Co., New York, on pages 25, 26.

FOREWORD

WITHIN RECENT years the study of the *Lives* of medieval saints has found a new birth in interest, both among writers who know the history of the Middle Ages and readers who want to learn from them. This has induced a constant stream of literature, a fact in no way surprising to those who have seen in these years a new quickening of the religious thought and practice in which these saints were specialists.

The many books, articles, papers and poems which follow one after another in the course of this stream are sharply divided in aim and in content. On the one hand we meet simple narratives, stories and legends. On the other side lies the work of the modern expert in hagiology who hunts in the haystack of legend for the slender needle of historical truth. Both these sharply divided varieties of instruction hold virtue, merit, and delight for readers; in both cases, however, the delight is limited in its appeal.

The simple narratives of the *Lives* of the medieval saints carry with them, indeed, deep spiritual truth; they are full of heartening lessons; the general reader rejoices in them, as well he may. But the student who has received some training in history, who is accustomed to criticise, finds himself asking questions at page after page, trying to discover what facts of history lie behind these tales of miracle and wonder.

Foreword

At last in his dilemma he turns to the work of the specialist, the expert in hagiology. This expert is a worker in many fields. He carries with him his knowledge of history, of annals, of archæology and of architecture, of languages—Old and Middle Irish, medieval Welsh, British dialect, Norse and Anglo-Saxon, Greek and Latin, French and German. He travels to the lands, the scenes, where lie the ruins, visible or to the lay eye invisible, once perhaps the homes of these saints of his pursuit, the graves in which they were laid. He pores over inscriptions; he notes carefully the dedications of churches, in their locating, in their grouping, always aware that there are countless dedications of churches to saints in places which they never saw. He ponders well—and this is most important —the names of places connected with his story, looking at these through the microscope of geographical awareness, of etymology, of ethnic science.

Finally, this scholar writes his book, and upon it depends all our knowledge of such reasonably factual matter as lies imbedded in the *Lives* of our early saints. But general readers cannot follow with quiet enjoyment his iconoclastic pages. Dedicated to discussion of knotty questions, while he gathers the wholesome grains of truth the scholar repudiates, as lies, romance, fiction, the delightful chaff of legend. Add to this the fact that his footnotes refer his readers to sources, primary and secondary, in Latin, Irish, French and German, and your amateur may well confess himself beaten and lost.

There remains, however, a company of writers who would gladly find themselves in a middle way. They acknowledge with great gratitude their debt to the expert and scholar, and under his guidance they endeavour with all conscience to separate historical truth from imaginative story. Yet they venture to paint their saints in something of the colour which ages past have given them, hoping in this way to make more clear a picture of the spirit of these men and women who really lived and are now so widely unknown.

It is in the desire of fellowship with the company of this middle way that I have written here about some of Europe's wayfaring saints, of Celtic and Saxon and Frankish race, of the early Middle Ages.

CHAPTER ONE

THE WAYFARING CELTIC SAINTS

EARLIER in time, and therefore first to be considered in our thought, are the Celtic saints, the saints of early Irish, British, Breton descent, who lived in Ireland, Wales, Cornwall, Brittany, in the fifth and sixth centuries after Christ.

What manner of men were these saints?

Not " saints " in the modern sense of lay conversation: those who are always doing the things which no one else wants to do. Nor, either, the Celtic saint as he is pictured in his *Life*, written, in Latin or in Irish, centuries after his time on earth. For in this *Life* he is truly a formidable being, of power far beyond the frailty of common man. He is a man of God set apart from his fellows by Divine destiny; a " Wonder Child," whose birth is heralded for his mother by vision and dream, by marvels of the heavens and of Nature, seeking to honour him; one who blesses and heals with his right hand and curses and paralyses and slays with his left; who fights with demons until they flee, sways battles, raises the dead, and holds beast and bird subject to his God-given authority.

All creatures hasten to serve this man of countless stories and legends. A bird drops a feather to make a pen for St. Molaisse of Devenish when he wants to write a book; a wild boar of the forest tears with its tusks twigs and grass to build a cell for St. Ciaran of Saigir; a stag holds wide open on its antlers the book of St. Cainnech of Aghaboe as he seeks to study in the forest. St. Colman of Kilmacduagh is attended by a mouse, a cock, and a mosquito; the mouse nibbles at his ear to wake him for the hour of Office at noon, the cock rouses him before dawn, the mosquito settles down to mark the place in the saint's book when he is called away from his reading or his prayer. These are Irish saints, of the fifth and sixth centuries; and perhaps the liveliest story here is of St. Moling, abbot in the seventh century at St. Mullins, Co. Carlow. One day, it was told, as he sat deep in meditation he caught sight of a wren happily feasting on a fly. Just at that moment a cat leaped upon the wren and killed it. St. Moling rose to his feet, made the holy sign, brought the wren again to life, and ordered it to show the same mercy it had received, to disgorge, still alive, the fly it had devoured.

But, we read, creatures that brought fear or discomfort to man fled before a saint's command. We all know the tradition that St. Patrick banished the snakes from Ireland; perhaps this story had its root in the linking of serpents with evil through the picture of Satan in the third chapter of Genesis. Of St. Columba, too, we read in his *Life* by Adamnan that at the end of his days he lifted his hands to bless Iona and told his monks that " from this moment no serpent shall have power to hurt by poison either man or beast upon this isle, so long as its dwellers obey the rule of Christ." Finnian of Clonard drove out the sparrows and snakes and fleas which troubled the peace of prayer upon the English isle of Flatholm; Cainnech of Aghaboe on a Sunday morning reviled the mice which were devouring his sandals and sent them rushing into the Shannon's outlet to the sea. Above all, the Venerable Bede in his English monastery wrote of Ireland that " many times have serpents been shipped there from Britain; but directly the boat draws towards shore they perish and die when they catch a breath of Irish air." No wonder that Ireland has been called the " Isle of Saints," if this was held its power!

Such, at any rate, was the power of Celtic saints as the

writers of their *Lives* in the later Middle Ages pictured it. These writers worked in monasteries that held libraries; that held, also, each and every one of them, the deepest reverence for their own particular Founder and Patron. In each medieval abbey the Founder's relics rested enshrined in all honour, and were the first treasure to be rescued and carried away in flight, should attack by fury of man or of Nature drive the monks forth from their walls. Surely, these monastic scribes knew, the *Life* of this, their own holy man, must be adorned with all due laudation. If sufficient matter for his praise was at hand in their archives, in their traditions, in hearsay carried down the years, well and good; if not, the compilers must borrow, borrow without scruple rich and wondrous substance from the *Lives* of other reverend saints of other monasteries. Did not all know that Christian men in earlier days possessed all things in common? And certainly the saint of one's own monastery could not have been inferior in the gifts of God to the Founders of other holy houses. It was all of good purpose for edification, for the ears of pilgrims, aspirants, and novices. The science of criticism of documents and their evaluation as historic truth is, after all, a very modern gift to men.

But we are not concerned at the moment with miracle done by holy men through beast or bird or elements of Nature. Rather, with the aid of modern scholarship, we shall look here at our saints in their lives as human beings, in their failures and their success, in their struggles, their disappointments, their problems; at saints not yet canonised, saints in the making, seen, so far as possible, in the light of their own words and against the history of their times; men angry, worried, homesick, men happy and full of hope, always moving forward. Such men were well described in a lament, written by an unknown author, perhaps in the eleventh century. Here are some of its words:

The saints who did God's will at the beginning of time were uneasy and naked, scurvy, muddy; they were not stout and fat.

The men of keen learning. . .
Scanty shirts, clumsy cloaks, hearts sad and piteous, short rough
shocks of hair—and very rough monastic rules.

2

A second question follows. What, consciously or unconsciously, impelled these Celtic saints of the early Middle Ages
to seek places remote from their own world?

It is well here, first, to look back at their world's history,
at the time before their birth, and at their own time. For it
was this secular course of past and present days which in the
first instance was moving them to flee the Devil, the lusts and
vanities of the flesh, to leave a world of confusion and uncertainty, of sin and of danger, to try to find hope and sure
reality in a dedicated life apart.

In the minds of these men we can see the long decline of
the Roman Empire in the West; the struggle to hold this
Empire, in Spain, in Gaul, in Italy, against the menace of
barbarian raid; the crushing expense of maintenance of
Imperial armies, manned, as time went on, ever more and more
by mercenaries and by those newly freed from the chains of
captive slaves. We see the appalling contrast between the luxury
of nobles throughout the Empire, the wealth poured out for
the sport of public games, for the winning of public office, for
private luxury, country houses, vineyards and gardens,
banquets and rich attire—and the wretchedness, the utter need
of the poor, crowded in the alleys of great cities, picking up their
daily crust by theft and violence. Between the very rich and
the very poor the middle man could scarcely hope to live in
decency; ground down by taxes, buffeted by officials, eternally
confronted by disciplinary laws, he knew not how to hold his
own. Behind these economic factors lay debauchery and
corruption, steadily increasing as the old Roman morale sank
lower. And, lastly, for those who dared in the common life

of the world to follow that Christianity which from the fourth century was, indeed, the professed religion of the Roman Empire governed from Rome, there remained the vigorous, the deep hostility of the multitude who still rejoiced in pagan cults brought from the East, from Persia, from Syria, from Egypt, cults still firmly entrenched in Western lands.

In the fifth century this Roman Empire awoke to the realisation that the barbarian hordes of German race were no longer making occasional raids across the Rhine and the Danube into Roman territory. They were marching steadily, to occupy, to conquer, to settle. Their men wanted land, homes for themselves, their women and their children. Not only on the Continent, but in remote Britain the German Saxons, who already in the fourth century had crossed the North Sea to raid British shores, were now arriving to make permanent their stay. Roman soldiers at the same time were being withdrawn from this far-off part of the Empire in the desperate need to defend the frontiers nearer Rome. Now the Gothic invaders under Alaric, their chieftain, swept down from the North upon Italy; Goths, too, marched from Germany into Gaul, and from Gaul crossed the border to ravage Spain. The Vandals seized Roman Africa and made in it their own kingdom; Huns and Vandals in their turn entered Italy to sack and plunder. At the end of this fifth century the Roman Empire in the West was no more. A barbarian of Gothic blood, Theodoric by name, sat as king on his throne in Italy, holding his power by consent of his superior Lord, a Lord still Emperor of Rome in the East, ruled from Constantinople.

Comparative peace now lasted for a while in Italy. The next, the sixth century, saw its land ravaged and torn from north to south by civil war between the Emperor of Rome in the East and the barbarian kings who succeeded Theodoric. It saw Roman Gaul become barbarian Frankland, divided for rule among Frankish kings, descendants of the conqueror Clovis; it saw Spain in the hands of the Visigoths. The seventh century found another barbarian people, the Lombards, who had long been coming from the North to attack, now established in their own kingdom of northern Italy, the ancient city of Pavia now their capital. And, as all know, the eighth century saw the beginning of those twin scourges of barbarian inroad, the Vikings and the Saracens, who made the ninth a time of horror for Italy, France, the Netherlands, and the British Isles alike.

3

To give men the security in heart, if not in body, for which they longed, in the first century of the Year of the Lord had come forth the Christian faith. This, as we remember, had flowed, in the time that followed, from Asia Minor to Rome, from Rome to Gaul, to Britain, and to Ireland, through Christian missionaries, through traders and travellers, fighting men and sailors, envoys and messengers, through captives, carried off in pirate raids or in battle, through fugitives from war-stricken lands. The earlier years of the fourth century had already found Christian bishops in Gaul and in Britain; archæology has given evidence in Britain of Christian dwellers there in those early days. The fifth century found men in both countries studying Christian principles, teaching their belief, labouring to root out the weeds of heresy already springing into growth.

Hard on the heels of Christian bishops, priests, and missionaries followed Christian monks, opening a door of flight from the evil, anxious world. From the deserts of Egypt came word of an ascetic life of fasting and prayer, far removed from the crowded streets of Alexandria. Already when the third century was nearing its end, St. Anthony of Egypt had crossed the Nile to dwell twenty years in the wilderness; in the first years of the fourth century he had broken down the wall of his enclosure to admit the disciples who came, one after another, to learn from him the practice of his prayer in solitude.

Around St. Pachomius, in this fourth century in Egypt, gathered those who would unite with other men for prayer in community, equally set apart from the life without. A community needs a lawgiver, and Pachomius drew up for his disciples a *Rule* to guide and keep stable their daily living.

From Egypt the new movement spread, carried by travellers who told of their own knowledge. So, also in the fourth century, Rome caught its spirit through St. Athanasius, a fugitive from Egyptian Alexandria. Written documents added their persuasion; among them that story of a monk's life in the desert called *The Life of St. Anthony*. Women in Rome were quick to feel the power of this call; soon they, too, were giving their days and their nights to prayer, to fasting, withdrawn from society in the enclosure of their own homes. This new-born enthusiasm was fostered in this same fourth century by St. Jerome, coming to the City from the solitude of the Syrian desert, full of desire for monastic conversion, for himself and for others, as many as he could reach. Some eight years before, he had written to his young friend Heliodorus fiery words for a discouraged spirit: "What are you doing, deserter, loitering in your father's house? Depart! Though your mother tear her hair and rend her garments, though your father lie flat upon the threshold of his house to stay your going, trample your way forth over him, hasten without one sigh to the banner of the Cross! Your only love and duty in this business is to be cruel." Jerome was no man of half-measures, or even of common sense.

The fifth century found men and women learning this same forsaking of one's familiar round, less impetuously but as thoroughly, from St. Augustine in northern Africa. It found a Spanish priest, Orosius by name, crossing the sea in search of Augustine and writing his creed that "in this passing world every country of Christian faith is to me my native land." It found, in the Roman province of Noricum, the land of Bavaria and Austria south of the Danube, a man of God suddenly appearing to comfort the Roman citizens left there to face barbarian hordes, left alone and terrified, deprived of protection through the failing power of Rome. He would never tell whence he came. " What matters it," said he, " to a servant of God, where or of what family he was born? If you think me worthy to be called a citizen of our native land on high, why should you know from what earthly land I come? I am here because God bade me dwell here, among men in their perils." His name was Severinus.

Other men, equally nameless and lost to the world, turned, when their prayer day by day and night by night was fulfilled, to zealous study of the Scriptures. Reading led to writing; from the cells of monks came letters, commentaries on books of the Bible, refutations of heresy, explanations of spiritual problems, which filled many hours of their time. Under Jerome in Roman houses his disciples, including women, eagerly learned Greek and Hebrew, and pursued with passionate energy problems of Biblical text without end.

The monastic tide flowed, then, from the East to the West, and in the West it reached Gaul. Gaul already in the fourth century had been aroused in a vision of the monastic ideal through the example and teaching of St. Martin of Tours, who founded his monasteries at Ligugé, near Poitiers, and at Marmoutier, on the outskirts of Tours. Everywhere men heard of his prayers, of miracles traced to his working, and those who lived after his time were incited to follow his lead by a narrative of his life and acts written in the fifth century by his friend and follower, Sulpicius Severus, also of Gaul. From Italy, from Gaul, enthusiasm for the dedication to prayer and to the study of religion crossed the Channel to Britain and to Ireland.

4

Enthusiasm easily led to journeying in its behalf. Now men, both of Latin and of Celtic blood, went far distances in search of a place where they might be alone to pray and to think. Others went on long and perilous journeys far from home to care for the souls of their fellow-countrymen who had migrated in time of danger to foreign shores. Others sought out some place renowned for its holiness, that by dwelling there a while they might learn something of the same. Others went to these holy scenes in atonement for their sin.

Pilgrimages imposed as penance meet us in the *Lives* of Celtic saints again and again. The Irish St. Enda, who lived, probably in the sixth century, in Cell Enda, upon the largest of the Aran Islands at the entrance to the Bay of Galway, was told in rebuke by his sister, herself a nun, to go on pilgrimage of penitence to the monastery of Whithorn in Galloway, Scotland. In a fit of rage (so the story runs) he had snatched up a pole to strike the heads of robbers trying to enter his cell. " Touch *your* head with your hand, Enda," she said, " and remember the tonsure of your calling, the mark of Christ which rests there." St. Columba of Ireland and of Iona was one day —as Adamnan, his historian, tells—rebuking a woman who lived on an island near the Irish coast. " Every penance you give me, Father," she answered, " I am ready to do, however hard: attend to my housekeeping, get me to a nunnery, or even, if you bid me, journey as pilgrim across the sea. But I will *not* live with that man, my husband! "

The longing for solitude as part of the ascetic life, common as it has always been in followers of monastic rule, was inherent in the very nature, the temperament and character of the Celt. For the saints of Ireland and of Wales in the fifth and sixth centuries, for the British who held the remote parts of Britain while the Germanic invaders from overseas were fighting to make it England, for all these Celtic peoples the primary impulse, the depth of the spirit of wandering is reached in the word *peregrinatio*. To become a *peregrinus*, a stranger and an exile, was " for the love of Christ "—*pro amore Christi*—to leave one's home, to strip oneself of family and possessions, to root out from heart and mind all one's own aims and desires, and —for a Celt the uttermost self-denial—to forsake one's native land for some lonely, far remote spot, there to abide with no thought of return, with no plan, not even a plan of mission of penance or of pilgrimage. It was to hear in one's own ears the words spoken by the Lord to Abraham: " Go forth from thy land and thy kin and thy father's house into a land which I shall show thee of." Nothing must stay the adventurer; not even his entire ignorance of the time or place at which his wandering was to end. Such wandering into exile was, it was said, born in the Irish spirit, so common was it among their men of sterner discipline. So, too, it was written of a Welshman, St. Brynach, who held his church at Nevern, in Pembrokeshire, that " by thinking nothing of the place of his birth, by forsaking his own land, he sought to find it; by living in exile he hoped to reach home."

There were, it is true, other forces, minor ones, playing upon the Celts to intensify this impulse of wandering in search of their soul's rest. The Irish had never known the constraint of Roman governors and their officials and cohorts; the Celtic British developed their monastic life in its fullness amid their mountains, valleys, and moors in Wales and Cornwall, after the Romans had abandoned Britain. The monk trained in Roman ways of order and government, in Italy, in Gaul, might well attain what he sought for his life in a community disciplined by a common rule. The Celt dedicated to religion felt himself, instead, an individual free to wander. And not only was he free. He was inspired by the voice of God Himself, bidding him to travel from place to place, over earth and sea, pursuing new knowledge, new love of things spiritual, ever seeking that ideal "place of resurrection," that Land of Promise, in which, having won his fill of wisdom in the measure possible for him on earth, he might pitch his tent and build his cell, gather around him others of like mind, and give his latter days to passing on to them of his gathered store.

Nor should we forget that the Irish lived on an island, and knew and loved the sea. Irish literature, pagan before it was Christian, from an early time knew tales of voyaging and of peril, in the narratives, the *immrama*, of their *filid*, the keepers of Ireland's early records and the early makers of her verse. It was not so difficult to turn the Irish spirit of adventure to a Christian purpose. There is joy in Kenneth Jackson's rendering of the twelfth century Irish words which picture St. Columba's thought as he sat alone on the shore of his Scottish island of Iona:

> *Delightful I think it to be in the bosom of an isle, on the peak of a rock, that I might often see there the calm of the sea.*
>
> *That I might see its heavy waves over the glittering ocean, as they chant a melody to their Father on their eternal course.*
>
> *That I might see its ebb and its flood-tide in their flow; that this may be my name, a secret I tell, " He who turned his back on Ireland."*

But there is sadness in the Celt, too, a sadness such as the Roman never felt, in those words imagined, probably in the twelfth century, of this same St. Columba as he said farewell to his Irish monastic home and made his way towards the isles of Alba, the early Scotland:

> *Great is the speed of my coracle,*
> *And its stern turned upon Derry:*
> *Grievous is my errand over the main,*
> *Travelling to Alba of the beetling brows.*

The Wandering Saints

Were all Alba mine
From its centre to its border,
I would rather have the site of a house
In the middle of fair Derry.

It is for this I love Derry,
For its smoothness, for its purity:
All full of angels
Is every leaf on the oaks of Derry.

My Derry, my little oak-grove,
My dwelling and my little cell,
O living God that art in Heaven above,
Woe to him who violates it!

From the fifth century to the ninth, Celtic monks travelled to seek in the unknown after solitude for their prayer. On Achill and the Arans, on the Great Skellig of St. Michael and the Great Blasket, on countless islands and lonely rocks off Ireland's western coast; on the Hebrides and the Orkney Isles of northern Scotland; on the English islets of the Bristol Channel, Steepholm and Flatholm; off England's northern shores, on the Farnes and on the Isle of Man; on tiny islands in the English Lakes; on islets near the coast of Wales, we mark or we imagine their hermit homes, their cells with rounded roofs, like old-fashioned beehives, their distant communities. As late as the ninth century, when Irish wandering saints were turning into Irish wandering scholars and the ascetic life of solitude was giving way to resounding debate and controversy on matters of doctrine and of grammar, we find three Irishmen drifting over the sea from Ireland for seven days in a boat without any oars, its framework made secure by hides tightly drawn, coming to shore in British Cornwall and going thence to King Alfred of Wessex, to tell him that " we stole away because we wanted for the love of God to be on pilgrimage, we cared not where." Dicuil, an

Irish scholar of this same ninth century, dwelling in France at the Court of Louis the Pious, son of Charlemagne, tells that he himself knew of anchorites who had made their way to the islands of northern Europe before the Vikings of Scandinavia descended upon these to plunder and to settle. These islands near the Arctic Ocean allowed them the solitude for which they longed. When at last the coming of the Vikings drove them out, Dicuil writes that " they left behind them books and bells and pastoral staffs, from which one could conclude that they were Irishmen."

Release from the world; solitude for the following of the ways of prayer; a lively seeking after knowledge; a passion for sacrifice and self-denial; a driving concern for the souls of their fellow-men—these were the marks of early medieval saints. For these ends they wandered wherever their time called them.

5

They might be seen, sometimes in small companies of two or three, often alone, tramping along the lanes and trails, struggling through the forest, plunging through the stretches of bog and marsh, climbing the mountains. On their feet they wore sandals of hide; their monkish habit was of skins roughly sewn together, with a hood to protect them from cold and rain; in their hands they carried a staff, and from their shoulders hung the pack which held the small store of food, the cup, the books of prayer for Mass and Office. Their food they begged from the peasants of the cottages they passed, who often willingly gave a meal to a holy man in return for his blessing upon them and their home. In lonely and inhospitable places they sat in the evening to eat what they had gathered as they walked from fruit trees growing wild, from bark, from the leaves of some wholesome plant. At night they made a bed of boughs under the open sky; sometimes a cottager gave them a lodging upon the hay of his barn and a drink of milk from his cow before they left at dawn. A pool or a stream by the path on the moor or in the forest was welcome for washing away the stains of travel and—a worse evil—the plagues of itching stings and bites gathered in the sun, in the woods, or in their host's thatched barn amid the straw. Often they halted a while for the prayers of their monastic round of Office, and if the wayfarer was a priest, a flat rock made for him an altar on holy days.

Now and again the pilgrims found rest at some monastery upon their way. The pattern of these monasteries was usually the same: a group of buildings, perhaps few, perhaps many, surrounded by a strong wall as protection from roaming thieves. The walls and roofs of these buildings within the enclosure were made of stout stakes intertwined with twigs and branches; sometimes they were thatched with straw, cemented by hardened mud. Here were the cells of the brethren, often shared by several monks, and holding little but beds of straw and coarse blankets. Each cell stood separately; as, at short distances, stood the refectory, the kitchen, the guest house, the infirmary, and the huts set apart for manifold and varied handiwork, from the baking of bread to the skilled labour of carpentry or the making of clothes for the brethren and of woven adornments for the church, to the creative art wrought in metal, in colour on parchment, or in ink. Not only the work, but all the necessities for life and work—tools, pigments, utensils, parchment, hide and linen, timber, food and drink— were found, grown, fashioned, designed, executed, brewed and baked by the monks themselves.

The monastery was built by them near a lake or river which not only gave them fish for their evening meal (fish was not by any means a common luxury), but allowed them the bathing which their laborious living and rough cells made a necessity in frequent use. Near the monastery, also, was a wide space of level land which the brethren cleared, dug up, and planted with grain for bread, with vegetables, with herbs for use in sickness. In the midst of all stood the church, built of wood, and, as time went on, made for permanent use in stone.

Among the brethren of these settlements, then, our pilgrims rested from time to time, talked and prayed. Then, again they took the road, bearing with renewed hope the vision of a future day when, their search ended, their experience ripe, they, too, would finally build a house of prayer and settle down.

We shall now turn to follow some of them in their wayfaring years.

CHAPTER TWO

SAINT PATRICK

Ireland in the Fifth Century

THE STORY of St. Patrick opens in Britain at the beginning of the fifth century of our era, when over the Roman military government which had controlled Britain with strong discipline for three hundred and fifty years there lay the shadow of its end. Rome was already hard pressed by the Gothic invaders of Italy; she needed all the soldiers she could summon from more distant parts of her Empire. In the winter of 401 Stilicho, Rome's great general, as his poet Claudian tells us, called back from the north-west of Britain the troops which had been guarding that land, for the Gothic chieftain Alaric was already at the gates of Milan. In 410 Stilicho was dead, and the Emperor Honorius informed the British that, at least for the time, they must defend themselves from barbarian invasion by their own resources.

Ireland, as we have noted, had not come under Roman control. From 379 until 405 the Irish were under the rule of Niall of the Nine Hostages, a High King famous in history for his constant raids upon Gaul and Britain. It was one of these raids, coming down from across the sea upon Britain's west coast in or soon after 401, that caught and carried off a boy of some sixteen years, named Patricius, or Patrick.

We do not know at what part of the coast he was captured. The pirates, we read, seized him in the open country at his father's home, perhaps a farm; but where this home was, or whether he was born there, is still uncertain. Perhaps it was

MAP ONE: Journeys of the Welsh and Irish Saints
in the Sixth Century

in Cumberland, near Ravenglass, opposite the Isle of Man; perhaps it was in the south-west, near the Severn. We do know that Patrick had been brought up in Roman Britain, educated in Roman ways and taught the Christian faith. His grandfather, he tells us, was a priest; his father, Calpurnius, was a deacon of the Church. He also describes his father as a " decurion," which probably means that he was a member of the municipal council of some town near his farm; it might, however, mean that he held a small military command. In either case, as an official of standing, possessed of land and substance, he was able to give his son such education as the schools in Roman Britain could still supply, some training in Latin grammar and writing, some knowledge of history and philosophy, some reading of the Bible.

Yet even this seems to have been for Patrick and his family a matter of form and custom. We get the impression of a home that was happy, but in no sense intellectual or deeply religious; one that followed the conventions of its Celtic-Roman world, including Christian observance, after no carefully marked pattern. Young Patrick at sixteen was thinking little of Latin rhetoric or of his Church. He was enjoying life among his friends; and problems of the future did not worry his mind.

Now the pirates hurried him to their boat, carried him back with them to Ireland, and sold him as a slave to a man of wealth, named Miliuc, who set him to tend swine and sheep on the mountain Sliabh Mis, Slemish, near Broughshane, Co. Antrim, in north-east Ireland. On the hill and in the forest day and night Patrick kept watch; often he tried to sleep and could not because of snow or frost or rain. At last in this new misery he thought of God; God, he remembered, never slept; to Him in the cold dark night, in that silence and loneliness, he could pour out his troubles. After a time he began to feel that he was no longer alone. This was an immense comfort, and soon he was praying constantly; a hundred times a day, he tells us, and almost as often in the night.

2

Winters and summers went by, one after another, until six years had gone and Patrick was twenty-two. Then one night, as he lay asleep, words of a voice in a dream came to him: " It is good for you to fast," said the voice; " for soon you will go to your own land." After a moment, it went on: " See! Your ship is ready."

Perhaps, thought Patrick when he awoke, this really was a voice from Heaven. At any rate, he decided to take the risk, to break away then and there from these silent hills. It was a bold step, born of desperation. Death or chains fell on those caught as runaway slaves. Patrick had no friends, no money; he knew little enough about roads to the coast, nothing about ships. But he started out, as he writes, " in the strength of God who directed my path towards good." He wandered some two hundred miles, came to the coast in the darkness of night, found a lodging in a hut and at dawn a ship about to leave. He hurried to its captain. Would the ship take him on, to work his passage anywhere, wherever it was bound? The captain snapped back that he certainly would not; no doubt he suspected a slave, escaped from his owner. Patrick turned away, again in despair. But that ship had need of a strong young man, and the captain remembered this just in time. There came a shout: " Hurry on board! " In a moment he was there, one of the crew.

There was a cargo on board, of fierce Irish hounds, and it was Patrick's job to keep and feed them. Such hounds were in constant demand in Gaul and Italy, not only for use by those who loved to hunt wild game, but, even more, for the entertainment of the crowds that filled the amphitheatres of towns on festive days. Men of noble and wealthy family celebrated their election to office in Roman Gaul or Italy with sumptuous public sports. The successful candidate, or his relatives, would give the show free of cost to the multitude; and search was therefore made far and wide for novel features to interest and excite the mob, especially for gladiators or for wild, savage animals which would fight one another to the death: bears, lions, leopards, wolf-hounds. We can still read letters from a leading Roman senator of the later fourth century, named Symmachus, begging his friend Flavian to help him get hold of some fierce beasts for the glory of his own particular show in the Circus of Rome:

" The great day is upon me and those bears have not come —so often promised, so long expected! Only a few cubs have I got, and they are worn to the bone by starvation on the journey. Not one word, either, about my lions!" Then, a few days later: " Thank you from my heart for those seven Irish hounds. Rome was thrilled beyond words!"

For three days Patrick lived with his charges on the Atlantic. Then the ship came to shore in France, perhaps at Bordeaux, perhaps at Nantes after edging its way up the mouth of the Loire. From the port the captain and his crew, with the dogs, set out on foot towards their destination, whether in Gaul or in Italy, we cannot say. It was a long journey; Patrick tells that for twenty-eight days they travelled through country empty and deserted, that for ten days they met no one. Fortunately the weather was good. But their store of food gave out, and they were terribly worried because many of those precious hounds which were to fetch so high a price were falling along the road, sick and half-dead. Suddenly one day, when things were at their worst, a herd of pigs ran across the way. Everyone rushed to seize and kill, and everyone, including the dogs, feasted for two days of rest.

The reason for the deserted state of the roads across Gaul at this time has been sought in much discussion. The voyage of Patrick from Ireland may be dated some time between 407 and 409. On the last day of December, 406, a host of barbarians, Alans, Suevians, Vandals, had poured from Germany across the Rhine to plunder Gaul; perhaps before the terrifying news had reached Ireland Patrick's ship had already set sail. By the time it reached harbour, fear of these barbarian raiders may have driven men of Gaul to distant parts of the country, far from the highways. Perhaps, again, peasant bandits were seizing this time of terror to make raids of their own. Or, it has been thought, the reason may lie with Constantine the Third, declared in 407 " Emperor " by the Roman military forces still left in Britain. The usurper had promptly crossed the Channel in the hope of seizing at least some part of Gaul; perhaps the thought of his soldiers was keeping travellers at home. Or, in truth, the reason may be far simpler: that Patrick's captain deliberately took lonely byways to keep his hounds secure from seizure by anyone.

At length the destination was reached and Patrick was discharged, to get himself as best he could to the sea and across it to his home in Britain. This took a long time; but its story is not told.

His family, of course, rejoiced in his return and shuddered at his experience; they begged him now to stay with them. For a while he was happy. Then, to his surprise, he found he could not rest. Day and night, in his thoughts, even in his dreams, he heard Ireland calling. Long he struggled, and then he knew it was no good. The Irish people were heathen and ignorant. They needed teachers; they needed him. He had learned all this in those six years among the Irish hills, and now he had to go.

3

But not straight back to Ireland. He himself was ignorant; he had never really worked at his books. He could do far more in Ireland if he were a priest, and that needed much preparation. He went back across the Channel to Gaul.

The preparation was to take far longer than he thought. Some time, as he tells in the first of the *Dicta*, the " Sayings " which bear his name, and this one we may believe to be his own, he spent travelling " through Gaul and Italy and the islands of the Tyrrhenian Sea," the waters of the Mediterranean upon the west coast of Italy. Some of these islands were inhabited by anchorites, solitary men of prayer. Perhaps, however, this wandering among the islands may rather belong to the " long time " which we have noted, between his leaving his ship's crew in Gaul and his coming home to his family in Britain.

There is no certain evidence that at any time he stayed in the monastic school of Lérins, lying on those islands of Saint-Honorat and Sainte-Marguerite in the Mediterranean near Cannes. This school was founded at the beginning of the fifth century by Honoratus, in later years bishop of Arles, and it quickly attracted men of Gaul. But at this early time of its history, when Patrick was wandering here and there, its renown was hardly great enough to draw him there for study.

At Auxerre, the city on the Yonne in central France, seat of a bishopric since the fourth century and already growing in repute of scholarship, he settled and worked hard to gain the culture, the knowledge which he lacked. Here he was welcomed by the bishop, Amator, and here, after Amator died in 418, he stayed on to learn from Amator's successor, the great St. Germanus. Here he was ordained deacon; we are told nothing in regard to his ordination as priest.

So the years went by, while he worked and hoped, until it was 429. In that year Germanus, this bishop of Auxerre, was sent to Britain by the Pope of the time, Celestine the First, at the urging of Palladius, Archdeacon of Rome. Heresy was spreading among British Christians; Saxons were invading Britain from across the sea, Picts were coming down from the North; there was treachery at work among the British themselves. While, then, Germanus was busy with these troubles in Britain, he grew increasingly aware of the problem of Ireland and its people. Reports reached him of its many heathen, of the need of teaching, of organisation, of a bishop for Ireland. Who, he asked the priests in his company, who should be sent? Someone who had known Patrick in Auxerre put forward his name. He had lived in Ireland and knew Irish speech. The suggestion was rejected.

Nor did it find more favour when it again came up for discussion after Germanus had returned to Auxerre. Patrick's thought of his mission to Ireland seemed, indeed, to vanish in smoke. The disappointment was so great that he was ready to give up in despair. " I was almost lost," he wrote long afterwards. It was not, he admitted, the malice of enemies which had rejected him. It was not even that friend of his, that very close friend, he remembered in bitterness, who had seemed so eager for his election, and then had betrayed to those concerned in it a confession which Patrick had once made to him in confidence, of sin committed long before, in his careless youth. The real reason for his rejecting was, he knew well, his lack of long and strict training in Roman rhetoric and the liberal arts, his ignorance, his " rusticity," as he called it, those years of neglected schooling which could never be regained. The Cathedral clergy of Auxerre, accustomed to Roman-Continental standards of Gaul, could not think of a bishop who had not been entirely familiar from his school days with Latin rules of grammar, with the polished writing of Latin prose. In 431, Palladius, probably the same Archdeacon of Rome, was consecrated by Pope Celestine and sent to Ireland as bishop for its people. For Patrick all now seemed to be over, at least so far as the Irish were concerned.

Then suddenly things changed. The bishop Germanus and his clergy held another conference at Auxerre; they decided, it would seem, that Patrick might do good service in Ireland in a minor way, as assistant to Palladius. Perhaps Palladius was having his own difficulties with the Irish. Once decided upon, action followed quickly. In 432 Patrick was sent off on his way to Ireland, accompanied by one Segitius, a senior priest of Auxerre, as " witness " of his progress and " companion " for his aid.

Our information now comes, among other sources, from the Irish Muirchú, who wrote of St. Patrick's life in a narrative of the late seventh century. The two travellers had gone only about sixteen miles on their way to the coast when, where now the little town of Avrolles stands, they met two of the clergy who had gone with Palladius to Ireland and were now hurrying back to Auxerre with the news that Palladius was dead. Probably he had died in Ireland, perhaps as a martyr; one traditior vaguely suggests that he had set out on a journey to preach among the Picts and that he had died in Pictish land. Patrick returned to Auxerre with the messengers. Now there was no rejection, no delay. Germanus consecrated him bishop for the Irish, very possibly in a church dedicated to Amator, just outside the city in the suburb known as St.-Amâtre. Then he set out for the work for which he had waited so long. He arrived in Ireland in 432, when he was nearly fifty years of age.

Here we mark that Patrick did not wander forth from Britain without definite aim of destination and design, as did so many Celtic wanderers, awaiting the Lord's pleasure unknown. Patrick was a Celt; but he had received Roman training, Roman-inspired education, little as it had been, in a country administered after the Roman manner. All this made for definite, ordered action. So now we see him going, after due preparation, to teach and to organise in Ireland according to Roman use and discipline.

And such was sorely needed. Ireland in this earlier fifth century was a country of wild tribes, warring one against another, ruled by kings under the supreme lordship of the High King, who held his Court at Tara, his capital as ruler of Meath in North Leinster. Under these kings lived and worked, first, nobles, owners of wide lands; next, men of wealth whose cattle browsed on the acres which they held in rented tenure from these nobles, their landlords; next, farmers who ploughed and sowed their allotments as tenants of those richer than themselves; next, free-born labourers; and, finally, slaves, either born in slavery or brought to it by capture in war or in raids, like young Patrick himself.

Muirchú tells that after his ship reached Ireland Patrick sought out the northern country of Antrim where he had lived as a slave, and that then he made his way to County Down and began his missionary work near Downpatrick, where now stand the ruins of Saul Abbey. We find him in tradition later on at work farther south, in County Meath of Leinster in the east; in Connaught of the west; and at last establishing his Chief Bishop's seat at Armagh in Ulster, in the north-east.

4

Did he find Christianity already at work when he arrived in Ireland, a foundation on which he might build anew? Our best, and most reliable evidence for this is the statement of that chronicler, Prosper of Aquitaine, who lived in this same fifth century and wrote against its year 431 that Palladius was sent by Pope Celestine as " the first bishop for the Irish believing in Christ."

Christianity, as we have already said, doubtless passed to the Irish from Roman Britain and Gaul early in our era. Tradition has connected its early practice in Ireland with the south, south-east, and south-west. Medieval *Lives* of Irish saints tell of four holy men who, as the later Middle Ages believed, taught their religion and administered its sacraments before Patrick came to their land. They were Ailbe, founder of a church at Emly, now a village near Tipperary, and Patron Saint of Munster in the south-west; Ibar, renowned as head of a monastic school on Becc-Erin, Beggery island (now no longer an island), in Wexford harbour of the south-east; Declan, founder of a church at Ardmore, near Youghal in the south, a saint still held in honour by the people of Munster; and Sean-

Ciaran, Ciaran the Elder, of Saigir, the ancient name for Seirkieran, which still holds ruins marked by his name near Birr, in County Offaly (Ui Failghe), of Leinster.

Of these we may dismiss Ailbe and Ibar as belonging to a later time. But there is a slender possibility that Declan and Ciaran were in Ireland before Patrick and that after his coming they yielded to his authority and worked under him as their Chief Father in God. The *Life* of St. Declan has interesting matter of legend: " Now the most blessed bishop Patrick, hearing that the ruler of the Dèssi " (a people of Munster) " would not believe holy Declan, came to them to preach the word of God. Four bishops there were in Ireland before Patrick, sent from Rome even as he. They were Ailbe, Declan, Ciaran, and Ibar, and they held not unity with holy Patrick, but diversity of will; nevertheless in the end they came to one mind with him." Ailbe, Declan, and Ciaran, according to this story, before long submitted. " Ibar, however, in no manner would consent to holy Patrick nor be subject to him; he did not want Ireland to have as Chief Bishop a man born of British, or any un-Irish people. So Ibar and Patrick carried on great battles with one another. But afterwards, by bidding of an angel, they made peace in brotherly love."

St. Ciaran the Elder was said to be bishop over the Osraige, dwellers in that ancient kingdom where now Kilkenny and the diocese of Ossory lie. *Lives* of this Ciaran, in Irish and in Latin, are still in our libraries. We read that at the time of his birth all the Irish were heathen. Then comes the story that Ciaran himself was not baptized until he was thirty years old, when he heard that the Christian religion was to be found in Rome; that he journeyed there, was converted, and consecrated bishop. In Rome, so we find in this happy legend, he met St. Patrick. " And Patrick said to Ciaran: ' Go thou to Ireland before me, and journey therein until thou come to a little spring of cooling water, Uarán, that runs between the Irish of the south and of the north. There build thee a monastery; for there shall be thine honour and thy place of resurrection.' And Ciaran said:

' I know it not.' And Patrick answered him: ' Dear brother, thou shalt go in peace, and the Lord shall be with thee. Take this bell as thy fellow on thy way. Never a sound will it utter until thou come to that place of the spring, and there shall it ring out clear and sweet.' " So it came about, and the first beginning of the famous abbey of Saigir, or Seirkieran, was made by Ciaran for the greater glory of God.

At first, our tale continues, Ciaran had no monks to serve his cloister, for he had journeyed alone. We have seen that a savage boar tore saplings from the forest for the building of his cell. Presently other dwellers of the forest came out in curiosity from their holes and dens to see what was going on and stayed to do what they could to keep him company: a fox, a badger, and a wolf. Soon, we read, they were for him his " monks," meekly obeying his word as in monastic rule. They were for him his first " community," and he was their Father in God.

Occasionally alas! as in all holy houses, there was a lapse from discipline. " One day the fox, who was more cunning and crafty than his brethren, stole the sandals of Abbot Ciaran, contrary to holy vow and profession, and carried them off to his old haunt in the forest, intending to devour them there. When the Father heard of this, he sent Brother Badger into the forest after Brother Fox, to bring him back to his cell. Now Brother Badger had right good skill at finding his way in the woods, and quickly came straight to the hollow which was home to Brother Fox. There he sat, enjoying breakfast on those sandals. Nor would he move. So Brother Badger bit the ears and the tail of his brother in holy rule, plucked out his fur and forced him to start back to his monastery that he might do penance for his sin. At the hour of Nones they arrived. And St. Ciaran said to the fox: ' Why hast thou wrought this evil, brother, such as it becomes not a monk to do? See now, our water of the spring is sweet and pure and free to all, and so is the food we share in common alike. If thou didst desire meat after thine own craving, from the bark of trees Almighty God would have given it thee.' Then Brother Fox prayed for mercy, did his penance, and had nothing at all to eat until Ciaran gave him leave."

In the heart of all this charming story there lies a kernel of truth, that St. Ciaran ruled a monastery at Seirkieran. On the other hand, it is certainly true that Patrick found much of Ireland still pagan when he came there. He tells us that he journeyed to its remote parts, where no man had come before him, to baptize and confirm and ordain; that at his coming many Irishmen were still worshipping idols in foul rites, with no knowledge of the Christian God.

5

There were other hardships for him, and many of them. Very often he was in danger from those who hated Christian teachings and clung to their gods of ancient time; the very rulers in whose kingdoms he hoped to carry on his mission work often had to be won by gifts before they would allow him within their land. " Daily," he writes, " I expect for myself either murder or capture and slavery. Once I was seized by enemies who longed to kill me. But my time had not yet come. They took from me all I had and bound me in iron. After two weeks the Lord delivered me from their power and gave me back what I had lost."

Then, too, there was the scorn which cultured scholars, bishops and priests of Gaul, had spoken against this man, so unfit to sit in a bishop's seat, they had told one another, when he had been elected for Ireland. Patrick feared that they still felt the same, in spite of his long and splendid work as bishop. " I am despised by many," are his own words. " I have been afraid to put what I want to say into writing, for Latin is still to me a foreign tongue; anyone can see that, from the way I speak and write it. I am still seeking that skill which should have been mine long ago. Did not many men speak against me as bishop for Ireland? ' Why does *he* go out to deal with those who know not God? How can he defeat trouble? ' These things they said behind my back." They felt sure, and Patrick knew their feeling, that he could never hold his own against the Irish who, naturally quick and intelligent, had picked up learning of various sorts from men of Gaul, traders who had come to their shores.

Much of Patrick's insistence on his shortcoming, or on what he held his shortcoming, was due of course to his own sincere humility; and part, we may suspect, to that convention among medieval writers of letters and autobiographies which prescribed such assertions of unworthiness. Yet his words show that his real humility was deepened by his remembrance of the opposition to his election as bishop for the Irish people.

Last of all, Patrick was often homesick. He longed, as he says, for his own native land, for his family, for his friends in Gaul. Among his last words are those of all the wandering saints: " I live among untaught clansmen, a stranger and an exile for the love of God."

But he tells also of baptizing many thousands; he converted chieftains; he fostered in Ireland the love of the religious life brought by him from his experience in Auxerre. The sons and daughters of Irish chieftains, he writes, entered monasteries under his preaching, against the will and with the fierce anger of their kinsfolk. He organised Ireland under episcopal rule, as he had known and watched it in Gaul, and he ruled his bishops, few though they were in number, from his own Chief See of Armagh.

6

Among the bishops who may reliably be held to have worked under Patrick in Ireland, the Irish Annals tell of three who were there with him from 439 onwards: Secundinus (more often known as Sechnall), Auxilius, and Iserninus. Articles of *Canons*, declared to have been drawn up by Patrick, Auxilius, and Iserninus, throw light on the ordering of the Church in Ireland in these early days. They tell of the Irish heathen, feeling the first appeal of the Christian faith; the heathen are forbidden here to give alms to the Christian Church, and must fast forty days before receiving Christian baptism. The *Canons* tell, too, of Christian converts who fall into sin, who dishonour Christian marriage for their own profiting, who refuse to pay their just debts, who fall back into pagan rites of witchcraft. Such sins, if not repented of, brought excommunication, and those cut off might not even enter the church on Easter Eve to see the solemn ceremony of baptism. Murder brought to the sinner, once baptized, a year of penance; the same punishment fell to adultery of the less heinous sort; theft met six months of discipline, with severe fasting for twenty days.

Under Patrick, according to this same code of regulation, Irish clergy were of necessity at all times decently attired; they were bound under pain of excommunication to say their Office morning and evening. Special care was here taken against the illegal functioning of stranger priests, a common trouble in the Church of the Middle Ages. These, in the *Canons* we are examining, could carry out no function of any kind unless they had been formally recognised by the proper authority, the bishop; they might neither baptize, nor offer the Holy Sacrifice, nor give a blessing, nor build a church. Those who disobeyed this order were cast out from Christian men. And no priest at all could say Mass in a new church until his bishop had come to hallow it.

Sechnall, among these bishops, wrote a hymn in praise of Patrick which illustrates the first beginning of Latin religious verse in Ireland. It is named from its opening words, *Audite omnes*, " Hearken all! "; its verses declare Patrick's virtue as bishop, as worker among the heathen, as student of sacred writings, and as man of God.

This brings us to a last word, on Patrick as writer. It is true that his Latin style, in spite of long study, remained imperfect to the end. But he knew his Bible thoroughly, and he was constantly a student of Church law and order and doctrine for the right ruling of his clergy and people. Two important documents from his pen (in addition to the *Dicta*, the " Sayings," which must be examined critically as to authorship) have come down to us. The first is a *Letter*. It was written to the soldiers of one Coroticus, a British chieftain; in a raid upon the Irish coast they had killed Christian converts of Patrick, only recently baptized. In his wrath Patrick demanded that these murderers be driven from that Christian Church in which they, too, had been baptized; and he met defiant, insulting words for his courage. The second writing, sent out when he was an old man, he called his *Confession*. It was a reply to his critics, one and all, whether those who looked down on him for his " rusticity " or those who disapproved of his acts as bishop. From this " Confession " we learn much of what we know concerning his life.

The *Lorica*, the " Breastplate of St. Patrick," known to scholars as " The Deer's Cry," is a prayer to Heaven for its guarding of body and soul against the perils of this world, a girding on at daybreak of the power and grace of the Spirit, in the Christ, in angels, in all holy saints, in the strength of God's heaven and His earth. The language here is Old Irish, of the early Middle Ages; but whether the hymn comes actually from Patrick himself or from his time is a matter of question.

Patrick never returned home to Britain. The care of his Irish people held him firmly, and from the day he landed for the second time in Ireland his journeyings were for them. Among them, however, he was constantly travelling, on his way to visit, to teach, to receive, to confirm and to consecrate, for nearly thirty years. The *Annals of Ulster* state, against the year 441, that " Patrick, the bishop, was approved in the Catholic faith," which would mean that his work in Ireland received the official blessing of Rome; but there is no evidence that he went from Ireland to Rome for this confirmation.

Tradition places his death on March the seventeenth, 461,

and gives his burial to Saul, near Downpatrick, in that north-east to which it gave the beginning of his work. Years before this time he had made his prayer: " I ask of God that He give it me to persevere and to render myself to Him a faithful witness until the day of my crossing hence." His prayer was fulfilled; he left a sowing which was to grow into rich harvest in Ireland of the next, the sixth century.

CHAPTER THREE

SAINT NINIAN OF SCOTLAND; SAINTS OF WALES, CORNWALL AND BRITTANY

Britain and Brittany in the Fifth and Six Centuries

ONE OF the most interesting names in the records of wayfaring saints of Northern Britain is that of Nynnyaw, known to us as St. Ninian. Unhappily in the course of medieval centuries a mist of tradition has gathered round this name, and scholars even now are working to clear the air.

In the evidence before us we find reason to think that St. Ninian lived in the early fifth century; that he was a bishop of the British people dwelling in southern Scotland, in territory long ruled by Roman military power; that he also taught his Christian faith to the " Picts of the South."

These Southern Picts, barbarian invaders of North British land, lived in eastern Scotland, in the region lying between the Tay and the Dee: in Perthshire, Angus, and Kincardine. On their west lay the mountain range of Druim Alban; on the north they were divided by the mountains of the Mounth from their kinsmen, the Northern Picts, who hunted the lands of the Ness and the Spey.

Our earliest authority on Ninian is St. Bede, who wrote of him, as bishop of the British and missionary to the Southern Picts, in his *Church History of the English People* some three hundred years after Ninian lived. Moreover, the cautious Bede observed that his information came from " hearsay "—*ut perhibent*. He went on to state that in his own eighth century and in his own day a bishop was holding a see in the place where, long before, Ninian had built a church of stone, a building " uncommon among the British "; that for this reason the church of the eighth century was itself known far and wide as " The White House."

According to Irish story Irish monks, probably from the later fifth century onwards, crossed the sea to study and practise their faith in a monastery which they called for its fame *Magnum Monasterium*, " The Great Monastery," and also *Alba*, " The White House." Tradition has identified this monastery with the bishop's seat of which Bede wrote, and that was undoubtedly at Whithorn in Galloway, on Scotland's south-western coast. By this eighth century, of course, the British had long yielded in occupation and rule to their Anglo-Saxon conquerors, and the bishop of Whithorn in Bede's time was an Anglo-Saxon, Pecthelm by name, installed about 730.

Recent scholarship has pointed out that although Ninian may have built his church at Whithorn in Galloway, there is no actual proof that he did build it in that place. We do not know how far he journeyed in his desire to convert those Southern Picts.

There are other details concerning Ninian which rest unproved. From Bede we gather that he travelled to Rome for the training and discipline which the Church could give him there. In other tradition, embodied in a twelfth century *Life* of Ninian by St. Ailred of Rievaulx, we are told that on his way back he passed through Gaul and brought back to Britain with him from Gaul masons to work on the building of a stone church; that he stayed in Gaul at Tours to learn from its famous monk, Martin; that he dedicated his church in Martin's honour.

That a church was built of stone by Ninian somewhere in North Britain in the fifth century under Roman, under Continental influence, may be a fact. Such building was known there at that time. But the mention of pilgrimage to Rome occurs too often in the records of these early saints to allow one to believe it of Ninian with any certainty. Moreover, in the fifth century dedications of British churches were offered, not in honour of holy men or women of current or recent days, but of those told of in the Scriptures and revered by the whole Catholic Church from its founding.

Men, however, down the centuries honoured Ninian in the church at Whithorn. There they believed he lay buried. Pilgrims came there to pray before his shrine; many miracles, they reported, were done there through his presence and his power, both while he lived and after his death. Early in the ninth century detailed evidence for the succession of Anglo-Saxon bishops at Whithorn fails us, and we wait until the twelfth, when the diocese was revived and Ailred of Rievaulx wrote his *Life of Ninian*, a labour of love full of legend, for a revival of Ninian's cult in the hallowing of churches and their parishes under his name. That name is still held in memory at many places: in churches and chapels of towns and villages, in the countryside at well and bay and cliff, in Scotland and in northern England.

2

From Scotland, which gained its name through the " Scots," who were Irishmen and who from the fourth century invaded North Britain constantly and settled there in permanence, we come to Wales. Wales, also, had received much from Ireland. In the third century of our era people of the Irish tribe of the Dèssi had come, as tradition told, to settle in Pembrokeshire in Wales. From that time onwards there was a strong connection between South Wales and Ireland.

Irish invaders also settled in North Wales at an early time, perhaps shortly after A.D. 400. But about the middle of the fifth century a chieftain, Cunedda, of the tribe of Gododdin, came with eight of his nine sons and many of his people from Manaw Gododdin, a region lying along the Firth of Forth in south-east Scotland, near North Berwick, to fight and to drive out these Irishmen. He did this with so great force and slaughter that he and his tribesmen settled in Wales in their stead. So we are told in that *History of Britain*, which Nennius the Briton, who described himself as of Welsh training, is said to have edited about A.D. 800. The suggestion has been made that this Cunedda was an official of the Roman administration still in practice in North Britain after the departure of Roman military power, and that he was sent by this administration into Wales to occupy and to rule its northern lands. The thought naturally follows that he was of the Christian faith. If this is true, he was of importance for the conversion of Wales. He founded the royal line of Gwynedd, in a realm of northern Wales; in the following, the sixth century, his great-grandson, the famous Maelgwn, was its king. Maelgwn's sons, too, were chieftains of various tribal divisions of Wales, from the north as far south as Cardigan.

Doubtless in the earlier years of the fifth century dwellers in Wales were escaping much of the evil of the Picts and the Irish Scots of Scotland, who were always on the march southwards to plunder and carry off spoils from British land south of the Tweed. Most people of Wales had little enough to tempt pirates bent on plunder. They were poor, clustered in villages around the forts built on their hills for their defence. Their mountains and their valleys made bitter going for intruders.

But those of the Welsh, and of the British outside Wales, who lived in regions easier of access, suffered long and deeply. At last the terror could no longer be borne, and, we are told, British leaders, with one Vortigern, a ruler in east-central Wales, at their head, invited men of Germanic race to cross the Channel for their aid. Thus in the end they brought " wolves into the sheepfolds for the destruction of Britain." The " coming of Hengist and Horsa " is traditionally placed in 449.

For a time there was harmony between the British and these strangers. Soon, however, smouldering tension burst into blaze of war. Across Britain the blaze spread, " until it licked the western ocean with its fierce red tongue." Romans of military training, still living in Britain, and the British who had learned military skill from them, fought the enemy with all their might. At last, about 500, the British won the decisive victory of Badon Mount, Mons Badonicus, and for a while the German Saxons ceased their troubling. The place of the battle is not known, and its hero, Arthur, is seen but dimly as a British leader through the clouds of legend. But there was peace in Wales from foreign menace for nearly the first fifty years of the sixth century.

3

And so we come to our wayfaring Celtic saints of Wales in this sixth century which saw their work rise and grow into fulfilment. It did so with difficulty; for if, indeed, there was peace from without during these first fifty years, there was trouble enough within Welsh marches. Through a writer, probably taught in Wales and known as Gildas Sapiens, Gildas the Wise, who was at work during these years of relief from foreign terror, we learn of the Five Kings of Britain in this earlier sixth century and of their wickedness. They ruled in the West Country of Britain; and their acts show that not only Christianity, but monastic dedication was already vigorous in their lands.

There was Constantine, who held his power over Devon and part of Somerset and Cornwall. He was a man of blasphemy. Had he not taken upon himself the very array, the vestment of a holy Father Abbot, that he might murder at the altar itself two little princes of royal blood? There was Voteporix, whose tombstone reveals him a Christian, " the protector." He was king of Dyfed, the land of modern Pembrokeshire, and foul with the lust of impure living. There was Cynlas, ruler of some kingdom in Wales unnamed by Gildas, possibly in its central part: " the tawny butcher, scorner of God and enemy of His

Church, steeped in evil from his youth; he who not only cast away his own wife, but looked with eyes of desire upon her sister, vowed in holy order of continence." Above them all, both in leadership among these princes of the Welsh and in hateful deeds, stood that descendant of Cunedda, Maelgwn Gwynedd, " the Dragon of the Island " (Anglesey)," rolling in the black abyss of wickedness of many years as though drunk with wine from the vineyards of Sodom." He once, in brief and sudden penitence, had entered a monastery to pray night and day, but he had left it again for sin and the Devil.

About 547 Maelgwn died; it was said, in an outbreak of the Yellow Plague, an epidemic which raged in Europe in these early Middle Ages as the Black Death was to rage in the fourteenth century. Now the Germanic hordes renewed their battle, and the last fifty years of the sixth century were full of conflict; obscure in detail as it reaches us, but surely building up in firmness the kingdoms of the Anglo-Saxon rulers to come, in Britain of the south-west, of the north, of the east and the south-east, of the country around the Thames. It was against this turbulent background that monastic life and learning grew in Wales and that its monks went forth abroad to teach those who knew less than they. No doubt the very anxiety and turmoil of their days led them to seek a way of sure and lasting hope in the hereafter.

As in Ireland under Patrick in the fifth century, so in Wales in the sixth, the Church was ruled by bishops who watched over and ordered its religious houses and schools. The story of its monastic discipline begins in the late fifth century with two men working hand in hand in South Wales. One of them was a bishop, St. Dubricius or Dyfrig, who ruled his clergy and monks in the region of Glamorgan which was afterwards to hold the cathedral of Llandaff. At times, we may believe, he journeyed into Herefordshire; its land, at least, shows four dedications of churches in his name. He lived in a monastery, and often, men said, he sought still deeper retreat during Lent

" in his own house " upon the isle of Inys Pyr, now generally identified with Caldy Island off the Pembroke coast.

His friend and fellow worker was Illtud, who has come down to us as *magister*, a " master " or head of a monastic school, settled, it would seem, in the present village of Llantwit Major, twenty miles from Cardiff. As time went on, the school became known as Llanilltud, " the enclosed church of Illtud." The master was very learned and very famous for his learning; we read in a record of the early seventh century, the *Life of St. Samson*, that he " knew thoroughly all the Scriptures, both of the Old and the New Testament, the various branches of philosophy, the arts of metric, of rhetoric, of grammar, of arithmetic. No man of Britain was skilled as he, and," the writer ends in his pride, " I myself have been in his splendid monastery." The belief came naturally to men of later days that a scholar of this reputation must have been taught, had perhaps even been ordained priest, by the great St. Germanus himself during his stay in Britain; too simple a belief, however, to be accepted, especially if one has regard for dates. Many young men, we are told, came to Illtud's school for their training; famous among these in later days were Samson, Gildas, and Paul Aurelian.

The monastery stood in the midst of meadows and fields which gave pasture to its cattle and corn to its monks; but work on the fields was often hindered by the tidal water of the river nearby as it rose from the sea to drown the springing seed and to make marshland of the farm. In dry weather birds arrived in flocks to settle and devour. Two legends describe the master's working against these troubles. Illtud, we read, had hoped to conquer the flowing tide by building a great wall of stone, cemented with clay. The force of the sea was too great, and the first wall broke down; so did a second, and a third. At last in despair he decided that the monastery must be moved farther inland, since not only its fields, but its houses and church were in danger. On the night before the moving was to begin, as he lay asleep, a voice forbade him to leave. Directly after

Matins, this voice said, he was to hasten to the shore and hold out his abbot's staff against the rising tide. He did so; and this first of his problems was solved.

In harvest time the gulls began to devour the corn, and Illtud set his students on watch. All day long they stood in the fields throwing stones at the invaders. After a while one of them—now it is Samson, in another story it is Paul—grew impatient. Prayer is better than watching, he decided. So he fell to prayer, and again an idea was born. Why not drive these pesky gulls into the monastery barn? Soon all the monks were horrified at the noise in their silent hours, as the prisoners shrieked and squawked their penitence for their crime. Illtud came hurrying from his study. When he learned what had been done, he freed the birds, with proper rebuke, as St. Francis was to rebuke long afterwards; and the gulls in gratitude for his mercy never came again.

4

One of the names given in such stories of Illtud's school, however, should not be credited. We have no good reason for thinking that St. David of Wales was a student there. His *Life*, written in Latin in the late eleventh century by Rhygyvarch, gives us some vividly imagined fiction concerning David's travels from Wales, the land of his birth. He went, it says, to Glastonbury, " where he built a church "; to Bath, " where by his benediction he changed its death-dealing water to a stream, always hot, that brought health to those who bathed therein "; to Crowland in Lincolnshire, to Repton in Derbyshire, to Leominster in Herefordshire; to various parts of Wales; and to Jerusalem. There, the story goes, he was consecrated Archbishop by its Patriarch, a detail obviously added to enhance David's dignity among the saints of Wales.

Other tales in this *Life of St. David* are even more wonderful. We read that an Irish abbot, one among the many pilgrims described as journeying from Ireland to visit David and his monastery, asked the holy man to lend him a horse to carry him to his ship, bound for his Irish shore. David gave him his own horse and a blessing upon his way. When the traveller— his name was Bairre—reached the sea, no ship was in sight; his start had been delayed. It did not matter. Strong in the thought of David's benediction, Bairre headed David's horse for the waves and came safe and sound to shore on the other side. "There is still in Ireland," Rhygyvarch declares, " a painted image of this horse, all covered with gold, to keep in men's minds one of Ireland's many wonders."

Another tale of pleasant fancy is told of one of David's own monks who also crossed the Irish Sea. He was a visitor, travelling to learn from Ireland's men of religion. His name was Modomnoc, and he was bee-keeper for his Welsh brethren. When, also blessed by David's hand, he went on board his boat, his bees followed him and settled on the prow. Thus, so the story goes, Ireland won her bees, just as through Patrick she lost her snakes.

We turn from these legends of marvel to look at a sober picture of the Celtic monk's discipline in the sixth century, as it is shown in this same *Life of St. David*. Here we may trust its detail. His monastery stood at Mynyw—in the Latin, Menevia—where now St. David's village and Cathedral stand in Pembrokeshire of South Wales, near that far western point of its coast looking out upon St. George's Channel.

The keynote of daily life was hard work, shared by every brother alike; for " he who does not labour, may not eat." In fear of that enemy ever lying in wait for monks, that depression which poisons the sap of a life of negligent round and order, David " laid upon the shoulders of his brethren the yoke of Divine toils."

Their monastic day opened at cockcrow before dawn, with prayer of Office in church. This over, and it was long, all went out into the fields. There was no ox at Mynyw for heavy service; " each monk was as an ox to his fellows," pulling the plough across the earth; in the hands of all were saw and hoe, spade and mattock, for cutting timber, for breaking up the soil, for the sowing of the corn. Thus passed the morning. Back in the cloister at noon, all prayed, all worked at household necessities, or wrote, or read until the hour for Vespers. Reading included the study of Latin, of the text of the Bible, of the books of Latin Fathers of the West, of secular arts. The medieval world owed much later on to this reading and writing of the early monks of Wales.

At the sound of the Vespers bell each in silence rose from his work; even the writer, absorbed in tracing line or curve of some letter in his script, left it ragged and unfinished in his haste to obey. Chanting of psalms filled the church until the stars came out at dusk. For a brief time there was rest, while the Father Abbot remained alone, still at prayer. Then all gathered, in the rough room that served as refectory, for the frugal, the only meal of the day, of bread and vegetables seasoned with salt, and, at its ending, a cup of water, or milk and water. Grace was said. Once again the bell for Office; and now some three hours of watch and prayer and bowing of the knee. No one dared throughout these hours to yawn, or sneeze, or spit. And so to bed. Once a week, from the last prayer of Friday until after the prayer of dawn on Sunday, strict and continual vigil was kept, except for one hour of rest after Matins in the little hours of Saturday.

The habit worn by these Celtic monks of Wales was made from animal hides; and all things, of course, were shared in common. In matters slight as well as important, counsel and permission were asked of the abbot: priest, confessor, " soul-friend," as the Celtic picture has it, for all his sons in the Lord.

Admission to this austere life was strictly guarded. He who knocked upon the monastery's gate in hope must wait ten days as a suppliant outside its doors, neglected and alone, as if a criminal deserving the censure of all. Should he persist, he was at last admitted, to be put in charge of a senior monk who kept him at hard labour, sharpened by dour commands, until the brethren decided that they might safely call him to their common life.

We can see here the influence upon these monks in early medieval Wales of the Fathers of the fourth and fifth centuries in the deserts of Egypt. Tradition holds St. David not only as abbot but as bishop in his seat at Mynyw. But it is as founder of this early monastic rule that he is of chief importance to history. From Mynyw—St. David's—men went out to found daughter monasteries in other parts of Wales and abroad.

. 5

From St. David and his monks we come to other saints of Wales, famous for their travels. The *Life of St. Cadoc*, written late in the eleventh century by Lifris, probably Archdeacon of Glamorgan, would have us believe that he visited Jerusalem three times and Rome seven, as well as going on his way from Wales to Cornwall, Scotland, Ireland, Brittany, and Greece; that often he spent the Lenten weeks in retreat upon Barry Island, off the coast of Glamorgan near Cardiff, or upon Flatholm, that islet in the Bristol Channel near Weston-super-Mare.

Very possibly he did retire for Lent; but much of this wider journeying must be looked upon as a tale of pious imagination. Cadoc of Wales in this sixth century is himself, however, very real. He founded a monastery at Llancarfan, near Llanwit Major, in which he taught his monks to live as strictly and to learn as eagerly as did Illtud and David. We read that once he went into Brecknockshire, north of Glamorgan, " because he had heard that a famous professor of rhetoric, Bachan, had recently come to Wales from Italy, and he longed greatly to gain from this scholar Latin learning after the Roman style." The same *Life of Cadoc* also tells that he was once the cause of great fear even to the terrible Maelgwn himself, the king in North Wales. He heard that Maelgwn had marched south and was ravaging land near his monastery, and he swiftly went out to stop this insult. He did stop it, with the help of the Lord, for sudden darkness fell over the king's whole army as it lay encamped, and out of the darkness thundered Cadoc's voice. Maelgwn in terror, probably believing that the Last Judgment had arrived, confessed his sin, and promptly there was light.

6

Both the *Life* of Cadoc by Lifris, and another by Caradoc of Llancarfan, probably of the early twelfth century and preserved for us in the *Codex Gothanus*, picture him bringing home to Britain water from the River Jordan to mingle with that of a Cornish well for the well's honour and blessing. This again is legend. Yet it is reasonable to think of Cadoc and of other wanderers among his fellow saints, in search of solitude or in pursuit of souls to teach, crossing the mouth of the Severn from South Wales to land in Somerset or Devon, even if dedications in these shires prove little.

We may think, too, of monks from Wales venturing out in their wicker boats covered with hides to edge their way along the Cornish coast and up the estuaries of its rivers. St. Samson, we read in his earliest *Life*, written perhaps in the seventh century, said good-bye to his mourning brethren of Glamorgan, visited his mother and his aunt, both of them nuns, consecrated the churches in which they prayed, found out that his sister had run away from home and was living in sin, promptly excommunicated her when she refused to repent (in the story he is already a bishop), healed and blessed a multitude of the sick and sad, and with a few followers departed " in prosperous voyage across the Severn Sea." Once across, he entered the mouth of the river Camel in northern Cornwall and came to shore at " Docco," where a monastery was already standing, itself named in honour of a " Saint Docco " of Wales. The place once known as " Docco " is now St. Kew, near Padstow.

Alas! the brethren had become somewhat slothful of practice, and Samson, this energetic adventurer for God, "received scanty welcome." "Hasten," he barked, "and bring to me someone among you who has some sense!" They hurried to find Father Winniavus, who came with a deep sense of shame to meet the holy visitor. With reverence he bowed, and prayed to know the reason for this visit. "I am going to preach the Gospel to heathen men," said Samson, "and I should be glad to rest a while here on my way." "Most good in God's eyes, beloved Father, is your intent," replied Winniavus, who was both prudent and shrewd, "but your stay here, I greatly fear, would not be of comfort to your soul. Go, Father, go farther, and in peace, and show forth to this Cornish land the living power of God."

Samson journeyed on, driving a rough wagon along the bank of the Camel. As he came towards a village near Bodmin, he heard loud sound of revel, and saw at a distance men dancing and shouting in heathen ritual before the image of their god, set up on the summit of a hill upon the moor. "Stay here," he said to the monks who were his companions, "don't move and don't make a noise." Then, taking two of them with him, he walked straight to the crowd, brandishing the knife which he, as did other monks, always carried for use in daily work. He thrust back the peasants, who in their surprise stood still and made no attempt to stop him, climbed the hill and cut the sign of the Cross upon the rude heathen image. "I myself have seen and touched that carving," declared the author of his *Life*. By this time the crowd had lost its fear. Some of the peasants broke into angry shouts, some mocked with laughter, some, the older and better part, warned Samson to get speedily away. "It is only a game we learned from our fathers," they muttered. Just then a boy who was riding wildly round fell from his horse, struck the earth, hard and dry, and lay motionless. The noisy peasants again were silent, gathering around him. Samson seized his chance. He shouted to the crowd that their god could do no good, knelt down beside the lad, saw that he was only unconscious and already awaking, revived him with that rough skill which wandering monks of early days were often called upon to use, and won from these pagans a howl of praise for the power of the Christian magic.

Another of Cornwall's monks is St. Petroc. To those who study the *Lives* of St. Petroc and St. Cadoc it may well seem that Petroc, too, came from Wales to find the estuary of the Camel, to build his church at Padstow—Petroc-stow—to teach heathen men in Devon, as in Cornwall, and to convert Cornish chieftains. St. Carantoc, we may think, journeyed from Cardigan in Wales to found his church at Carhampton in Somerset, then onward to Cornwall, to reach by the estuary of the Gannel the Cornish coast near West Pentire headland, where the present village of Crantock honours him on the sixteenth of May. St. Mawgan may have come from Pembrokeshire to teach on the shore of Mawgan Porth, near the Bedruthan Steps to which Newquay now sends her visitors on holiday. And likewise a succession of monks from Wales crossed the water, to be honoured long afterwards in Cornwall as holy men.

7

Many Welshmen went, too, across the sea to the Channel Islands and thence to Brittany, the famous home of medieval saints. The fourth and fifth centuries had seen a constant going forth of British emigrants to this new Britain—Armorica, Brittany—lying across the Channel in France. Partly they went for the sake of adventure, partly in hope of trade and better living, and some in flight from Pictish, Scottish, or Saxon menace. Some had already fled before the Roman power long ago, when it settled in Britain. Life was hard in the new land; and monks in Welsh and Cornish monasteries felt a call to cross the Channel in the path of these fellow-countrymen, left without care for their souls.

In this work we find St. Samson of Wales a pioneer traveller and missionary. In Brittany he founded his monastery of Dol, and went on to build another at Pental, near Rouen, on the Lower Seine. Dol, where Samson was both abbot and bishop, later was to grow into a famous Breton see. Paul, known as Paul Aurelian and described, with Samson, in the tradition of South Wales as a student under Illtud, went from Wales to found the abbey which was to give birth to the diocese of Saint Pol-de-Léon. From Wales to Cornwall came also, we may think, St. Brioc, who then went on to Brittany to build his monastic centre, afterwards the bishopric of Saint-Brieuc.

These names, of course, are but a few among the multitude. The number of the wayfaring saints of Britain is uncounted, and there were very many who can find no mention here. Their *Lives*, written by those who looked back to them for inspiration are still at hand for our reading; but they are full of details certainly or probably untrue. Yet even though the detail is out of perspective, the background of the picture and its figures themselves come to us from a very real life.

CHAPTER FOUR

SAINTS OF CLONARD, MOVILLE, BANGOR AND CLONMACNOIS

Ireland in the Sixth Century

WHILE THE monastic life of saints was thus rising in Wales, history was also moving swiftly forward in the Irish Church. From the late fifth century, which saw the death of St. Patrick, to the seventh, we find a most remarkable change in Ireland. Gradually the rule of bishops in their dioceses yielded to the rule of Father Abbots, very many in number, exercising authority in monasteries settled here and there and everywhere, from the north to the south of the country. Each of these abbots held his own chief foundation: a mother house from which he journeyed constantly to visit and to order his whole *paruchia*, his family of daughter houses scattered over the land. Bishops, of course, there still were; but these bishops for the most part were attached to monasteries for the due carrying out of episcopal rites, for the celebration of sacraments proper to their function in the Church. They, with priests, clerics in minor orders, and lay brothers, made up the *familia*, the community under rule of the abbot in charge of all.

Not seldom, however, this abbot himself was in bishop's ordering. The Father Founder of a *paruchia* at his death frequently handed down his power, ecclesiastical and secular— and his secular power was very real—to the heir he chose as his successor, his *comarba*, a succession which in many cases lived on in a long line of all-important influence. These Father Abbots, too, not only ruled the mother house and its daughter communities. To them and to the priests under their monastic authority the layfolk of varying degrees within their districts, noble or artisan, farmer or peasant, looked for the sacraments, the guidance and the maintenance of their spiritual life, and very often for aid in earthly needs as well. Authority was shown, also, by the Father Abbot's marks of office. Each lived in his own " abbot's house " and was distinguished by his *bachall*, his pastoral staff, which he used at times with miraculous effect upon the hostile or insubordinate, and by the bell which he always carried with him to summon his monks to their prayer.

Thus the use and tenure of spiritual authority in Ireland differed in the sixth century from that of the episcopal rule in Wales. Yet the growth of monastic life was similar in each of these Celtic lands; and we may believe that both Wales and Scotland aided the Irish in their rising to that height of monastic order which was to be their glory in these early Middle Ages. Other regions of Britain, the lands which were to be called English, were too heavily beset at this time by the heathen Anglo-Saxon chieftains, the Anglo-Saxon kings of the future, to find peace or place for the developing of a stable monastic life within their own borders, to say nothing of the gift of aid elsewhere.

From Ireland Irish novices went across the sea to stay and to learn in Whithorn in Scotland, to train their minds and their bodies in the discipline of South Wales, under David at Menevia, under Cadoc at Llancarfan. Welsh monks also guided their boats towards Ireland. We read that Gildas of Wales went at the call of Ainmire, High King of Ireland about the mid-sixth century, to help the Irish Church; but not, as the monk of Ruis in Brittany who wrote the *Life* of Gildas in the eleventh century declared, because Ireland after St. Patrick's death had become a heathen land. Tradition likewise records that the Irish Church in this sixth century received a Liturgy of the Mass from saints of Wales, from David and Gildas, and probably from Cadoc also.

The monk's life, in Ireland as in Wales, was a hard one. Here, again, the hours of the day and many of the night were given, first, to prayer; secondly, to teaching, and to learning from word of mouth or from books; thirdly, to work with the hands. Prayer, of course, was always in the monk's mind. That nun of bold and firm counsel, St. Samthann, abbess of Clonbroney in Meath, once made brief answer to one who asked her what was the proper posture for prayer, prostrate on the floor, sitting, or standing? " Each and all of them," she said. But to a scholar who confided to her his resolution: " I am going to put away study and give my time to prayer," she retorted, " How then will you be able to learn concentration for prayer if you never keep your mind on books? "

Around the monastery lay the farm, where corn was planted and reaped, where browsed and roamed the cows, sheep, pigs and goats tended by the brethren. Lessons were doubtless often given in the open air to novices sitting on the grass of the fields. Here, as in Wales, they learned of the Scriptures, interpreted by the Latin Fathers, of the doctrine, law, liturgy, ritual, and monastic rulings of the Church. Latin was read by those who could absorb it, and monks skilled in art were glad to find young men who could be trained to add to the number of their manuscripts, written and illuminated in an art then rising to its own beauty and skill.

Here in Ireland, also, we find one daily meal of bread and vegetables, served in the afternoon. Fasting was not only observed at the proper seasons of the Church, but was very often welcomed at other times, either by the whole community or by individual members, as the twin sister of prayer, prayer in times of trouble, for themselves or for others in need. Confession of sin to the Father Abbot or, in the case of a novice, to the " senior " priest who directed his life, was a matter of frequent, sometimes of daily, practice. As Comgall, the abbot of Bangor on Belfast Lough, declared, for all these early Irish monks: " a man without an *anmchara*, a soul-friend, is a body without a head."

2

Ireland has always been a land of imagination, of vision, of fairies and pixies, of story and legend. It is very hard for those who now read the *Lives* of individual Irish monks of this early age to root out the poppies from the wheat, to separate legend from truth. Truth there is, in the record of names, of places, of journeyings. And even among the legends there lies truth in the background. From them we gain not only light upon the character of our saints, but light upon their customs, their way of living, their dwellings and their communities.

In general, these saints are described after a common pattern. Miracles attend their years on earth and the years that follow. The child, his early promise recognised, is given into the care of some good and learned man for his first training; the boy, if of noble birth, speedily and wonderfully exercises authority; if his parents are poor, he lives with them, at least from time to time, to guard the cattle on the home farm from straying, from attack by wolves; the youth leaves home, whether farm or noble castle or royal court, and wanders from monastery to monastery in search of his soul's ideal place of progress; he receives tonsure and habit as monk; he founds houses or cells of religion here and there, on an island, in a forest, or on a hilltop; at last, in his older years, he builds the monastery ever afterwards known by his name, and settles there to become Father, abbot and counsellor, of unnumbered souls.

3

The leader of these sixth century Irish saints in point of time was that Enda who owed his conversion of life to the teaching of his sister, the nun St. Faenchea. His name still lives on Aranmore, one of the Aran islands some thirty miles from

Galway. Tradition claims that Aengus mac Nadfraich, king of Munster, gave it to him for the founding of his religious house. Many monks of future fame lived and learned there under his stern direction. He himself, it was said, was taught at Whithorn.

He is now little but a name. A far clearer figure is St. Finnian, abbot of Clonard in Meath, on the river Boyne; renown knew him as " tutor of the saints of Ireland." Little thought he took for his body's comfort. His only indulgence was, now and then, a piece of broiled fish; his drink was a cup of beer, or milk and water; his bed was the bare earth, and a stone served him as pillow. One of his friends burst into tears as he sat by the Father, reading, and suddenly looked up to see as never before those bones bare of flesh, pressing hard against the thin habit, that robe filthy and unkempt.

Penitence was his delight. Very possibly it was he who wrote a document which we still have, called *The Penitential of Finnian*. A " Penitential " was a long list of penances, drawn up for the guidance of a confessor in assessing due and proper remedy for the sins told in his ear by his many and different penitents. Such lists formed a prominent part of the discipline of the churches of the early Middle Ages, among the Celts of Wales and Ireland and, later on, among the converted heathen, the Anglo-Saxons of England and the Germanic peoples of the Continent. It is very likely that Finnian drew Gildas of Wales into consultation regarding this work of his. The sins for which penance was here assessed make dark reading. They range from evil thoughts and quarrelling, from anger, envy, and greed, to perjury, theft, murder, lust and black magic. This Finnian of Clonard died in 549 and gave his life, men said, that he might save others in one of those recurring visitations of the Yellow Plague.

There is another St. Finnian in Irish records of this century. He was abbot of Magh-Bile, Moville, in County Down, north of Strangford Lough, and he was almost as famous as Finnian of Clonard. Books and study were his joy. Some modern scholars, indeed, believe that it was he who drew up that *Penitential of Finnian*.

More familiar among Irish monasteries, however, is the name of Bangor. Here, on Belfast Lough, St. Comgall ruled a monastery known in later time for a collection of prayers and hymns which we still can read, the *Bangor Antiphonary*. For fifty years, it was said, until about 602, Comgall was monk and abbot here; and his *paruchia* held three thousand men in various parts of Ireland. For a while he was head of a little house on Ely Island in Lough Erne, that lake which stretches northwards from Enniskillen in County Fermanagh of Ulster. There he set so severe an example of ascetic living that even his long-suffering monks could not survive; seven of them died from hunger and cold. Abbots of neighbouring houses finally came to beg him, for holy charity, to remit somewhat of his rule, and he listened to them. He allowed his community henceforward " to live and work as other monks were doing," but he made no concession to himself.

Every day as he went to work in the fields with his brethren he carried with him, as did many, his " chrismal," the little receptacle in which rested the sacred Host from the altar. Robbers refused to steal it from him, for they had heard that his God dwelt within it, and they feared the vengeance of this unknown Power. When he lay dying, nearly ninety years old, his monks wanted to bring him Communion every day; but he asked them instead to send for his " soul-friend," St. Fiachra, abbot at Ullard in Kilkenny, that from him he might receive strength and solace for the road. He loved all his monks, and he was sometimes troubled by the wide spreading of his charge. " Stronger is an army of many soldiers," he is said to have replied to those who urged him to build more houses, " acting in harmony on one field under the eye of their leader, than fighters scattered leaderless in many places throughout the land."

4

If the name of Bangor, Comgall's abbey, is more familiar, the story of the younger Ciaran is perhaps the most interesting in the monastic tradition of sixth century Ireland. He is not to be confused with Ciaran the Elder, whom we have seen as abbot of Saigir in Offaly, bound up in the tradition of St. Patrick's time. This younger Ciaran was born in Connaught shortly before the elder one died. He was the son of a skilled wheelwright or carpenter, and as a boy he watched carefully the cows and sheep on his parents' farm. But he was a sore trial, nevertheless, to his family, good and Christian as it was, for he was more than Irish in his hospitality and was for ever giving away the family property—a cow, a calf, a knife, a vessel of valuable workmanship—to the poor people who came to beg from him as he sat on a boulder in the meadow. The Lord, it must be said, regularly returned Ciaran's kindness in fourfold measure, and Ciaran could not change his ways. One evening, as he was coming home to supper from the fields, he met strangers who complained that they had asked his mother for food and had received but rude words. Her son strode rapidly on to the house and threw out all the food he could find, milk, butter and bread, to the dogs in the yard. It had been soured by the Devil's malice, he said, and was not fit for men.

His home was in County Roscommon of Connaught. Soon after this battle with his mother he fell into another difficulty. He was longing to join the pupils of Finnian of Clonard, for he had heard much of his wisdom in teaching the Scriptures. He therefore asked his mother to give him a cow to take to school with him, that he might have milk, at least, for he did not expect at once, he said, to be received within Finnian's monastery. His mother answered: " No; other boys in school don't have cows of their own." Ciaran said good-bye and started off on his long march. As he passed his parents' herd in the meadow, he laid his hand upon his favourite cow, and she followed him. The boy and his dun cow trekked across Ireland to Finnian's enclosure, and many hungry schoolfellows enjoyed her milk.

At Clonard he made rapid progress and received tonsure and habit as monk. Gradually Abbot Finnian began to ask aid from him in matters unusual and new, such as confront any monastery, ancient or modern. One day the abbot came with a problem not at all familiar. " Brother Ciaran," he said, " the daughter of the High King has journeyed to us from the Court at Tara. She is hoping to become a nun, and she wants to get some understanding of the psalms and other holy books. As you know, we have no guesthouse for women, and I am sending her to stay with a dependable, kindly widow who lives near. But would you for dear charity's sake let her read with you a while, until we can plan some sort of convent for nuns? "

So the two sat together day by day, the princess asking her questions and the monk explaining his Latin. After a long time Finnian remembered her, and he asked Ciaran what he thought of his pupil? " In truth, Father," said Ciaran, " I can tell nothing of her ways or her appearance; never, as God knows, have I looked upon her face or seen aught of her save the hem of her dress. Nor have we spoken one word to one another except in the reading."

At last Ciaran decided to move on to other schools. First he went to study under St. Enda upon his island of Aranmore, and then he crossed again to the mainland and journeyed south until he reached the estuary of the Shannon. There he stayed to learn in a monastery upon Scattery Island. Its abbot, who is also described as bishop, was St. Senan, a very learned scholar. He is still remembered on the island. Monks as visitors and men as aspirants he welcomed gladly to his abbey, but, unlike Finnian of Clonard, he would have nothing to do with women. His story tells that once a woman, a very holy one,

St. Cannera, as she drew near to death, asked of the Lord of heaven that she might receive the last sacraments and her burial on Scattery's shore, since Scattery had a great reputation for holiness as well as learning. Comforted in her belief that the Lord looked kindly upon her petition, she crossed the water. At his island's edge stood the abbot, for he had been told of this coming intruder by one of his monks, doubtless thrilled at the sight. With hand uplifted, holding firm his pastoral staff, " Depart hence," he commanded, " and plague not our peace." " But Christ has promised to receive my soul," Cannera pleaded. " Could you not give my body a place of rest? " " Your soul may be pure," retorted Senan, " but you are a woman. What have monks to do with women? Begone! " " I will die first! " answered Cannera. And die she did, then and there, upon the island's bank. The abbot could hardly refuse to commend her soul to God, and burial naturally followed his prayer.

From Scattery Ciaran went to Isel, " the low-lying place," from which the senior monks of its cells begged him to depart; " for we cannot keep and feed our brethren as long as you are here. You give away too much! " He packed his books in his wallet, hung it from his shoulder, blessed his unwilling hosts, and made for Hare Island, in Lough Ree, a widening of the Shannon north of Athlone. But this, he soon decided, was not his destination. Nor was his next halting-place, Mountain Height, on the bank of the Shannon. The monastery there was too comfortable. " No home for monks," he said. " My novices would have a hard time getting to heaven if I tried to teach them here." For ten miles, turning south again, he followed the Shannon. Then on its left bank he came upon a meadow in the midst of fen and forest land. Water, timber, fuel and food were there in plenty. There he built his abbey of Clonmacnois, and there his Feast is still kept on September the ninth.

He lived in Clonmacnois only a year, a year full of toil and perplexities. Many men came to learn of him, but many in other houses were jealous of his growing fame. In his last hours his monks, standing around his bed, asked him what they should do if trouble came upon them? Should they stay at Clonmacnois or should they go to some other place? " Hasten quickly, if trouble threatens, to other places," he said, " places of peace, and leave my relics here, as the dry bones of a deer on the hill. It is better for you to dwell with my spirit in heaven than near my bones here on earth, with stumbling in your feet." Then he asked them to carry him out to the hill which rose outside the monastery. There, as he looked up into the sky above him, " It is a path of dread," his monks heard him say, " but one must go." " And behold "—so wrote one of his followers after his death—" angels filled the road between heaven and earth, rejoicing to meet holy Ciaran."

Clonmacnois was to be one of Ireland's most famous monasteries, and its family of daughter houses grew as time went on until, men declared, it seemed that they would cover half the land.

5

It is good to think that at least some part of these stories, although we do not know exactly how great a part, is true. But let us turn for a moment to look at the legends, pure and simple, which fill the pages of the *Lives* of the Irish saints and are themselves full of interest. We find dreams and visions. Upon his island of Aranmore, St. Enda, the master, and Ciaran, his novice, both see a great and fruitful tree spreading its shade from the bank of the river Shannon over all parts of Ireland, from its inner country to the sea. " What does it mean? " asks Ciaran. " My son," answers Enda, " that tree is you yourself; for your renown will fill Ireland, and the grace of God in you will avail for its people far and wide." Bangor, too, has its vision. A guest staying there at Eastertide sees angels present at High Mass in its church, blessing now its altar, now the hands and lips and head of Abbot Comgall as he offers the Holy Sacrifice.

We find, of course, stories without end that tell the attraction possessed by these men of God for creatures of earth and water. Finnian of Clonard, when oxen are lacking, harnesses wild deer in the forest to a wagon loaded with timber. Fish of their own accord hasten to the shore near Bangor's monastery at Comgall's call when he is making ready for guests; the swans on its lake sing for him and fly to settle on his knee as he sits in meditation. A fox carries the Psalter across the fields back and forward between Ciaran, the boy, who cannot leave his cows, and his teacher, who is a monk and cannot leave his cell; the wind carries question and answer. Later on, when Ciaran is travelling from school to school, a deer runs into his path from the forest and takes upon its antlers the burden of his books.

Other tales reveal the brotherhood, the friendship which bound together these early monks of Ireland. There is one about St. Colman of Elo which may well be true. Once, when he was a young monk, horribly discouraged and feeling that he never would be able to work in Ireland because the Irish, his countrymen, were so difficult, he decided to cross from Ireland to Scotland, to visit St. Columba in Iona's monastery. St. Columba, Irishman though he was, had left Ireland for Scotland; perhaps he, Colman, had better do the same? He started out by boat, and on the way was caught in the currents of the dreaded whirlpool known as " Brecan's Cauldron." After a terrible crossing he arrived safe, but soaked to the skin. He was dried, warmed, and given the best supper which Iona could provide. Then Columba took his guest to his abbot's house for talk. " I heard, brother," he said, " that you were coming, and I was afraid you would be tossed by the Cauldron. So I gathered my brethren in the church and we prayed diligently. Now, then, don't be upset by that folk of ours across the sea; don't forsake your own Irish people! Feed them with words of sound doctrine and give them of the grace given to you. It was sheer necessity which drove me myself from

Ireland to Iona. Do you go back, so that Ireland may not lack the word of God." Colman went back and in course of time founded his own monastery at Lann-Elo, where Lynally now stands near Tullamore in Offaly of Leinster.

Another story of Colman's petition for aid from a brother monk is less convincing to the logic of this twentieth century. One day, the story goes, as he was wandering in search of an ideal settling place, he arrived at a house of religion at Killeshin, near Carlow in Leinster. Its brethren welcomed him cordially, but he did not find in them men to whom he could talk of his problems. They really were lamentably ignorant, it seemed to him, and before he knew it he was thinking about himself, of his own learning and knowledge of books. The thoughts were very savoury, and he lingered over them for quite a long time. Then suddenly a shutter seemed to fall before him, cutting off all light. He could remember nothing; he could think of nothing deep; all he had known so well a few minutes before, all had vanished out of his mind. He wrestled and writhed, but nothing came. He fell to prayer, for at least he could remember God in this dark night of the soul. At last, tired out, he slept, and dreamed that an angel was telling him to go and find St. Mochua. " The Lord of his mercy has heard your prayer," said the angel, " and Mochua will give you release from this punishment of your folly."

Mochua was abbot of Tech-Mochua, "the House of Mochua," near Timahoe, County Leix. Colman somehow found his road there. When he arrived, the abbot was working on his monastery's fields, a load of wood in his arms. As Colman came up to greet him, a little bird perched upon these saplings and trilled its song. " Do you know what it is singing? " asked Mochua. " Not a note," answered Colman. " Well, that is strange," replied his host, " for you are a learned scholar and I know nothing. It is telling that you have lost all your wisdom." " So I have, Father," said Colman miserably. Then he confessed his sin of pride to St. Mochua and all his memory came back.

Sometimes, we are told in these legends, aid comes to those in need through their friends who have departed this earth. There is a pleasant story of another answer to prayer given to this same Colman, long after he had founded Elo. Now, it tells, he had worked for very many years; he was old and tired, and he longed for rest. So he went off to Clonard in Meath, where in its abbey church Finnian, its Founder, lay enshrined. Its monks received him with the hospitality of those who welcome in each guest the Lord Christ Himself, and he was duly conducted to the guesthouse. In the dark silence before the hour of Matins, while all lay asleep, he crept out and across to the church. Its door was locked fast. " Most reverend Finnian," he whispered, " please, open the door for your fellow-servant in God." The door swung open. There stood Finnian, and Colman fell at his feet. " Father," he prayed, " I beseech you, entreat for me of the Lord that I may leave earth for the land beyond, this very year." St. Finnian comforted him: " Your prayer is heard; this year you shall be with Christ on high." Next morning Colman said good-bye to the monks of Clonard, and they all wondered what joy had suddenly come to light up his weary face.

Often practical aid is given by miracle. St. Comgall of Bangor encourages one of his monastery's boys who is trying hard to learn to write and can only make marks like scratches from a bird's claw. He blesses the child's hands, and the marks begin to make sense. Another such blessing for a monk who knows nothing of metalwork produces from him a beautiful pan for broiling fish for dinner.

On the other hand, punishment, equally miraculous, is dealt out, speedy and severe, for evil doers, such as we read about in the stories of St. Gregory the Great's *Dialogues* of this same sixth century. Comgall blesses the garden at Bangor, and sudden blindness falls upon thieves who break in at night to steal its fruit and vegetables. " Let them wander helplessly, O Lord," the wrathful abbot prays, " that they may know their guilt." He fasts and prays long hours in the darkness after sunset at the gates of a wicked chieftain. At midnight the earth quakes, the fortress quivers from its foundations, and the chieftain falls to his knees.

Here punishment looks forward to the repenting of the guilty. Sometimes, however, sin is condemned without mercy, without hope of redemption in this life. We find St. Finnian of Moville hurling fearful words of excommunication at the head of a " son of iniquity " who has thrown a spear to wound one of Moville's monks: " Thy flesh the birds of heaven will devour; thy bones, scattered here and there, the earth will not receive; thy wretched soul will go down for endless eternity to hell." Soon afterwards a wind from the south blows the sinner into a deep valley near the sea; his body is caught upon a sharp wooden stake, and he hangs there impaled until he dies. So, also, when a young chieftain of royal blood impiously disturbs Finnian by irreverent remarks as he is saying Mass, the abbot suddenly stops in the Liturgy, raises his hands high, and implores vengeance of the Lord. At once a huge hammer falls from scaffolding above and crushes the interrupter beyond human repair. Not only irreverent words, but untimely ones, bring Finnian's curse on men. King Tualthal Maelgarbh, the " Bald-Rough," who really existed and was killed about 543, during Finnian's lifetime, incurs, so Finnian's *Life* declares, sentence and prophecy of evil shortly before his death. He has been worrying the abbot with silly questions. " Where is hell? " he asks. " Is it on high or is it on the earth or below the earth? How wide and how deep is it? Is there a long distance between it and us? " At last Finnian loses patience. " I have not measured hell," he answers shortly. " But you will. You will know very soon how long or how short is the road that leads to it. Before this day ends, you will be in it."

Of course, Satan and his demons appear in these stories. At Bangor one evening Comgall from his abbot's chair saw a devil sitting at the refectory table in the seat of the monk who had charge of the monastery's food and wine. At this horrid sight the abbot was shocked beyond description. " What sort of a cellarer have we here? " he cried. Just then the cellarer himself appeared, gave one look, lifted his hand, and the devil fled. Comgall, Lord Abbot though he was, made his apology to his humbler brother.

6

Most famous of all, however, from the point of view of both the wanderings and the legends told of early Irish saints, is the marvellous story of St. Brendan, founder of Clonfert Abbey in Galway, west of the Shannon near Lough Derg. There are two St. Brendans. One was head of a monastery at Birr, not far from Clonfert. He was a loyal friend of St. Columba of Iona, and Columba bade his monks chant requiem Mass for him a few hours after he died. Our Brendan of Clonfert was also Columba's friend, and, according to Columba's *Life*, visited him in Scotland. Such a relatively brief journey, however, yields no reason or basis for the many-coloured robe of fantasy which time and imagination have woven around the figure of Brendan the Navigator, in a myriad of tales described in nearly every language of European culture, and annotated, too, by learned papers innumerable.

In the *Codex Salmanticensis* there is a text—late, but derived from the original *Life* of Brendan—which is of interest. Its story seems simple, compared with the Navigation legend, and appealing in its lesson of the monastic reality. It shows St. Brendan as a young student in Ireland, looking out over the ocean from a high hill near his home, and seeming, so he thought, to catch sight far out at sea of a lovely island, ideal for the hermit's life. Whereupon, it goes on to tell, he fasted and prayed until a voice came to him, promising that he should obtain this land of his desire.

With a few companions in three hidebound boats he set out. Many islands they passed, but all were stark and inhospitable. For five years they wandered over the sea, and at last they came to an isle barred everywhere by high cliffs. No entrance to its centre could they find, though for fifteen days they searched round and round. Upon its height they could see a church, and from the church came a sound of human voices singing in delightful harmony. Then from the cliffs there floated out to them a plank, which they caught, and read, carved on it, this message: " Do not labour to enter the island; for this is not your promised country. That you shall reach, in the end. But now go home. Your family wants to see you."

So Brendan went back to Ireland, where by his teaching he turned many people to God. Once again at length the lust of wandering tempted him, and again he set out in his boat. And after two years of further seeking he came to another lovely island. " Here," said he, " I shall surely stay; here is my place of rest." This time there appeared an old man, who said: " God has given it me to dwell here thirty years, that I may give you this message. The man who seeks his own desire is fighting the will of Heaven. As soon as the ninth hour has passed, do you go home, and teach the Irish the way of life."

St. Brendan said his Office and again went back to Ireland and there worked for seven more years. Then St. Ite, abbess of a house of nuns where Killeedy now stands in County Limerick, drove him on mission abroad. She had known him as a boy and had herself taught him three things well-pleasing to God: the faith of a clean heart; a simple life guided by religion; generosity of love. Now she begged him to go across the water to teach the ignorant, and he went. For a time he visited Gildas, the wise scholar of Britain, and, of course, Gildas gave him an altar for his Mass. Alas! on the altar he found a missal written in Greek, and Brendan knew no Greek. Nor could he remember, try as he would, the Latin Proper of the day. There were monks in the church, waiting for him to begin, and Brendan could not think what to do. In this dilemma he fell to prayer. At once the Lord opened to him the meaning of those Greek words, and he chanted them as though they were the Latin he knew so well. The writer of this story must have remembered the morning of Pentecost.

For months Brendan taught well and valiantly. Then at last he went back to Ireland, founded Clonfert and said of it: " Here is my place of rest; here I will dwell for all the time to come."

In Ireland he died. As he lay dying, he said to his brethren: " Commend my going forth to your prayers." And his sister, Briga, abbess of Annaghdown in Galway, asked him: " Of what are you afraid, Father? " " I am afraid," he answered, " if I go forth alone, if the road be dark. I fear to come into a place I do not know, to see face to face the King, to hear the sentence of the Judge." Then he gave the kiss of peace to his monks and said once more to Briga: " Remember me to my friends, and tell them to keep from unkind words, even be they true. For such are children of hell." So he went forth on his way, ninety-six years old.

Far different from this *Life* of St. Brendan, legendary as it is, appears the full-blown fable, the Christian *immram*, the romance of his voyaging. Here, in his long and baffling search for the Land of the Saints, the Land of Promise, Brendan comes to the Country of Fruit-trees and Perpetual Day, where no darkness falls; he passes the Isle of Mice; he reaches the Paradise of Birds; he sees an ocean full of monster fish; he is terrified by the griffin with great claws flying above his head; he hears the clang of the demon forges on the isle from which devils hurl molten iron at his boat; he anchors off the Isle of Dwarfs, little men with faces black as coal; he looks up at Satan alighting upon the prow of his boat; he comforts, by power of prayer, the tormented dwellers on the Isle of Fleas, fleas more numerous than the grains of sand along the seashore; he keeps Easter upon the back of a whale, mistaken for an island; in mid-ocean he comes upon Judas Iscariot floating upon a rock, tortured by demons from hell, and only of God's mercy given rest of peace on every Sunday, on the days of Christmas and Epiphanytide, of Easter and Pentecost, and on all Feasts of

Mary. Brendan prays, too, for him, and wins him one extra night of deliverance, while the devils in their fury swear to double their malice, once the holy man has gone.

It is interesting that St. Malo is said to have voyaged with St. Brendan in his search for this Land of Man's Desiring. His earliest *Life* declares him born in Wales. Story tells that it was he who kept everyone quiet on the supposed island during that Easter Mass, which happily had reached the *oratio Dominica* when the whale began to toss and shake. Later on, Malo took his boat to the coast of Brittany and became bishop of Aleth, the old Roman town, where now Saint-Servan stands in the estuary of the Rance. In after years the diocese was known by Malo's name, as is still known the Channel seaport familiar to all. There is still at St. Malo a chapel of St. Aaron, the hermit with whom Malo stayed, according to the story, when first he came to Brittany. Malo is usually identified with the St. Machutus whose Feast is celebrated on the fifteenth of November.

CHAPTER FIVE

SAINT COLUMBA; SAINT KENNETH; SAINT KENTIGERN

Scotland in the Sixth Century

THE SAINTS of sixth century Ireland not only travelled from place to place in Ireland, and from Ireland to Whithorn in Scotland, to Menevia and Llancarfan in Wales. It was in 563 that St. Columba left the Ireland of his birth to journey northwards in his boat and to land on that Scottish isle of Iona to which one sails from Argyll. Like his fellow Irish *peregrini*, he was seeking an island because he wanted solitude. Yet not complete solitude; for twelve of his followers went with him, since by this time he was an experienced monk and abbot.

With the *Life* of Columba, although much story of miracle and marvel still meets us, we are entering the plains of history. Now, indeed, we find ourselves on ground mapped out by scholarship, ground easier to follow than the hills and valleys of medieval tale. The description of Columba's youth and earlier manhood, spent in his own Ireland, shows us a man of character intensely mixed, caught in a turmoil of aims and longings which were constantly at war one with another. On the one hand, he came of the blood of Ireland's High Kings, and he never forgot it. Anger in his time rose high and fierce between Irish chieftains; and Columba, born among the glens of Donegal in the north, passionately proud of his lineage and of his northern kinsmen of the clan of Niall, vitally concerned in all that concerned them and in nothing of a neutral mind, was always ready to defend, probably with excess of zeal, what he held right and just.

We are told of a quarrel of his with Diarmait, High King, and head of the southern branch of the Niall. Diarmait, we read, had put to death a youth who in his wrath had killed one of the king's nobles and had fled to Columba for sanctuary. Diarmait, also, as we read in a tale perhaps more famous than true, had forced Columba to yield his precious copy of a manuscript, a copy of a roll belonging to St. Finnian of Moville. Columba had carried off this roll to copy it for his own benefit, and had done the work in secret, no permission asked or given. The manuscript was doubtless very precious; perhaps it was one of the Vulgate text of St. Jerome, for the *Life* of St. Finnian declares that he " first brought the Gospel to Ireland." At any rate, Finnian was exceedingly angry at this presumption. He referred the matter to the High King himself, and Diarmait gave judgment that Columba must return this copy to the owner of the original, adding those words so well known: " To every cow belongs its calf, to every book its copy."

Tension, the story goes on, between the rival clansmen of North and South rose in Ireland to pitched battle, fought probably at Cooldrevne, near Sligo. So horrified were Irish churchmen at this war between the folk of one and the same race, and this their own, that they gathered in judgment at Teltown in Meath to excommunicate Columba for inciting his followers to the crime of murder. In this assembly St. Brendan of Birr rose with angry protest to defend his friend: " If you knew how God honours this man," he stormed, " you would never have done this to him."

How much of this story is true? We shall do well to see what Adamnan, ninth abbot of Iona, wrote between 679 and 704, in his *Life* of Columba. Here he does tell of a battle of clansmen in Ireland. He even tells of sentence of excommunication passed upon Columba. But he declares it was due to " certain venial and very excusable reasons," and says nothing of the battle as its cause. Nor does he give the legend, told elsewhere, that

St. Molaisse, the hermit of Devenish, " Ox Island," in Lough Erne, bade Columba leave his native Ireland in penance for his sin. He merely writes: " In the second year after the battle of Cooldrevne, and the forty-second of his life, Columba set out for Britain, *pro Christo peregrinari volens*—willing for the love of Christ to live as a stranger abroad."

One would gladly believe, then, that it was the other side of Columba's character which sent him across the water to his Scottish isle, the free will of a dedicated spirit rather than the force of condemnation and of penance prescribed. From childhood he had been eagerly Christian. He, too, had wandered from school to school in Ireland, seeking his " place of resurrection," at Moville, at Clonard, at Glasnevin, near Dublin. When he held himself ready, he had founded his own Irish abbeys, of Derry on the Foyle and of Durrow, near Tullamore. Derry, Daire-Calgaich, " the Oak-Wood of Calgach," was built in the country of the northern descendants of Niall, where Londonderry stands in Ulster. Durrow, Dair-mag, " Oak-Plain," held its monks amid the clansmen of the southern branch, in Offaly. Its name is remembered for the *Book of Durrow*, a text of the Gospels first written, it would seem, by Columba himself, and now represented for us by a copy made in the eighth century, in Northumbria, but under Irish influence.

2

In 563, then, Columba reached his little island of Iona, separated from Mull by a strait only a mile wide. He was never an exile from his own land as St. Patrick had been. Repeatedly he journeyed back from Scotland across the narrow sea to care for the Irish portion of his scattered *paruchia*. He never lost his part in the history of the Ireland of his time, secular as well as churchly. In 575, some twelve years after he had left his native country, he was there at the Assembly of Druim Ceat, near Derry, to take action for the settling of the boundaries of

Ireland's kingdoms, to fight with all his power in defence of Ireland's bards, the *filid*, to defend their Irish annals and the poetry which he loved.

A second reason which may well have been in Columba's mind as he left his Irish home for Iona in 563 springs from history. In the last years of the previous, the fifth century, chieftains of the House of the High Kings of Ireland had come with their followers from its north-east, from a region of County Antrim known as Dalriada, northwards by sea to Scotland, to conquer and to found in Argyll a new Irish-Scottish kingdom, a new Dalriada. These chieftains were of Columba's kindred. It was natural that in seeking an island monastery he should settle on one off Argyll's coast, one from which he could teach and minister to these kinsmen of his. His interest was rewarded. It was Conall, king of this Scottish Dalriada in Argyll, who allowed him to possess Iona in peace; and at a later time, about 574, Columba himself in his own Abbey Church on the island blessed and consecrated Conall's successor, Aedan, son of Gabran, as Dalriada's king. He did more. As time went on, kings fell to quarrelling, in Ireland and in Scotland, over the rule of this newer Dalriada in Argyll; and Columba worked hard to bring about harmony between them as he journeyed to and fro.

There was yet a third motive, a third labour. These men of Dalriada in Argyll had lately been attacked by the Picts of the North, who occupied the land stretching northwards from the Tay valley to Loch Ness. We have already met the Picts of the South, converted by St. Ninian in the fifth century. These northern Picts were still pagan when Columba came to Scotland, and, as St. Bede tells us, he was for them " the first teacher of the Christian faith."

Their king at this time was fierce and powerful, Brude by name. He held his stronghold near Inverness. There he was surrounded by his men of war, and—far more formidable for Columba in his zealous thought of teaching heathen Picts—by the Druids, who were Brude's counsellors, his wise men, entirely determined to keep untouched by outside interference their pagan ritual and its mystery of magic.

But neither mountain barriers nor Druid magic deterred one of a royal house of Ireland. Moreover, as Columba well knew, Brude was not only a heathen soul. He was a chieftain who held power of menace over the monastic settlement upon Iona; at any time he might descend upon its monks to pillage and to drive them from their rising walls. Almost directly, then, after his landing on the island, Columba started out on his long, most difficult and dangerous journey north, partly by boat, partly by mountain trails. Story has it that two friends from Ireland went with him. One was St. Comgall, whom we have seen as abbot of Bangor. The other was St. Cainnech, another Irish monk, a great friend of Columba and Comgall, often welcomed in Bangor and in Iona. His *Life*, full of legend, tells of their adventures. Once, it relates, when they were together, whether in Ireland or in Scotland we do not hear, the three were caught in a storm of rain and sleet. Soon Comgall and Columba were wet through; but, to their great surprise, Cainnech, who was standing beside them, was entirely dry and warm. " What does this mean? " they asked. " Tell me," said Cainnech, " what were you thinking about when the storm broke over us? " " I," said Columba, " was concerned for my monks, in danger on the sea." " My mind," said Comgall, " was worrying over my brethren at work upon the harvest." " Well," said Cainnech, " the Son of Mary knows that my mind was with the angels in heaven."

St. Cainnech, who is known in Scotland as Kenneth, founded abbeys in both Ireland and Scotland. His chief monastery was built at Aghaboe, once Achad-bo, " the field of the cow," in the land of Ossory where Ciaran the Elder had worked.

On the bank of the river Ness the three abbots came to the great gates of Brude's fortress, held by sentinels and fast barred. But the guards knew a chieftain when they saw him, even in a monk's habit. When they heard Columba's short, sharp command, the gates flew open. Behind them stood King Brude himself, his sword raised to strike, and behind him his Druid priests and his warrior lords. Columba looked at St. Cainnech. "Your turn," he said. Cainnech lifted his hand and slowly in the air made the sign of the Cross. The Pictish king, overcome by this ritual, in fear of some deadly spell, lowered his sword, drew back, and the visitors entered.

No such easy victory could be won over the Druids, counsellors of Brude, as they had been counsellors for his forerunners on the Pictish throne. Most formidable of all was their leader, Broichan the Magus, weaver of magic. Victory was to come at last, but only after long time and effort. Its story is a lively one: of Columba again and again crossing sea and loch and mountains on his way north; of his power shown among the Picts, against sickness, against evil spirits of storm on lake or sea; of his voice like a peal of thunder chanting the psalms of the Church, chants of which the Picts did not understand one word, which they heard as incantations drawing down some dread fate upon themselves and their possessions; of Columba at other times trying with gentle and kindly manner, with an interpreter at his side, to make them understand what he was so anxious to tell. At last, however, the Christian faith took root among Brude's people, and the king allowed Columba's monks to hold Iona in peace.

3

When we turn to look at Columba himself, we see in him everywhere the man of Celtic race, in Iona as in Ireland, his mind quick to reflect both darkness and light. Darkness often knew his wrath. With loud blast of anger he terrified even the monster of the Ness, which not long before had torn to pieces one of the Picts who was swimming the river. Columba arrived at the river and found that its boat was moored to the bank opposite; at once he told one of his monks to swim across and get it. The brother was in mid-course when suddenly to the horror of those who were watching, this shark, serpent, or dragon rose to the surface and rushed to devour. Columba did not hesitate a moment. He sent up to the Lord the quick fury of his prayer, shouted with all his might, saw the monster stop in its course, taken by surprise, and his fellow-monk scrambling in safety up the other side. It was Columba, too, who rushed straight into the sea off Ardnamurchan in Argyll, up to his knees, calling to Heaven to fall upon the man, the criminal, even then with mocking laughter rowing away from him with plunder stolen from one of Iona's friends, one who could ill afford such loss. The man of murder, the man of evil lust, the treacherous, the niggardly, he clearly saw and denounced as the victim of demons, in dire danger of hell through his own fault.

Often Columba sat on the beach of Iona, copying the script which was his joy, and, it was said, writing his own verse now and then. The verse, if it be his, reflects his thought on God and man. In the hymn *Altus Prosator*, which has come down to us under his name in a Latin barbarous and confused, self-conscious and laboured, such as the Celts toiled happily to write, there is no passage more vivid than that which describes the Day of Doom:

> *The Day of God's provings, King over kings,*
> *The Day of His anger loud, darkness and cloud,*
> *The Day of the thunder's sound, heard in the heavens around,*
> *The Day in mourning clad, bitter and sour and sad.*
> *When women's love lies dead, and men now have fled*
> *All lust and petition of this world's ambition.*

> *Then stand we shall trembling before the Lord's judging*
> *To account for our actions, our sins, law's infractions;*
> *Then shall we see nearby our wickedness clearly,*
> *The book of our conscience shall look in our face.*
> *Into weeping we break forth, all hope we forsake,*
> *Gone now is the hour once held in our power.*

When we think of the splendour of the *Dies Irae* of the thirteenth century, these lines, even in Columba's Latin, are uncouth, their rhyming is crude, their whole runs joltingly with strange and jarring sound. Yet their fear-compelling thought is entirely the same.

From his monks Columba exacted strict obedience to the letter, as to the spirit, of rule. Once, we read, the hour of prayer in Iona's church was at hand, and search was made for him. It was the ritual that he, as abbot, should ring his abbot's bell. But he could not be found. At last the brother next in rank, Baithene, a kinsmen of Columba who afterwards succeeded him as abbot, ordered that the Office should begin. All were busily chanting psalms when Columba entered the church, his face red as fire and his eyes flashing in anger. Baithene fell to his knees. " I will not judge you," said the abbot; " go to Father Cainnech for judgment."

Cainnech was in his Irish monastery; long and painfully the unhappy Baithene travelled to find him. There Cainnech bade him return home in peace. " Your journey," he said, " has been penance enough. But remind your abbot, Columba, of that day when he and Comgall and I in Ireland were furiously fighting the Devil for the soul of a bishop, yes, a bishop, falling right before our very eyes into mortal sin, and how upset we were when just as we seemed to be getting the victory, our abbot rang his bell and we had to turn to the prayers laid down for the day."

Yet, when his monks were tired or worried, it was Columba who encouraged them. When they came in weary from the fields, he was there, ready with refreshment. He was always anxious if they were late in returning from a mission, especially if they had gone by sea. He held out peace to the penitent, help to the poor. He sent men to hunt from his hiding-place the robber who had killed and carried off some of the seals fed by Iona's monks on a little isle near their home. The thief pleaded hunger; and Columba at once ordered several of Iona's sheep to be killed and carried to his boat as a gift.

Scholarship, which kills as readily as it gives life, has not left untouched the story of Columba's last day on earth, the story of the old white horse which carried Iona's milk-pails from its cowshed to its cloister and which on this Saturday afternoon came up to him as he sat under the Cross near the barn and laid its head on his breast, its eyes full of tears. Did not the horses of Achilles, the scholars remind us, weep that their charioteer was slain by Hector? Did not Xanthus, his favourite of all horses, warn Achilles himself that soon he, too, must die?

One wonders whether Adamnan, who told Columba's story, was thinking of Greek epic when he wrote it down. Anyone who for long has owned a horse, or a dog, or a cat, has felt its uncanny sense of trouble in the air. These early monks knew beasts and birds better than most of us who walk in streets and market-place. Perhaps we may believe the story of the bird, the crane, driven by winds upon Iona's shore. One of the brothers found it, almost dead, and by his abbot's command gave it special care. Columba was sure, he said, that it had come from his own Irish land. After three days, it was set at liberty, rose on its wings, wheeled a moment in the air, and then flew off towards the Irish coast.

4

Many times we are reminded of the affection Columba's friends bore him. St. Cainnech was one day sitting at dinner in his Irish abbey when word came that Columba was on his way there from Scotland and that a storm was blowing hard. Cainnech so quickly left his dinner for his prayers in the church that he left one of his shoes behind him.

Another friend of Columba was of Scotland by birth, St. Kentigern, famous as the founder of Glasgow's church. Tradition, written down towards the end of the twelfth century in Kentigern's *Life* by Jocelin of Furness, a *Life* also full of legend, told that as a boy Kentigern had been taught by St. Servan, who had a school at Culross on the Firth of Forth. Those schooldays are pictured in the legends which men of Glasgow still remember: the tale of the bough of hazel, which burst into fire in Kentigern's hands to rekindle the lamps of the church at Culross, extinguished by his jealous mates; the tale of the robin redbreast, Servan's special joy, which the same boys in malice had torn to pieces, its head from its body, and declared it was Kentigern's doing, until Kentigern by his prayer gave back to the robin healing and life.

As a child, we are told, Servan called him " Munghu." Professor Jackson, in his article, *The Sources for the Life of Rt. Kentigern*," page 301 (see the Bibliography at the end of this book), suggests that " *Munghu* is a Cumbric ecclesiastical nickname." It is still recalled in Kentigern's other and more familiar name of " Mungo."

The legends given by Jocelin relate that Kentigern at last left his master, Servan, and journeyed south towards Glasgow, where he is found a bishop, established in his episcopal seat on the bank of the little stream of the Molendinar. At some time, we read, a king in southern Scotland, Morcant by name, drives him forth to cross the border and to stay a while in Cumberland. From Cumberland he is said to have gone on to visit St. David at Menevia, and to dwell in Wales in a monastery where now the Cathedral of St. Asaph stands. Further story, in no way founded on fact, adds that the Cathedral gained its dedication from an Asaph who was a pupil of Kentigern and eventually became bishop in that place. Under the protection of a friendly ruler, Rhydderch Hael, king of Dumbarton, he is enabled to return to Scotland and to work as bishop on the bank of the Annan river, near its flowing into Solway Firth. After some time he is found once more in his own see at Glasgow.

There another legend finds him receiving a visit from Columba, who has come from Iona to talk on many things with this man of wisdom and renown. It is, we are assured, a wonderful meeting. Unhappily, as the two sit, deep in their problems, some of Columba's company, smitten with envy, steal and kill the very choicest ram from Kentigern's flocks. Kentigern is, however, a saint. All ends well; and the two pioneers, of Iona and of Glasgow, give each to the other his pastoral staff when they say good-bye. The staff which Columba has given to Kentigern is found afterwards among the treasures of St. Wilfrid's abbey at Ripon.

Further story of this saint of Glasgow is wrought into the arms of the city; a story common in ancient fairy tale. A queen yields to temptation and bestows upon her young lover the ring of her true and royal lord's gift. Her guilt is revealed to this monarch, who draws the ring from the young man's finger as he lies asleep, throws it into the Clyde, and his queen into prison. In her despair, doomed to death by her king and husband, she sends a message to Kentigern, imploring him to save her. Kentigern orders the messenger to go fishing in the Clyde; a salmon is caught and within it is found the ring. This is at once taken in triumph by the wife to her husband, who promptly sets her free.

For a thorough sifting of the small amount of truth from this mass of legend which has grown up around the name of Saint Kentigern, founder of the church of Glasgow, the reader is referred to Professor Jackson's study.

5

We come to Columba's last days. Twice, we are told, he had longed to die but his hour had not yet arrived. Two of his monks, standing one morning at the door of his cell at Iona, saw his face light up with joy, then quickly cloud over in sadness. " What is it, Father? " they asked. For a while there was no answer. Then at last, because he saw that they were much concerned, he said: " Thirty years to-day I have been in Britain, and long ago I prayed that at this time God would call me hence. Only a moment since His angels were near, ready to bear my soul on its way. But even while they waited just now He ordered them to turn back heavenwards. The prayers of my churches are stronger than mine; they will keep me here on earth four more years." The literal truth, probably, is that in 593 Columba, while his monks in Scotland and Ireland prayed for him day and night, nearly died of some grave sickness.

The four years passed, and now it was May, 597. Old and weary, for he had passed his seventy-fifth year, Columba drove in the monastery's wagon to see the work of his monks on the western side of his island. "A month ago," he said to them, "at Paschaltide, I longed to go forth; but I would not make your Easter sad." Then, turning his face to the east, he blessed Iona for all time to come.

On his last Saturday, June the eighth, he sat over his copying of script, and reached verse eleven of the thirty-third Psalm:

Inquirentes autem Dominum non minuentur omni bono;

They that seek the Lord shall not lack any good thing.

"Here," he said, "is the place for me to stop. Let Baithene write the rest." Just after the midnight bell had sounded for Office, the monk Diormit, who watched over him continually, found him lying alone in the darkness before the altar of the church. He took him in his arms as he lay. The brethren entered and stood around them, lanterns in their hands. Diormit helped Columba to raise his hand in a last blessing, and then on this Sunday morning he went to his rest.

Adamnan, in his *Life* of Iona's founder, has described for us Iona's memory of its Saint:

"Of mind most acute and exceedingly shrewd, he lived and fought upon the island for thirty-four years. Not an hour passed that was not spent in prayer, or reading, or writing, or work of some kind. In fastings and watchings unwearied, he laboured by day and by night, under burdens so heavy that each single one seemed beyond the power of man. And amid all this he was loved by all, his face always gay, glad in his secret heart with the joy of the Holy Spirit of God."

Columba's monastery of Iona lived on to win wide renown; to carry on long conflict with the Rome it revered, and in 716 to submit, at least in part, to Roman ruling; to send its teachers southwards to convert the English of Northumbria.

CHAPTER SIX

SAINT OSWALD; SAINT AIDAN;
SAINT CUTHBERT

Northern England in the Seventh Century

WE COME, then, from Scotland to the land of the English in Northumbria, to trace the influence of the monastery of Iona upon northern England, and therefore to look at three of the saints of this English North Country: a king, Oswald, who worked hand in hand with his bishop, Aidan, and Cuthbert, who at a later time owed much to Aidan's work and its legacy in his own life as monk and bishop.

The land of Northumbria, reaching north of the Humber to include a considerable part of southern Scotland, especially on the east, consisted in the late sixth and the early seventh century of two kingdoms, Deira and Bernicia, at times held separately by two English rulers, at other times united in the hands of one king. The union of the two kingdoms under one ruler was first brought about in the early seventh century by Ethelfrith, a man of high ambition. He had founded his power by marrying the daughter of a king of Deira and by driving into exile her brother, Edwin, Deira's rightful heir. Then he had proceeded to extend his rule over Bernicia. Under him Northumbria was still heathen, clinging to the religion of its Saxon kinsmen on the Continent.

While Ethelfrith was thus securing this northern kingdom, young Edwin was steadily waiting for his hour of revenge. In his exile from his own Deira he had wandered for long years, a fugitive in remote places, until at last he had come into East

Anglia, the land of Norfolk and Suffolk. He had found hospitality in the household of its King Raedwald, just at this time reaching his long cherished aim of becoming the most powerful ruler in southern England. Raedwald decided that it was well to protect and to aid this young heir; and Edwin remained safe, in spite of repeated attempts on the part of Ethelfrith to get hold of the refugee whom he feared and hated. At last, in 616, Raedwald judged that his power might reach out over the North. He marched against Ethelfrith, to defeat and to kill him in a great battle near the river Idle, on the borders of the shires of Nottingham and York.

In this way by Raedwald's strength Edwin became king of all Northumbria; but by his own, after Raedwald's death, he gradually gained supremacy of power among English rulers, both of north and south. He married a daughter of Ethelbert, to whose kingdom of Kent Augustine, known later on as saint of Canterbury, had come in 597 bringing the Christian faith from Rome to England. The bride came northwards with her Christian bishop, Paulinus, and in 627, partly through the persuasion of his wife, partly of Paulinus, partly of the Pope himself, Boniface the fifth, and partly because he believed that aid from a Christian Heaven had delivered him from his enemy, Ethelfrith, Edwin received Christian baptism.

It is not surprising that he, too, had enemies. His English neighbours hated his increasing power; the British hated the English who had occupied Britain; the heathen longed to drive out this new Christian religion. In 632 Edwin lay dead, and very many of his strong men were either dead with him or scattered in flight after a desperate battle in Hatfield Chase, part of the land of the Idle and other streams flowing to the Humber, the land which had seen Edwin's victory over Ethelfrith. The march against him had been led by Cadwallon, " King of the British," who held his seat of rule in Gwynedd, North Wales, and was " vowing that he would blot out the whole race of the English within the borders of Britain "; and by Penda, the heathen king of Mercia, the English

94

midlands. It was the twelfth of October, and Edwin was forty-seven years old.

Upon this tragedy the newly born Church of Northumbria was threatened with collapse. Its work had only gone on for five years under the consent of its king, and very many men of its land were still pagan. Paulinus, its bishop, fled back to Kent with Edwin's widowed queen; two kings, who had been Christian but hastened now to renounce their allegiance, succeeded to Edwin's rule, one in Deira, one in Bernicia; only one man, James, a deacon of the Church, remained at his post to uphold Christian work beyond the Humber. The next year, 633, Cadwallon struck again, and killed, one after the other, both those "apostate kings." Northumbria was thus left without ruler both in Court and in Church.

2

Now Oswald rises before us. He was not, it is true, a wayfaring saint; yet some picture of him is needed to throw added light on those many wayfarers for whom he made Christian journeyings not only fruitful but possible.

He was a son of the King Ethelfrith whom Raedwald had killed in war, and since that day he had judged it wise to live in exile. Some of this time of exile he had spent with the monks of Iona, who had led and baptized him into the Christian faith. Now he saw the two kings of Northumbria—one was his brother, the other his cousin—dead at the Welsh Cadwallon's hands. It was an opportunity for great daring. Towards the end of 633 he gathered all the fighting men he could muster, and they were few, and led them out to meet the British king and his great army.

Long afterwards folk of the North remembered and told the story of the battle. Its field lay on the moorland hard by the Roman Wall, not far from Hexham; its name has come down to us as *Hefenfelth*, "Heavenfield." Here Oswald encamped.

This done, he bade his men cut wood from trees on the moor and fashion it into a Cross, then dig a pit for its securing. He himself held the Cross in both hands while they made firm and fast the earth around its base. Then, as all looked upon their work standing high upon the moor, he gave the word: " Let us all kneel and together pray the Lord of life and truth and power that in His pity He defend us from this proud and savage enemy. Well does He know that for the saving of our people we have come to this just war."

Dreams of leaders who face their fate in battle are frequently described in legends of the past. None the less it may well be true, as we read, that while Oswald was asleep in his tent upon the moor that night, it seemed to him that a great light shone around, and in the midst of it was standing the revered Founder at whose grave on Iona he himself had so often knelt in prayer. " To-morrow night go forth from thy camp to war," St. Columba said in this dream. " The Lord has promised me that your enemies shall be driven to flight, that Cadwallon shall be given into your hands, that you shall return home with victory and shall reign in joy." In the morning Oswald told his chieftains of the vision, and all his men, pressing around him, shouted aloud that, did it so come to pass, they would receive forthwith the Christian God in baptism.

In the darkness before dawn on the next day they rushed to the fight, and all came about as the dream had foretold. Failbe, abbot of Iona forty years later, solemnly declared that he had heard Oswald telling this vision to one of his predecessors, Abbot Seghine, who was ruling Iona when the battle took place. Cadwallon's army of Welshmen was completely defeated; Penda and his men of the English midlands were given cause to fear; and all Northumbria in its joy of victory promptly crowned Oswald, one of its own royal house, as its ruler and king.

3

For eight years he ruled, and then Penda found his chance. In 641 he met Oswald in battle at " Maserfelth," possibly Oswestry, " Oswald's Tree," in Shropshire, killed him and crushed his army.

It is natural to compare the thought of Oswald of the seventh century in Northumbria with that of Alfred of the ninth in Wessex of south-west England. Both delivered their lands and their people from enemies in noteworthy and decisive battles; Oswald was honoured by sainthood; Alfred deserved it. We hear, however, much of Alfred's enlightened work for the secular governing, protecting, ruling, and educating of his West Saxons; of this we do not read much in Bede's description of Oswald. Bede is instead deeply concerned with Oswald as one of England's holy men; but even so we miss in his narrative the precise details which Alfred's *Life* gives us of his spiritual custom and practice. Oswald, however, was only thirty-seven when he fell in battle. It is true, also, that we find in Bede this king of Northumbria travelling south to Wessex to receive from the font of baptism as his spiritual son in the Lord its king, Cynegils, whose daughter he then took as his bride. We read how he held communion with God day after day in the dark hours of the morning, from shortly after midnight until sunrise; how his spare moments, snatched here and there, were given to the same devotion, in petition, in offering of thanks; how, whenever he was sitting, whatever his business, all unconsciously he held his hands palms upwards on his knees, as though in prayer. At the last moment of that last battle, the story went, when his soldiers were surrounded by Penda's army and he knew that he must die, he commended to the Lord of Heaven the men who fell at his side. English folk as they looked back upon the battle spoke of this: " ' God have mercy on men's souls,' said King Oswald, as he was struck down on that day."

At once Oswald was honoured as hero, saint, and martyr. Every year on the day before he died the brethren of the church of Hexham came to the place of battle to keep the Vigils of the Dead, and early on the morning of the day itself, the fifth of August, there on the moor they offered their Eucharist in thanksgiving for his work among them. There a church was built. Miracles without number were told of as brought about by his intercession. And not only in Britain and in Ireland, but on the Continent, in Germany, Italy, Switzerland, the Netherlands. More than sixty churches since his time have been dedicated in England in his name.

As king, indeed, all men did not own his power, even in land bordering on Northumbria and subject to its influence. Some thirty or more years after his death his niece, Osthryth, wife of Ethelred, king of Mercia since 675, wanted to lay his relics, for the homage of monks and pilgrims, in Bardney Abbey, Lincolnshire, a monastery held by both the king and his queen in special reverence and affection. At sunset, Bede tells us, the wagon carrying the relics arrived at the Abbey gates. Its monks flatly refused to receive them. They knew quite well, they said, that Oswald was a saint. But as a king he had acted like no saint; he had come from outside their borders to take rule over them, and even after his death they still felt him an alien to them and their land. Lindsey, the old kingdom which covered northern Lincolnshire, did not care for control by the neighbours, Northumbria and Mercia, which in turn seized its rule.

Darkness came on at Bardney, and the escorts spread a rough tent of protection over the precious relics, left them in their wagon outside the Abbey gates, slept and kept watch in turn. For the monks, however, there was no dark for sleep, no peace for prayer. All night long they saw a radiance of splendour glowing from earth to heaven above the wagon outside. At break of day they went to the escorts to beg and implore that King Oswald's bones might be enshrined among them; for now they were certain that he was beloved by God. Their prayer was welcome; the monks laid the relics to rest and hung a banner woven of purple and gold high above the holy place.

4

It is Oswald's work for the conversion of his people to Christianity which especially draws our interest in the pages of Bede. Very soon after he had been acclaimed king in the lands of Northumbria during the winter of 633-634, he began the labour which, he hoped, would bring not only his fighting men to the fulfilment of the pledge made by them on the eve of Cadwallon's slaying, but all his kingdom into the Christian Church. He sent, therefore, a request to the monks of Iona, in whose abbey he himself had been baptized. Would they give him a bishop who would travel around his lands to preach and to win the heathen?

Promptly Iona did as he asked. But the man whom its monks sent to Northumberland was strict in his demands and hard upon the mass of the ignorant and the indifferent. He could not win them; soon hardly anyone was listening to him or heeding his words. After a while he returned to the island monastery and reported to its elder brethren that he could do no good in Oswald's kingdom, that its people were dour, stubborn, and barbarous. The report struck dismay. What was to be done? What other man could be sent to such discouragement? In the worried silence one of those present looked towards the speaker. " It seems to me, brother," he said quietly, " that you were too hard upon those unlearned folk who came to hear you; that you did not do as the apostles did, feed them first on the milk of easier lessons, so that step by step they might grow strong to receive more perfect doctrine and carry out the higher biddings of God."

The monk's name was Aidan. All eyes at once turned to him; and soon he was consecrated bishop for King Oswald and his Northumbria.

5

Under its last bishop, Paulinus, the people converted in Northumbria had received the teachings and the custom, in matters both great and small, of the Church of Rome, as followed by the daughter Church of Canterbury from which, as we saw, Paulinus had come. Aidan, however, trained and taught in the monastery of Iona, brought to Northumbria, not a different faith, but a different practice and discipline.

The monastery of Iona, with its daughter houses, and these became many as time went on, belonged to what is called the Celtic Church of the sixth and following centuries, the Church found in Ireland, in Wales, in Scotland. In matters of doctrine, in reverence, it acknowledged the headship of Rome; it acknowledged and confessed the Christian, Catholic faith taught from Rome, and from Canterbury, a see of Rome's making. In lesser matters, however, in those of ritual, of calendar, it held its own independent practice. The Celts also held themselves independent in the governing of their abbeys; we read nowhere that Columba appealed to Rome for permission, for guidance, in the building of Iona's monastic settlement. As is well known, they kept their Easter at a different date, obtained by different calculation from that observed by Rome, and by Canterbury in following Rome. Their monks were at once recognised by their different manner of tonsure; the Roman use prescribed a rounded shaving of the crown of the head, the Celtic use made a shaven path across the head, from ear to ear.

These points seem slight. Nevertheless, obedience was obedience; it was a matter of the spirit, not of the importance to men's minds of the detail concerned. Deeper division was made by the Celtic insistence upon intensity of ascetic discipline for monks, by the Celtic austerity which forbade richness and a splendour of adornment in churches, and by the relative simplicity of Celtic ritual. All these diversities were passionately prescribed by Celtic ordinance and followed by British and Irish alike.

It was this difference from Roman ritual and discipline, this British and Irish usage, which now under Aidan marked the Christianity, the monasticism, of Northumbria, and which he taught men to practise in a kingdom where once, under Edwin and his bishop Paulinus, the Roman way had been the rule.

6

Aidan arrived in Northumbria, probably in 635. The friendship which grew firm and lasting between him and his king is described by Bede in his *History*. Soon he was journeying around his great see, through town and country, and always on foot, never yielding to the comfort of riding on horseback unless serious emergency called him—preaching, baptizing, doing all a mission bishop's work. " He left to his clergy a most wholesome example of abstinence and self-denial; his words appealed to all because all that he taught he himself followed day by day."

Like Columba, like so many of the Irish saints, Aidan longed for solitude that he might pray and study in peace from the world's tumult. Paulinus had made his bishop's seat in the city of York; Aidan asked Oswald to give him as his " bishop's stool " a monastery upon the isle of Lindisfarne off Northumbria's coast. At low tide this could be reached on foot or on horseback by way of the sands on the shore, for a little while laid bare. The monastery was built after the Irish manner which we have seen. In it Aidan lived as a monk—and he had been professed as one of Iona's monks before he had been consecrated bishop for Northumbria—among the monks and novices and boys whom he gathered there.

Here we note a matter of high importance, a breaking away on the part of Aidan from the Irish monastic custom in which he had been trained. He was not abbot over Lindisfarne. He was not an Irish bishop carrying out his episcopal functions in obedience to the abbot of Lindisfarne. He himself appointed Lindisfarne's abbot; he presided over the life of its monks. He was, on Lindisfarne as everywhere else, the bishop set over Northumbria, over its monks, its priests, its people.

On the island the monastic Offices of day and of night were observed; monks meditated on Bible truths, learned by heart the psalms, carried out the manual work of the monastery, wrote or copied texts, and tried their hand at adornment, if they had the gift, even although the days of beauty of illumination were to come in the future. Every Wednesday and Friday throughout the year, except during the fifty days between Easter and Pentecost, all fasted until the ninth hour. Only the boys of Aidan's little school were excused from this duty. We read of twelve boys who were to be known afterwards as trained under his charge.

Of course the bishop frequently went forth to minister to the world outside his island retreat. For this purpose, as a resting-place when he was tired after his long walks, he had an oratory and a room of his own in a country seat of King Oswald near Bamburgh, the royal fortress of Northumbria's rulers, standing high upon its rock above the North Sea. From social gatherings Aidan fled, only joining the feast if he were bidden by the king or if he had serious occasion for talk and for conference with the wealthy and noble of Northumbria. Usually he left the dining-hall after a few minutes of time and very little food.

As often as his own work made it possible, the king would attend the preaching of his bishop, especially in Aidan's early days in England; for at first Aidan had difficulty with the

English language. His own was Irish, as of one born in Ireland or in Irish Scotland and brought up in the Irish-Scottish Iona. Oswald himself had learned to understand and to speak Irish during his years upon the island. Bede tells us that " it was a joy to his people to see their king interpreting the message of Heaven to his generals and ministers." He continues: " Churches were built here and there; the people gladly flocked to hear; by royal gift sites and property were given for the founding of monasteries; the English, children and grown men and women, peasants and nobles, were trained by their Irish-Scottish instructors, Aidan and his monks, in the practice and discipline of life under religious rule."

Oswald, indeed, was full of generous impulse. Once, so men said (thus writes Bede in his careful way), at Easter he sat down to feast with his bishop. The long fast of Lent was over. A delicious fragrance of hot meat rose from the table; the king was hungry, and he gave fervent " Amen " to Aidan's blessing. Just at that moment his almoner came up and spoke a word in his ear. A crowd of poor, starving men had come this Feast Day from various directions to the royal castle and were now sitting in its courtyard outside, begging to be given of the king's charity. Oswald did not hesitate. " Take the meat outside and give to all," he ordered, " and take this silver dish and break it into little pieces, and divide them, too, among these poor men." Aidan was delighted. He seized the king's hand and cried: " May this hand never see corruption! " Men believed afterwards that this petition really came true, that Oswald's right hand and arm were kept as holy relics in the royal fortress of Bamburgh.

At times Aidan felt the need of even deeper solitude than he could find with his monks upon Lindisfarne. Then he went off by himself to a cell which he had built upon the isle of Farne, one of a group of seventeen islets mingled with rocks and reefs, lying a mile and a half from Bamburgh, their nearest approach to the shore. Farne Island is, however, about seven miles by sea from Lindisfarne. In this longing for complete quiet from distraction we find the Irish instinct penetrating even more deeply this Irish bishop's mind.

7

For ten years after the death of Oswald Aidan lived on in Northumbria and saw trouble enough. The land which Oswald had held in his single control was again divided into two kingdoms, those of Bernicia and of Deira, ruled by two princes of the royal house: Bernicia by Oswy, brother of Oswald, and Deira by Oswine, son of one of those faithless kings killed in 633 by Cadwallon of Wales. Penda of Mercia was still watching for another chance to attack. Now that Oswald was dead at his hands and Northumbria lay divided in rule, his power overshadowed all this land north of the Humber.

Aidan worked with both rulers, Oswy and Oswine, in the same monastic living upon Lindisfarne, the same journeying up and down Northumbria. But it is his friendship with Oswine which comes to life in the pages of Bede. Bede, indeed, lingers over Oswine as he did over Oswald. " Good looking," he describes him, " tall, pleasant and gracious in talk and in manner, hospitable to every man, noble or simple, loved by all folk everywhere. Nobles of the highest rank hastened from almost every province to serve him in his Court. Above all, he was humble."

Here Bede adds a story. Oswine gave this bishop of his a horse, the best he could find, and this in spite of Aidan's known love of walking about his diocese. The king said that he would need the horse when he was in a hurry. Then, of course, Aidan gave this wonderful animal away to the first beggar who needed a lift, and, naturally, Oswine was deeply vexed. He heard about it just as he was going into his great hall for the midday meal, and he burst out in angry words when he met

Aidan at the entrance. " What induced you, Lord Bishop, to give away to a pauper a royal horse bestowed upon you for your own need? Have we not cheaper horses in plenty to give to beggars, and did I not give that one specially to you? " The bishop looked quietly at him a moment, and answered: " What say you, O King? Is a mare's colt of more value to you than a son of God? " With this he turned away and went to his place at table. It was a cold day, and Oswine, who had just come in from hunting, stood for a while with his thanes warming his hands before the fire on the hearth. Suddenly he ungirded the sword which hung at his belt, gave it to one of his nobles, and walked towards the bishop. Kneeling at his feet, he asked forgiveness for his rude anger. " Never again," he said, " will I say a word, however much of our money you give to these sons of God." Aidan raised him at once, and all seemed well again. But the bishop, as dinner went on, looked more and more worried and unhappy. At last one of his priests, a Scot from Iona, asked him, in that Irish-Scottish language which those around did not understand, what was troubling him. " I know," answered Aidan, " that the king will not live long. Never have I seen one so humble. This people is not worthy of their ruler."

His prophecy soon became true. Oswine's fellow-king, Oswy of Bernicia, had long been jealous of his success. In 651 Oswy invaded Deira, and on the twentieth of August Oswine was murdered by his will and command. It was the more horrid a deed in that Oswy, too, was a Christian king, and with Oswine himself had vigorously furthered Aidan's work. He repented bitterly when it was too late, and at the place of the murder he built a monastery. Its monks prayed daily both for the slayer and the slain.

Aidan had only a few days of mourning over this second tragedy. He died on the thirty-first of this same August, 651, and was buried on his isle of Lindisfarne. Bede, who praises him so generously, has only one note of censure. At the end of a long and glowing description of his character and his acts, he adds: "These things I warmly honour and love in this bishop, because indeed I doubt not that they pleased God. But that he kept Easter at the wrong time, either because he was ignorant of canon law, or was held from obeying his own knowledge by the will of his Irish people—this I neither approve nor praise."

Many men of note received their training in Aidan's monastic school on Lindisfarne. Among them was Cedd, who was to be bishop of the East Saxons, founder and abbot of the famous abbey of Lastingham in Yorkshire, " among mountains high and remote, seemingly rather fit for the refuge of robbers and the haunts of wild beasts than for the dwelling of law-abiding men." Here Cedd proved his own Celtic discipline. The lonely spot had a bad reputation, and, before he began to build, he stayed in it all one Lent, passing all its days except Sunday in prayer and unbroken fast from sunrise until sundown, that it might be cleansed from pollution of crime by the power of the Holy Spirit. Cedd's brother, Chad, who wrote a splendid page of history as bishop of Lichfield in Mercia, was also of Lindisfarne's school; and so was Eata, in later days abbot of Melrose and of Lindisfarne, bishop of Lindisfarne and of Hexham. Nor did women lack the guiding of Aidan. It was Aidan who gave the veil of a nun to Heiu of Hartlepool in Durham, and thus opened the way of the religious life for women in Northumbria. It was Aidan, also, who "loved devotedly, visited frequently, and diligently taught" Hilda in her earlier years as abbess of Hartlepool, before her rule in Yorkshire over the monastic life of both men and women at Streoneshalh, later known as the abbey of Whitby.

8

And, thirdly, in this line of Irish tradition among saints of Scotland and England we turn to think of Cuthbert, whose name is so renowned, whose story has so often been told, with its learning and its legend. We have marked that in his life he owed much to Aidan. As a lad, like St. Patrick and St. Ciaran of Clonmacnois, he tended flocks of sheep, browsing among the hills by the Scottish river Leader, a tributary of the Tweed. There, so we read, awake one night and saying his prayers, he saw through the darkness a vision of angels, ascending and descending as Jacob once had seen them in Bethel. As they went heavenwards, they bore in their hands the soul of Aidan. It is once more, of course, a vision common in the *Lives* of early saints. Cuthbert had been born about the time that Aidan began his work in Northumbria; he must often have heard of this bishop who had learned the monastic life in Scotland. Now he was some sixteen years old. Bede tells us that " handing over his master's sheep to his fellow-shepherds he then and there decided to seek a monastery."

The monastery was Melrose. It looked out upon the Tweed and up at the Eildon hills, standing, not on the site of those ruins of Melrose Abbey which we know, but nearly three miles away. If a dim tradition holds any truth, it had been founded by Aidan. Its abbot when Cuthbert entered was Eata, one of Aidan's pupils at Lindisfarne. Eata was away from the abbey at the time and Boisil, its prior, welcomed the youth as he rode up to begin his training. The pattern observed in this Scottish monastery was, as we might expect, that of Iona, with its simple ritual, its ascetic practice, its Celtic dating of Easter and its Celtic tonsure. Cuthbert was very content to keep within its common rule; he had no wish in this beginning to attempt extreme self-denial, " lest he should be unequal to his necessary labours." In due course, when he was ready, he offered his

vows as monk. Above all, it was old Prior Boisil who loved and
taught him well.

Often in his free hours he used to walk to the villages round
about Melrose and stop to talk with the peasants of the
countryside; and as he talked he told them what he believed
and why. Now and again he went farther afield. Once we find
him travelling with two of his monastic brothers, partly by land,
partly by sea, and probably along Scotland's south-east coast,
to the region of the Picts. It was winter; and the morning of
the Epiphany, the sixth of January, found the three in Pictish
land, perishing of hunger. Cuthbert, however, had spent all
night in prayer and felt cheerfully sure that something to eat
would soon turn up. Was not this the day on which the
Church celebrated a miracle, the changing of water into wine?
In a few moments, right before them on the sea shore, they
came upon three portions of dolphin's meat, carved carefully
as if by a knife.

Another time he was invited to visit the monastery of
Coldingham, on the coast between Berwick-on-Tweed and
Dunbar. It was a " double monastery " holding both monks
and nuns, and according to the usual practice in such settlements it was ruled by an abbess. This one was the Lady Aebbe,
half-sister of St. Oswald. Her name is still remembered in St.
Abb's Head, from which one can see Fife on the north, and
southwards catch sight of Lindisfarne. Her abbey may possibly
have stood upon this headland. Aebbe was a woman of out-
standing piety; her name, indeed, is found not only upon a
headland but in the calendar of saints. All the same, she does
not seem to have known very well how to rule. Her monks and
nuns, especially her nuns, fell into all kinds of slack and
unseemly ways. After her death things grew even worse, and at
last—through the wrath of God, it was said—Coldingham
Abbey caught fire and burned to the ground. One story told
that this happened in Cuthbert's lifetime. Another declared
that its cause, the wickedness of Coldingham's nuns, fostered
in him so deep a sense of women's unworthiness that he utterly

forbade any woman at all to put foot inside any church of his.

The latter story is certainly untrue. Cuthbert held high respect for women, and now he was visiting Aebbe in all friendliness and courtesy. To this visit belongs the well-known tale of the two little seals which came up out of the North Sea to warm with their breath and rub vigour into Cuthbert's feet as he stood absorbed in prayer and numbed with cold upon the shore under Coldingham's cliff.

About 658, when Cuthbert had been some seven years at Melrose, the young son of the Northumbrian King Oswy, one Alhfrith, whom his father had made ruler of Deira under himself, gave to Abbot Eata an estate at Ripon in Yorkshire, that there he might build a new monastery. Eata gladly did so, and became abbot of Ripon, though he still kept up his connection with Melrose. When he went to Ripon he took Cuthbert for his aid, and appointed him guest-master in this new house.

9

While they were living there and monks were coming to learn and to follow under them the Irish-Celtic rule which prevailed in Melrose, a change of thought gradually came about in regard to this rule. Some of the younger priests of Northumbria began more and more to resent the difference of custom which so sharply divided the Celtic Church of northern England not only from Rome, but from their brethren in England's southern kingdoms. The leader in this movement of the North was a young monk, Wilfrid, just back home again from long study in France and in Rome, and burning with devotion to the Church of Rome and all it commanded. Soon he won over to his way of thinking no less a supporter than Deira's king Alhfrith; the king, it is true, had already been feeling Rome's attraction. Action followed. Alhfrith decided that Wilfrid, so energetic and enthusiastic for the right cause, must have proper scope for his energy. He must have monasteries under his rule as abbot; he must teach his monks to follow Rome in discipline, in tonsure, in ritual. About 661 the monks of Ripon were given their choice: they were either to abandon their Irish-Celtic ways and adopt those of Rome, or to leave Ripon Abbey.

They chose to leave. Eata and Cuthbert went back to Melrose and Wilfrid became abbot of Ripon. Nor was this all. Some two years later, in 663, at Whitby Abbey in Yorkshire, now under the charge of Hilda as abbess, in the presence of King Oswy and a great assembly of Northumbria's leading men, spiritual and secular, Wilfrid passionately upheld the Roman use and won victory for Rome. Henceforth northern England was united in ritual and custom with Canterbury in the south. A few of the clergy refused to yield; among them was Colman, who had followed Aidan's Irish tradition and held on the island of Lindisfarne his seat as bishop over Northumbria. Now he went back to his home in Scotland, the monastery of Iona, and took with him from Lindisfarne for his comfort some of the bones of Aidan which were buried there.

At Melrose Cuthbert was now prior in the place of Boisil, who had died shortly before the decision of the Synod at Whitby. He and Eata finally decided that it was not for them to foster schism in the Church of Northumbria; they gave their adherence to the Roman dating of Easter and the Roman manner of tonsure, as did Cedd and his brother Chad.

Before he left Lindisfarne Colman had asked King Oswy that Eata might succeed him as abbot; for, as he pleaded, Eata had been brought up in its monastery. The king granted his petition, and once again Eata took Cuthbert with him, once more to rule under him as prior. The settlement upon Lindisfarne was very simple, they found, when they arrived in 663 or 664. Very few buildings stood there, and only the church was worth a moment's notice. The monks had no possessions except some cattle on its rough pasture land, a few tools, a few articles of domestic use, the necessary vestments and vessels for the altar, the books needed for prayer and study. Any money which Colman had received as gift had been at once handed over to men whom the monks held poorer than themselves. Sometimes the king or his nobles of Northumbria would visit the island; but they came to pay reverence to its church and usually went back to dine more comfortably at home. Should even the king of his courtesy ask that he might share the brethren's one meal in the afternoon, he supped as they did, on rough-made bread and vegetables and milk.

On the island Cuthbert lived twelve years. He had been ordained priest in Melrose or in Ripon, and now he said Mass for his monks, presided over all things connected with their daily life and tried hard to keep all in harmony. It was his business as prior to maintain discipline. And this was difficult; for there were still a number of elder brethren who heartily disliked the Roman customs and longed for their old Irish use. Sometimes when they met with him in monastic chapter they would hurl rude and angry words at him in answer to his instructions; all he did in return was to walk quietly out of the room and thus make an end of the quarrel. His instructions were carried out. Often he was seen absorbed in prayer in some place remote from the monastery's buildings; when no time was possible during the day, he spent in the church the hours of the night. Many of his monks found him labouring with his hands, in kitchen or outhouse, or, in his coarse habit of natural sheep's wool, undyed, walking around the island to make sure that all was in working order. As prior he had little patience with monks who grumbled that noise kept them awake at night. Work is better than sleep, he would good-naturedly retort; and nearly always he was heard singing psalms to drive off the curse of monotony and the weariness of labour continued too long.

10

At last, however, the longing for uninterrupted prayer became too strong to resist. There were far too many interruptions. At first, tradition tells, he tried to avoid them by moving to a little isle not far from Lindisfarne. But here he could easily be reached; people—monks and visitors—were always coming to talk. Then he asked his abbot, Eata, to allow him to move to the island of Farne, the island to which Aidan had gone for retreat in Lent. Eata understood, and in 676 Cuthbert went by boat the seven miles which were to lie in the days to come between him and Lindisfarne.

Here he spent some nine of the eleven years which remained to him; here " not only the living creatures of the air and the sea but the air and the sea themselves served him with reverence." Men were saying that the island was haunted by evil spirits; if so, they did not hinder Cuthbert. On the shore he made a dwelling for himself divided into two parts, one his oratory, the other his " house for common use "; around them ran a wall, in part made from natural stone and turf and rough planks of wood, and in part from the sheer cliff side. Its roof he put together from unshaped logs, and everywhere, in all the cracks and chinks, he thrust straw to keep the roar of wind and sea from disturbing his prayer on days of storm. At some distance, near the landing-place on the island, there was a larger building for the use of monks from Lindisfarne when they came to see him. Many, both monks and other men, did come, as before, and at first he worked hard to give them all counsel and comfort; but as time went on he had to be content to give only his blessing, unless there was a real necessity.

In the earlier months of his solitary life monks brought him bread from Lindisfarne. Then, as it seemed to him more honest to return to live with them than to live by their toil, he asked them to bring him tools for digging and wheat to sow in springtime. Spring passed, summer came, and not a shoot was seen. Well, would they bring him barley, he asked again. They did, and once more he sowed, although the proper season for sowing had long gone by. The sowing produced a fruitful harvest.

Cuthbert, like all solitaries of these early medieval centuries, was held most holy for his manner of life. But he himself had no pride. He simply felt that it was for him to live alone that he might do in the whole what most men could do only in part, might give all his time to communion with the God of heaven and earth and to entreaty for the souls and bodies of his suffering world. " Monks who live in community," he said to his brethren when they visited him, " who constantly obey their abbot in round of watching, praying, fasting and handiwork, as he bids them, are rightly to be praised; very many have I known who are purer in heart and more gifted in grace than I."

II

Therefore, when one day the king of Northumbria, then Egfrith, another son of Oswy, came with many of his nobles to the island of Farne and there knelt before Cuthbert and begged him to come forth to work as bishop, he could not refuse. He had known well directly he saw them why they had come. Messengers and letters had asked this from him in vain; but this entreaty broke down his will. He understood well the reason for the asking. The vast diocese of Northumbria had been cut up for its better administration into smaller areas; more bishops were needed. At Easter, 685, in the Cathedral of York, Cuthbert was consecrated to rule his portion of the Northumbrian Church, with his seat at his old monastery of Lindisfarne.

From this day until December, 686, for nearly two years Cuthbert was constantly travelling around his diocese, administering, preaching, talking to men and women of every

sort and condition, returning when he could find time for brief
quiet to Lindisfarne, where one Herefrith was now abbot.
Hardly had he known himself a leader of Northumbria's
Church when we find him on his way to Carlisle to give a
word of warning to a queen. Her husband, King Egfrith of
Northumbria, had marched out to fight the Picts, and Cuthbert
knew in his heart that he would die in the battle. It would
be her duty to return to the royal castle of Bamburgh as soon
as she could. " You cannot travel to-morrow," he said, " for
that is Sunday, and it is not right to travel by carriage on that
day. But on Monday take your carriage and travel with all
speed. To-morrow I have to dedicate a church here in Carlisle;
afterwards I will come to you at once."

Carlisle, though in Cumberland, was part of Cuthbert's
diocese, and again we see him on his way there, this time to
receive Egfrith's widowed queen—her name was Irminburg—
into the religious life as a nun. There, too, he talked with his
friend of many years, the hermit Herebert who lived alone on
one of the isles, still called St. Herbert's Isle, in Derwentwater,
amid the mountains of Cumberland. Every year Herebert
came out from his solitude to receive counsel and encouragement. Now Cuthbert said to him: " All that you need to
ask me, my brother, ask and do not delay. Say all you will,
for we shall not meet again. For I know well that the time of
my departure is at hand." In his grief Herebert implored his
friend to pray that he might not be left behind alone.

Not long after, when Christmas of 686 had passed, Cuthbert
felt that he could do no more. He was given release from his
duties as bishop and at once returned, not to Lindisfarne, but
to his little house on Farne, to live there his last three months
of pain and sickness. Much of the time he was alone, for in
winter the North Sea was rough with storm and kept the monks
of Lindisfarne from crossing those seven miles to care for him.
They did anxiously all they could, and their abbot, Herefrith,
was with him in his last hours, gave him the last sacraments,
and received his last words. Among them was a prophecy of

the future: "You must know, Herefrith, and keep in mind that if necessity shall force you to choose one of two evils, I desire very earnestly that you and your monks take up my bones and, carrying them with you, depart from these lands to dwell wheresoever the Lord shall provide, rather than in any manner to yield to iniquity and bow your necks to schism."

12

He died, a little over fifty years of age, on March the twentieth, 687, while some of his monks who watched outside his cell were saying their Office in the early hours before dawn. Two torches flashed a sign to the brother keeping watch upon Lindisfarne. There his body was carried, to be received by a procession of chanting monks, and to be laid in their island church. On the same day his old friend, the hermit Herebert, died on his isle at Derwentwater.

More than a hundred years went by, and the relics were still in the church. They were now on the floor of its sanctuary, enshrined since 698 in a new coffin of wood, especially made for the saint's honouring. Then in 793 raiders from Norway filled northern England with horror by landing upon this holy isle of Cuthbert to plunder and destroy. The saint, we read, was not slow to punish their insult to its church. In the next year, while they were attacking Bede's monastery of Jarrow in Durham, hoping to carry off riches offered there, their leader was killed, and soon afterwards some of their ships were lost in a storm at sea, their men either drowned or cut down as they were trying to gain the shore.

Nevertheless Lindisfarne could not survive the attack. As the years passed its community grew smaller and smaller, its life more and more relaxed through sickness and hunger of its monks, its buildings more and more unfit for their purpose. It may be that on account of these troubles Ecgred, who was bishop of Lindisfarne from 830 until 845, moved his seat and all the brethren of Lindisfarne inland to Norham-on-Tweed, some six or seven miles from Berwick on the same river. At any rate, whether from Lindisfarne or from Norham, late in this ninth century Eardulf, now bishop of Lindisfarne, decided that his monks must leave their home to seek safety elsewhere. The Danish chieftain Halfdene took up his quarters in the winter of 874-875 within Northumbria, planning, once spring should come, to ravage its country far and wide. Spring came, and Halfdene marched out. In the same spring Eardulf with his community fled forth, bearing for their protection on the way the relics from their church: the bones of Cuthbert, those of Aidan which had been left by Colman, and the head of King Oswald of Northumbria.

Tradition records that for seven years they wandered from place to place in flight before the invaders, drawing wherever they went homage and veneration from the Northumbrian people. The course their wanderings took is not clear, and name after name of some halting-place has been mentioned without bringing certainty. Most of the stories, of a stay at Craike in Yorkshire, at Whithorn in Galloway, of an attempt to go by sea from the coast of Cumberland to Ireland, a voyage cut short by storm, savour of legend. We may think of them crossing country southwards to the fells of Derwentwater and the hills of Cumberland. We know that at last they came to stay at Chester-le-Street near Durham, in 883, it would seem; and that there for more than another hundred years the bishop in charge of Northumbria, with the relics and the monks who guarded them, held his seat.

Some reason, probably the constant fear of the Scandinavian pirates, drove the community out again in 995, at the bidding of Ealdhun, then bishop in Chester-le-Street. For three or four months they stayed in Ripon, Yorkshire, and then they believed that they might safely return home. On the way, we read, the wagon bearing the relics suddenly stopped and could not be moved by any force. It was a sign, said one of the monks. They were near Durham, and to Durham they must go. The wagon was pushed firmly in that direction and in that direction it moved. In 995 Ealdhun established there his see, and there his monks built a church and laid once more the relics to rest.

In the Cathedral Library at Durham the fragments of the "light chest" of wood which was made to honour St. Cuthbert's relics in 698 are still guarded. Within its Cathedral, as belief, if not certainty, declares, his bones, with the head of St. Oswald beside them, still keep their peace.

CHAPTER SEVEN

SAINT COLUMBAN AND SAINT GALL

France, Switzerland, and Italy in the Sixth and Seventh Centuries

ABOUT THE year 590, when Columba had worked twenty-seven years in Britain and was to work yet seven more, another Irishman left his native land. He, too, was a monk, trained at Bangor under St. Comgall; he, too, was a priest of the Celtic Church in search of solitude; he, too, tried both to rule men in monasteries and to convert the heathen; he, too, was gay of heart with Irish joy, his heart finding place for monks, peasants, and the wild creatures of the forests among which he was to live. But, unlike Columba, he drove his Celtic passion for ascetic living too far; he fastened upon his monks a burden too heavy in the end for many of them to bear. He lived under lords whom he could not turn from evil to good; he quarrelled with bishops in defence of his Celtic usage; he wandered from land to land, driven by their anger; and in his wandering he sowed seed of harvest which was to last, part of it for a century, part in permanence. His name was Columbanus, or Columban.

With twelve followers—as in Columba's venture, the number of the Apostles—he set out across the sea, made his way to Gaul, perhaps by way of Britain, and on by land to Burgundy. He had already reached middle age, and doubtless he, too, was seeking his " place of resurrection," the quietness of ordered prayer.

But, and perhaps deliberately, that he might add mission

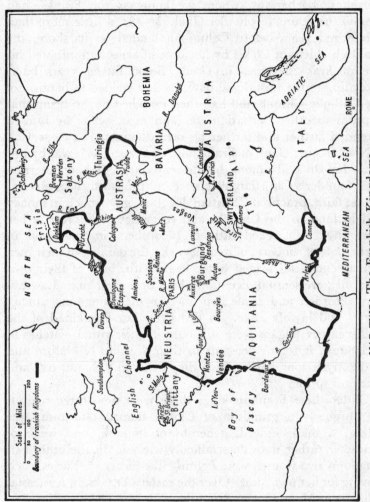

MAP TWO: The Frankish Kingdoms

work to prayer in solitude, he came to a troubled land. Roman military rule in Gaul had long ceased. In the fifth century the Germanic barbarians, whom we know as the Franks, had crossed the Rhine to plunder Gaul. In 481, a little more than a hundred years before Columban landed on its shore, the Frankish chieftain Clovis by his force of arms had initiated his line of Frankish kings in Gaul. Some fifteen years later, according to the traditional date, he had yielded to baptism of the Catholic Church and had then marched out to bring that baptism to other barbarians far and near, while he himself extended farther and farther his own dominion.

Now, in 591, Gaul, or Frankland, or France, as it was by this time, lay divided among his descendants. All had inherited their founder's Christian allegiance, all professed themselves as of that faith, practised Christian devotion, gave much in money and in land to the Church, and reverence of address to her hierarchy. All recked little of bloodshed, in mass and in particular, of robbery, of treachery, for the gaining of their own secular ends; all waged bitter feuds with those of their own kin; all were sensual, licentious, bent on indulgence. Lawlessness, disorder, and crime flourished in their kingdoms among clergy and layfolk alike. In this Christian Frankland of the sixth century pagans were still busy in their ritual, witches in their craft, ignorant peasants in their worship of Nature and of the mysterious spirits which they believed to haunt tree and lake and spring.

Under these Frankish kings there were now three realms. In Burgundy a grandson of Clovis, named Guntram, was ruling, a man, indeed, generous of impulse, and weak of character rather than determinedly wicked. In the other two kingdoms two women were fighting like incarnate Furies, each driving for her own aims. Over the eastern Franks, in Austrasia, ruled from Metz, Queen Brunhild, widow of its king, Sigebert, fiercely held on to its control, while her restless nobles awaited their chance to rise in revolt. Opposite her, at Soissons, capital of Neustria, region of the western Franks, another widowed

The Line of Merovingian Kings

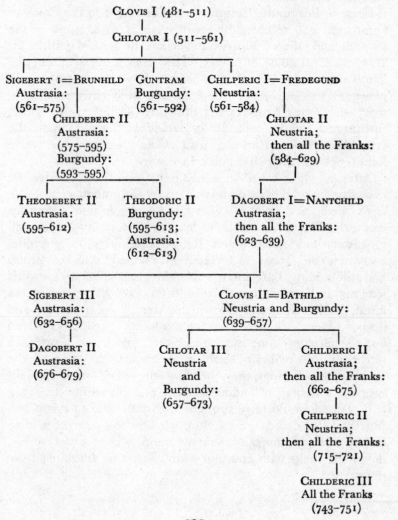

CLOVIS I (481–511)

CHLOTAR I (511–561)

SIGEBERT I = BRUNHILD
Austrasia:
(561–575)

CHILDEBERT II
Austrasia:
(575–595)
Burgundy:
(593–595)

GUNTRAM
Burgundy:
(561–592)

CHILPERIC I = FREDEGUND
Neustria:
(561–584)

CHLOTAR II
Neustria;
then all the Franks:
(584–629)

THEODEBERT II
Austrasia:
(595–612)

THEODORIC II
Burgundy:
(595–613;
Austrasia:
(612–613)

DAGOBERT I = NANTCHILD
Austrasia;
then all the Franks:
(623–639)

SIGEBERT III
Austrasia:
(632–656)

DAGOBERT II
Austrasia:
(676–679)

CLOVIS II = BATHILD
Neustria and Burgundy:
(639–657)

CHLOTAR III
Neustria
and
Burgundy:
(657–673)

CHILDERIC II
Austrasia;
then all the Franks:
(662–675)

CHILPERIC II
Neustria;
then all the Franks:
(715–721)

CHILDERIC III
All the Franks
(743–751)

queen, Fredegund, was feeding her lust for power on violence
and murder unrestrained. Each of these women was nominally
subject to the rule of a young son, the present king; each
nevertheless held the reins of government and kept the lands,
east and west, in fear.

Once in Burgundy, Columban went straight to the Court of
Guntram, who received him with respect as a monk of the
Church and offered him whatever site he wished within his
kingdom for a house of prayer. This, after some searching, he
found at Annegray, in Haute-Saône. It was a desolate, wild
place, a clearing in the woods among high cliffs and rocks,
reached by slow march along difficult, winding trails. Here,
surrounded by the solitude for which he longed, upon the
crumbling stones of an old castle, Columban and his twelve
followers built their first house in France.

After a while other men came to join them, drawn by
curiosity, by need of food and shelter, by Columban's name and
Irish birth, and not a few, indeed, by genuine desire for
monastic life. Some of them stayed. Before long a second
monastery had to be planned. This Columban built eight miles
away in an old fortress at Luxeuil, once famed for its hot springs
and still holding, bare and in ruins, the baths of luxury crowded
long ago in Roman times. Around its open space pressed the
forest, dark and grim, always threatening to overgrow and
devour. Here and there from the shadows of great trees peered
out the faces of stone idols, faces that struck the heart with
terror in this twilight, seeming in menace to demand the
worship, the offerings, they once had enjoyed. Only, one might
suppose, a despair of finding in those evil days a life they long
had wanted would have brought Christian men to this place.
But they still came, until Columban had to open yet a third
house, at Fontaines, also near at hand, where water rushed
down the rocks with constant sound and rose bubbling from
the earth.

2

In these three houses of his, Columban put into practice the Irish monasticism taught him by St. Comgall at Bangor. With the aid of the Irish who already knew and could endure, he pushed and pulled along the path of discipline his raw and ignorant Frankish novices who still neither knew nor could, but whom he unweariedly hoped to make monks for the glory of their God and his. In fervent, ringing words he strove to drive these men into the way which should be pleasing to Heaven:

" What is more blind than you, wretched man, you who wander with your eyes wide open, yet see not the path? As far as heaven's sky do you see, but never see what lies behind; as far as heaven's sky reaches your thought, and never seeks to penetrate beyond. O ignorance, hard and dry, who shall tell you of things that have no words for the telling? Poor, unhappy mankind, who shall rescue you? What have you of your own but your own soul? Do not, I beseech you, barter that one and only reality for things of naught. Think, think on death! Then shall pleasure and jest, lust and luxury, have fallen silent; then shall the body lie rotting in the clay. Shall then the soul, too, dwell in misery, delivered to torment without end? Better, of a truth, patient endurance of one hour here on earth than an awakening to pain that comes too late and lasts for all eternity! "

Driven by words such as these, amid the faces of the forest and the sound of many waters, Columban's disciples spent their days and nights in an almost unending round of prayer, fasting, and manual labour. Immediate and unquestioning obedience to a senior's word; silence except when necessity or daily routine called for speech; such food as they could find in the woods—roots, leaves, bark and berries—until they could gather their scanty harvest of vegetables, herbs, and grain; food served at the one meal in the evening, and little of that, " lest," their abbot warned them, " it overload the body and suffocate the mind." " Eating," he taught them, " is necessary every day simply and only because every day one must have strength for prayer, for labour, for reading. It is sin for a monk, not only to have, but even to want, anything beyond his actual need."

As stimulus on the road to perfection Columban held ready his own Irish *Rule*, his own prescription of penance, most carefully thought out by him on the basis of Irish precedent. Confession of sin, he insisted, must be made by his monks not only regularly, but frequently, followed by the fulfilling of penance assigned. For the monk who neglected grace before meals and did not say his " Amen " after the blessing of food, six strokes of the thong; for him who spoke at table without necessity, six strokes; for him who said of anything, " this is mine," six strokes. The same was measured out to him who forgot to make the sign of the Cross over his spoon at table, who raised his voice unduly, who coughed when he was chanting alone the first words of a psalm at Office, who smiled during Office in chapel. Twelve strokes fell on him who forgot his prayer before and after work; fifty on a brother who, when rebuked, refused to ask for pardon or dared to protest his innocence. Fasting of extra severity, and for various periods of time beyond the usual season, according to the degree of guilt, was imposed for foolish, unkind, or slanderous talk; special prayers, and many of them, were prescribed for those who had wasted precious food in kitchen or refectory. The monk who constantly by his careless or clumsy slip upset at table his cup of beer—the regular allowance in Irish monasteries—was ordered to drink water for as many days as he had sinned. Many of the brothers grumbled in their secret hearts. Some left Columban's rule; but most struggled along as best they could.

Yet there was now and then relief. Their abbot, like Columba, was always heroically cheerful, always ready with an encouraging word to the unhappy, the overburdened in body or mind. There were friends living not too far away, abbots of other, better-provided monasteries, who did what they could to help, especially in the earlier, harder days. There were fish in plenty in the streams and fruit on the brambles. An abbot, his monks knew, was not entirely dour and unfeeling when wild things allowed him near at hand. Often, as Columban walked in the forest, praying, thinking out his problems, its dwellers—fox, wolf, or bear—crossed his path and did him no harm. Birds and squirrels grew to know this familiar presence; often Columban's monks saw them come at his call and lie quiet under his hand.

3

So the years went by, and in them changes came for the three royal Courts of Frankland. Fredegund, the evil spirit of Neustria, its western part, died, and her son, Chlotar the Second, could then rule freely, no longer oppressed by her violence. He was, however, ambitious enough on his own account. Guntram of Burgundy, who had been kind to Columban, also by his death left royal power; his crown in 595 fell to a grandson of Brunhild, named Theodoric, or Thierry, the Second. His brother, Theodebert the Second, in the same year became king of Austrasia, the land of the eastern Franks. Both brothers were young; both were under Brunhild's control. Grandmother of both and advancing in age she might be, but she had lost none of her energy and little, so far, of her power. Her only fear, as ever, rose from those nobles of her land, always scheming for her fall.

Columban and his monks, since they were living in Burgundy, were now subject in political matters to its king, Theodoric, who often came to Luxeuil to talk with the abbot. Theodoric was weak in character and easily influenced. He had, too, his own share of the vice and folly of his Frankish royal line;

he lived freely with women and allowed himself whatever indulgence he would. Yet Columban won his respect and liking. One day in a burst of confidence the king spoke to him openly of his manner of life. " That is entirely wrong, my son, and you know it," answered the abbot. " Far better for you to marry and to gain for your kingdom a queen who would be held in honour and children who would be acknowledged as your lawful heirs."

This, of course, was the last thing which Brunhild's passion for ruling would allow. She wanted no Dower House for herself. When, after some years of persuasion, Theodoric actually yielded to Columban's words and brought to Burgundy as his queen a girl from Visigothic Spain, Brunhild's rage knew no bounds. This came about in 606; and after a year of unceasing quarrel in the Court of Burgundy, the unhappy wife, robbed of the treasure she had brought as her dowry, went back to her Spanish home.

Columban went to see Queen Brunhild, journeying through the wooded hills of the Vosges country. He gained nothing. Her rage descended on him when he refused outright to give his blessing to her two great-grandsons, little boys born out of wedlock in Theodoric's lawless life; when he struck unerringly upon the nerve of her pride, saying: " Sons begotten of evil will never win a Frankish crown." Henceforth, so she ordered, no one in Burgundy was in any way to aid Luxeuil or its monks. Under her torrent of wrath Theodoric himself soon gave way. His friendship with Columban turned sour, and he began to insist on demands which no abbot faithful to his rule could possibly allow. " All men have the right to go where they will in your abbey," he said. " I, the King, shall enter as and where I choose." " If you do, it will be to your peril," replied Columban.

A further influence, moreover, had now for years been urging Brunhild and her royal grandson of Burgundy to anger. It must always be remembered that, however weak and dissolute, evil and tyrannous it might be, the Frankish royal house always reverenced and feared the Catholic Church, the Church of their baptism. They consistently broke her laws; but they did the penance she imposed, and they exacted loyalty to her from their subjects. Columban, on the other hand, was as Irish in Burgundy as he had been in Bangor, as determined to keep the Celtic discipline and the Celtic practices which his Irish teachers had driven deep within his conscience. At this time, early in the seventh century, the Irish at home had not yet submitted to Rome in the matters of the dating of Easter and the monastic tonsure. The Irish of the south were to yield about 634; those of the north, always distinct from those of the south, were not to conform until the first years of the eighth century.

If, then, Columban and his monks fasted longer than the Frankish abbeys where Roman observance was the order, so, too, he kept his Easter and tonsured his monks according to the Celtic use of Ireland, Wales and Iona. He firmly refused to submit to the Roman usage followed by all the Frankish clergy. The Frankish bishops in course of time heard of this and were highly indignant; that monks claiming to follow the doctrine taught by Rome, claiming true membership in the Catholic Church, should be celebrating Easter while Rome was still keeping Lent was to these bishops a scandal speedily to be removed. Moreover, and this was even worse, according to his Irish tradition Columban had never once thought of submission to the bishop of the Frankish diocese in which his monasteries lay, built by him in serene independence. In these matters of ecclesiastical usage, of monastic routine, the Celtic Church prescribed, and the Irish abbots saw to it that the prescriptions of that Church were followed in their cloisters. Did not the abbots of Bangor, of Clonard, of Clonmacnois in Ireland govern without episcopal interference, each his own family of monks?

Some time before 601 Columban had written to plead with the Pope himself, then Gregory the Great, concerning this controversy of the date of Easter. Amid his pleading he argued in detail on the subject of Paschal calendars:

" I write, I know, with more frankness than humility," he added. " It is not of my place or my station to argue with you; it is absurd for me to worry you with dates of Easter, you who sit in the Chair of Peter, the Apostle, the keeper of the keys of Heaven. Yet you should be thinking, not of my littleness, but of the many learned scholars, of the past and the present time alike, who have firmly believed what I have written here. Gladly would I come to Rome—not to see Rome, but to talk with you. But I am frail now in body, and I have to care for my brethren in this foreign land."

To the Frankish bishops who gathered to judge this disobedient, stubborn Irish abbot in formal synod, and in these disturbed days synods rarely met, Columban in 603 wrote bolder words:

" Thank God that at least I have been the means of getting you together. Would you did it more often! I beseech you by our common Lord—if you want to be recognised by Him who will say to many in the hereafter, ' I never knew you '—of your peace and charity allow me and my monks to live in the silence of our forest, as we have lived for the past twelve years, and to offer our prayers for you, as we have always done. Our canons, our rules, are of the faith which is in us, the faith which brought us here from our own country, the faith in which we hope to live until we die. Take care, holy Fathers, how you treat us, men of exile, poor men and old. Better would it be for you, I think, to uphold than to upset us. For with you we are members of one Body in the knowledge of the Son of God, whether we be of Gaul or of Britain or of Ireland, or of whatsoever land we come."

4

Where the Frankish bishops condemned, the Frankish kings felt free to strike with angry hand. The years rolled on with increasing hostility of both Church and crown towards Columban, and at last the sentence fell, driving him from Burgundy, his home for nearly twenty years. He was ordered to return to Ireland. In 610 under strong guard he started on his journey to the coast. Part of the way the Frankish soldiers took him by land, part by boat on the river Loire. At Tours the river's strong current most happily drove his boat ashore, and he was able to spend a whole night in prayer before St. Martin's tomb, and in the morning to have breakfast with the bishop. " Why are you going home to Ireland, Father? " asked the bishop. " Because that dog Theodoric has driven me away from my monks," was the answer. At this one of those sitting at the table looked up and said, very courteously: " It is better, Father, to drink milk than wormwood. *I* shall keep my oath of loyalty to Theodoric, my king, with all my power." Columban turned to him. " Then, my son, if you are his friend," he replied with equal calm, " tell him this from the Lord God and from me. In three years he will be dead."

At Nantes Columban and his guards reached the sea, and a search was made for a trading vessel bound for Ireland. He was very tired, very glad of a rest, and he filled the time by writing to his monks, left in Burgundy without an abbot. We have his letter, and it is very enlightening.

" Athala " (one of these monks) " I name as my successor," he wrote. " Let all who think with me follow him in one mind. But if you cannot be of one mind, it is better that you cease to live in one community. Athala, you must resist those who oppose you, but do it with charity and in the peace of our Rule. I have tried to help all, to trust in all, but the burden has been too great for me. It has broken my strength and made me look almost a fool. Do you be wiser than I, and do not take upon yourself my load. You know now how little I understood; you have learned the lesson, that all cannot be taught alike, because men are so different in character, in spirit, and in mind. Treat differently one from the other the men who obey and love you, and remember that love, too, has its danger."

Again, in a last word to all: " A messenger has just come; the ship is ready. But my guards seem to understand how I feel. Perhaps if I ran for liberty, they would look the other way. I haven't told you all that is in my mind, for you think so differently among yourselves. That monk is my brother who loves peace and unity." From these words it would seem that already discord was rising in Columban's abbeys.

His work on the Continent, however, was by no means ended. The ship started, was driven by a great wave into the mud of the river-bed, and could not be cleared. After three days, so we read, the captain decided that God did not want Columban to return to Ireland; perhaps, he feared, the wrath of Heaven was keeping his ship stranded. With this thought he sent his captive ashore in a small boat, and promptly the ship floated seaward.

Columban's prophecy of evil for Theodoric, king of Burgundy, was to prove true. Just about this time a quarrel broke out between him and his brother, Theodebert of Austrasia. At last, in 612, Theodoric took his brother prisoner and handed him over to their grandmother Brunhild, who first sent him to a monastery and then put him to death. The next year Theodoric himself, now king of Austrasia as well as Burgundy, died of sudden sickness. Their kinsman, Chlotar the Second, son of Fredegund and king of the western Franks in Neustria, saw his chance.

First, he cleared the way by removing from any possibility of interference with his plans the four sons of Theodoric; and this he achieved by menace, by capture, and by murder. Then he did a deed which would have delighted Fredegund's jealous heart if she had been alive to see it. He marched out with a great army, joined forces with Brunhild's rebellious nobles, and captured Brunhild herself. Frankish chronicle tells that she was tortured for three days, mocked in parade as she sat on a camel, and then torn to pieces as she was dragged alive at the tail of a wild, rearing horse. Thus, in 613, Chlotar won his heart's desire, secure as king of all the Franks.

5

We return to follow the adventures of our wanderer, Columban. One of his monks was his companion in these journeys. His name was Gall, and he had known Columban in Ireland, for he had been Columban's pupil at Bangor. At Bangor Gall had been ordained priest, and from there he had started for France as one of Columban's twelve followers in his mission. And now he had joined Columban in exile from Burgundy, for King Theodoric had decreed that all of Columban's monks who were Irish by birth should share his banishment.

When Columban was freed from the ship at Nantes, Gall was set free with him, and the two friends started out for the Court of Chlotar of Neustria. Chlotar had no love for his cousin Theodoric of Burgundy, and he warmly invited them to settle in his land. Columban declined and Gall agreed with him. Italy was in their mind: a far-off country, they thought, where they might once more dwell in silent prayer and preach to heathen men, away from hostile Franks. So again they set out, and travelled to Austrasia, to eastern Frankland, the realm of Theodebert. It was still only 610 in date, and Theodebert was not yet a prisoner. He, too, offered Columban hospitality, and gave him a wide choice of places in which to settle. The region around Lake Constance was mentioned as especially wild and in need of mission work; it was under Theodebert's rule. Columban said he would gladly go and look it over, and once more he and Gall were on their way. After a halt at Mainz and a journey along the Rhine, they came to the shore of Lake

NORTH SEA

Heligoland

BALTIC SEA

Schleswig

Holstein

Wadden Zee

R. Elbe

Hamburg

Ijssel

Leeuwarden

Dokkum

Bremen

Saxony

S.R. Ems

Verden

Osnabrück

Katwijk

R. Weser

Utrecht

Münster

GERMANY

THE NETHERLANDS

Paderborn

THURINGIA

Antwerp

WESTFALEN

(Westphalia)

Fritzlar

BELGIUM

Cologne

HESSE

Erfurt

Maastricht

Marburg

Hersfeld

Rhine

Liège

Amöneburg

Fulda

Koblenz

Echternach

Frankfurt

Pfalzel

Mainz

Trier

R. Main

Würzburg

Austrasia

Meuse

Metz

FRANCE

Eichstätt

Regensburg

Vosges

R. Danube

BAVARIA

Passau

Luxeuil

Freising

Burgundy

Munich

AUSTRIA

Dijon

Besançon

Zürich

Bregenz

R. Inn

St. Gallen

Chalon sur Saône

Chur

SWITZERLAND

L. Geneva

THE ALPS

Milan

ITALY

Piacenza

Scale of Miles

Bobbio

0 20 40 60 80 100

MAP THREE: Journeys of Saint Columban, Saint Gall
and Saint Boniface

Zürich. Perhaps after all, they asked themselves, this might be the place for their working? The dwellers by the lake were savage, heathen, practising ritual of magic and superstition. But Gall spoiled their chance, if chance there was. He was enthusiastic and impetuous, and he believed in getting down to work. He at once set fire to one of the shrines of heathen sacrifice beloved by this people and threw into the lake all the sacred offerings he could find inside its walls. Naturally the heathen were furious; they hurled insults which fortunately Columban did not understand, seized and beat him, and gave Gall the run of his life.

Quickly the two shook off the thought of staying among this " sterile crowd of barren-hearted men " and wandered on to Arbon, on the south-west shore of the Boden See, Lake Constance. There they found welcome in the home of a kindly priest named Wilimar, with whom for a week they discussed problems of the Bible while he gave them dinner. " Do you know any really nice, solitary place near here," asked Columban, " where we could build our cells and say our Office in quiet? " " Just, I do believe, what you want," replied Wilimar. " Some ancient ruins, surrounded by high mountains, buried deep in the wilds."

They went, saw, were delighted, and settled down, where Bregenz is now found in the Vorarlberg of Austria at the east end of the Boden See. They reached the place by boat and stayed in it two years. The soil was fertile, and there was level ground for sowing and planting grain and fruit and vegetables. Their first act was to build a rough chapel and around it huts for their humbler needs. Soon they met some of the peasants who lived here and there in the mountains, and Gall was full of pride and joy when he discovered that they used a German dialect which he could both understand and speak. He was quick at languages and had been studying German of various kinds for some time. Columban at once handed over to him the work of preaching, probably with some feeling of self-sacrifice, for Columban liked preaching. These peasants had once, it seemed, been taught something of Christian belief, but had long ago fallen back into heathen ways. They had a temple not far away, in which Columban and Gall found three images of heathen gods, covered with gold and fastened to the wall. These were, of course, objects of great reverence.

On the day appointed for the first solemn celebration of Mass, a great crowd, men and women, young and old, gathered at the temple, now to be blessed as a Christian church. All were curious to find out what was to be done. At the proper moment Gall began to preach, and as he rose in the passion of his words, he gave them point by seizing the three heathen images, breaking them up and scattering their fragments. It was a critical moment. But just when an onrush of fury seemed imminent, Columban, who was chanting the Liturgy, began the procession and the singing of psalms for the consecration ceremony. All were so struck to silence by awe at this new experience that danger was routed.

It was Gall's duty to catch fish in the lake for supper, and he was famed for his skill as a fisherman. This was a necessary as well as a pleasant pursuit, since guests, travelling monks and pilgrims, sometimes came to stay a brief while. Often, perhaps through lack of time in the early days of building, he would carry on this fishing by night. Once, while he stood on the bank in the silence and darkness, the water spreading black at his feet and the mountains rising black around, a sudden storm broke over him. In its tumult he seemed to hear, high above the roll of the thunder, the voice of the Demon of the mountains, crying to the Demon of the lake below. " Come up to help me," wailed the spirit from the height, " that we may throw out the strangers who have driven me from my temple and destroyed my images and turned away my people from following me! "

Gall, trembling, crossed himself and hurried back to the little settlement. It was the hour of Matins, and the abbot gathered his house, guests and all, in church. As the torches flickered and the chant of psalms began, there came to their ears from without the howling as of devils in the wind and the rain, and all threw themselves upon the floor, imploring protection from the God they served.

For, although men were showing friendliness and converts were coming forward, there were still pagans in plenty who deeply resented the driving out of the old religion. Some of these went to a local chieftain, a man named Gunzo, and accused these newcomers, these Christians, of scaring away the big game on which trappers who dwelt by the lake depended for their living. The wrath of Gunzo rose high. About this time, also, two of Columban's household were lured into the forest and killed. Fear began to surround the Irish monks in their rude abbey.

But there was even more serious cause for fear. It was now the year 612, and Theodoric, that enemy of Columban, had just conquered his fellow-king and brother, Theodebert. The power of Theodoric, therefore, now reached as far as Lake Constance, and no one knew what he might do for the destruction of the Christian mission just begun. Columban, after much hesitation, decided to leave for Italy with Gall.

Then, just as they were ready for their journey, suddenly Gall begged leave to stay behind. He was sick with fever, he said, and could not travel, Columban, upset by this disaster, as he thought it, burst into angry words. " You want to stay here," he said, " because you are sick of wandering; you have had enough of trouble. Farewell then, and I give you leave to stay. But this is my last command to you: Never, so long as I live on this earth, do you dare to say Mass."

This is the story which comes to us from the ninth century *Life* of St. Gall. It does not hold, we may hope, the actual truth. Very probably Columban did believe that Gall wanted to stay behind. Yet he could hardly have left Gall burdened by such deprivation in the lack of priests, amid that solitude of heathen men.

6

At any rate, the two parted. We will follow Columban first, making his way across the mountains into Italy. Here the people from the North, the Lombards, were by this time in possession of their own kingdom; and in 590 one Agilulf had received its crown. He, like so many barbarian heathen, had been partly converted, partly taught in error. He was without doubt a heretic, but his wife, the Lombard Queen Theodelinda, was a Catholic. Now he, like the Frankish Theodebert and Chlotar, gave welcome to this exile and bade him build his cell where he would in his kingdom.

In the north country, near Piacenza, Columban made a last home, a cell which after his death was to grow into renown greater than that of any he had built in France. From King Agilulf he heard of a little church of St. Peter in a solitary spot amid the Apennine mountains. It was broken, desolate, and in ruins, but near it ran the stream of the Bobbio, lively with fish. Once more, then, Columban turned ruins into a house of religion and settled down, to teach and to train, to fight the growing weeds of heresy among the Lombards, to keep his Irish custom and ritual. A year only was given him for this last work of his. He died, on November the twenty-third, 615. His cell multiplied again and again, until at Bobbio, as the monastery's settlement was called from the stream flowing past, there stood one of the most famous abbeys and libraries of medieval times.

7

Gall, left alone in his sickness at Bregenz, struggled to his feet, put his nets and his few belongings into a boat, and crossed the lake to Arbon, to find his friend Wilimar, the priest. Wilimar once more received him gladly, and nursed him in his very real fever until he was again strong enough to work.

Among Wilimar's clergy there was a deacon who was continually exploring all the wild country around Arbon, on the hunt for food for his brethren. It was his special task. Once again Gall asked the question: Was there a solitary place where he might make his home? This time the answer was not so happy. " Father," said this deacon, " around us here there lies a wilderness as lonely as you could desire. Mountains and valleys, full of wild beasts, boars, bears, and wolves, await you, should you choose to dwell among them. I only fear that if I guide you to their haunts, they will speedily make an end of you." " If God be with us, who shall be against us? " was the cheerful reply.

Next morning at dawn, carrying their fishing gear and their packs on their shoulders, the two set out. All day they plodded on, and the sun was low on the horizon when they came to a little river, the Steinach, and walked along its bank until they saw a rocky cliff before them. Down its side, water was rushing into a tarn at its base. Here Gall caught his foot in briars and fell. " It is a sign," he declared. " Here I shall stay."

Here, then, Gall built his cell with help from two of Wilimar's clergy. Here he kept his monastic round, and other men came to share it. From here he went out often on mission to teach and convert, walking along the valley of the Rhine towards Chur, tramping the mountains of the Canton of St. Gall. We read that he brought healing to a daughter, grievously tormented

in mind, of the chieftain Gunzo who had been his enemy at
Bregenz, and that in his gratitude Gunzo offered to support
him as candidate for a bishop's seat in the region around Lake
Constance. But Gall refused, saying that he was alien in birth;
in his stead he put forward the merit of that deacon who had
guided him to the Steinach. The deacon, John by name, was
accepted, as one born at Chur. Gall preached the sermon
at his consecration, stayed with him a week, and then returned
to his cell. Ever afterwards John looked upon Gall as his
Father in God and helped him in every way to carry on his
work.

The mission prospered. Soon twelve disciples were around
Gall in this lonely place. In 615 he heard that Columban had
died. As a parting gift he had left Gall his pastoral staff, which
in course of time reached the monastery in the Swiss mountains;
and now, the story has it, Gall could at last say his Mass in
freedom and content.

In 629 Eustasius, the abbot of Luxeuil, where Gall had
worked so long in Burgundy under Columban, also died, and
its monks sent to Switzerland to beg him to become their head.
Six men came on this deputation, and every one of them was
Irish. But Gall refused also this call. He had chosen he
pleaded, the way of solitude, of a stranger in the wilds, and
he could not now return to the cares, even to the honour, of
the abbot's office in Luxeuil. Luxeuil was no longer a
humble, lonely monastery. The influence of Irish monks was
growing fast in France, and so was the number of Luxeuil's
novices.

He died, not long after 630, while he was on a visit to
Wilimar at Arbon. For forty-five years he had laboured, in
France and in Switzerland, and his *Life* records that he was
now well over ninety years old. He was buried in the church
of his monastery, between the wall and the altar.

There, on the bank of the Steinach, in the eighth century,
stood an abbey well disciplined, well endowed, Benedictine in
order, the home of many monks and the resort of many pilgrims.

The fame of miracles brought them to revere the tomb of the saint who had first pitched there his wandering tent. During the ninth century this cloister of Saint-Gall reached a glory of learning, of scholarship, of books, of teachers, and of skilled men of art, who designed and created there the marvellous illuminated manuscripts which bear its name.

CHAPTER EIGHT

SAINT OUEN OF ROUEN AND
SAINT FURSEY

France in the Seventh Century

WE COME now from Celtic saints—Irish, Scottish, Welsh, Breton—of the sixth century to Frankish saints of the seventh, though we still shall see Irish saints in France and the marks of Columban's life and work. The influence of his training lived long after his departure from Luxeuil. Under its abbot Athala, and still more under Eustasius, who succeeded Athala in office, Luxeuil's austerity of life, its devotion of monastic round, its record of courage in the face of loneliness and hunger, condemnation and exile, brought aspirants to the cloister and its sister houses and induced the building of other monasteries which followed Columban's code of discipline. Revolt, indeed, arose at times against its severity. Yet revolt faded away, the more readily in that, as it seems, Eustasius made peace with the bishops of the Franks. Henceforth Luxeuil, too, and her sister and daughter abbeys kept their Easter on the Roman date, although exemption from diocesan control was often granted for their life of prayer and for their missionary campaign. Eustasius and his monks worked hard to convert the heathen and heretics, especially in the region of the river Doubs and in Bavarian settlements.

The seventh century in France, then, was a time of the founding of many abbeys which practised the Columban discipline, and Frankish saints of this time were founders of these monasteries. In general, they were not dedicated to a life of wandering from place to place as were the Celts. They were rather men of affairs, absorbed as bishops or as priests in the work of a diocese, attending at Court upon the service of their Christian mission. Some of them, however, did journey from France to other countries, for pilgrimage, for teaching, and for political errands of peace and alliance between peoples. Their work whether in founding monasteries or in journeying abroad, was always closely associated with the powers which ruled the Franks during this seventh century. It will make for clearness, therefore, if we look briefly at these powers.

2

We last saw the Franks of both east and west united in 613 under one king, Chlotar the Second. Peace had descended for a while upon his house since he had ruthlessly removed all his kinsmen capable of opposing his ambition. Yet, as time went on, between the kingdoms which made up his rule peace was hardly found. The nobles of the eastern Franks, of Austrasia, were restive under his hand, the hand of a lord who originally had not belonged to them but to the Franks of the west, of Neustria. In 623 Chlotar decided to try to appease them by giving them as king his young son, Dagobert.

Another element pregnant with danger for the Frankish royal crown was the presence in each of the Frankish Courts, of Austrasia and of Neustria, of an official known as the Major-Domus, the " Chief of the king's household," " the Mayor of the Palace," as history was to describe him. The office of these two ministers allowed them, each in his own land of east or west, to organise and control the running of the royal domestic and social functions for the comfort and convenience of their kings, to superintend the royal households, to receive and welcome the royal councillors, the foreign ambassadors and guests from every quarter. As long as the Frankish kings held firm and strong rule, all was well. This the kings of the sixth century, in spite of their crime and offence against God and man, had at least done. As the seventh century progressed, however, the kings of Frankish lands became progressively more and more idle, more and more given to luxurious living, more and more worthless, until their rule lived no longer in reality, only in name.

The Mayors of the Palace, both in Austrasia and in Neustria, now seized their chance. As their control over matters of their Palaces came to include control of the royal estates, the royal courts of law, and the armies of their lands, through the lapse of the power of their kings, their road to dominion soon lay wide open before them. And not only this. The kingdoms, both in east and west, not only passed gradually from the rule of their kings to the rule of their mayors, but in the seventh and eighth centuries these kingdoms also suffered discord and tumult from the warring ambitions of these rival mayors. Each of these in his own land nominally acted for his sovereign lord, each in reality eagerly longed to gain power for himself over all the Frankish people.

Yet in one way the old tradition of these Frankish rulers held good. However worthless the Frankish kings of the seventh and following centuries, however ambitious and grasping their mayors, these kings and these mayors still professed allegiance to their Church. On their lands and with their money Frankish abbeys were built.

3

This brief description of the problems and the danger inherent in Frankish government of the early seventh century has prepared us to study one of the Frankish saints, known to us as St. Ouen. The story of his life will illustrate well the change which we have marked, from the Celtic to the Frankish pattern, from dedicated wandering to a dedicated going hither and thither in the service of Church and country. Ouen was a bishop, and there were others of his time, bishops and saints, whose lives in many respects resembled his, in their journeyings and their work. Like other men of note among the Franks of this age, he, too, was devoted to the Irish monastic tradition of Luxeuil and St. Columban. Above all, his life will reflect the weakness of the Frankish crown, the growing power of Frankish mayors, and the bitter rivalry between mayors of different kingdoms, rising high to end at last in victory for the strongest.

Neustria was Ouen's native land, and we meet him first at the Court of this Chlotar the Second. As the child of noble Frankish parents he was preparing here to take his part later on in Frankish political life. It was the custom among the Franks that peers of the realm should send their sons to "school" at Court, so that among the king's officials, councillors, and learned men they might gain the knowledge and experience proper for their rank and its future duties. Here, then, Ouen as boy and young man was rising into favour and notice. He was reading his Latin books, sacred and secular; he was studying the various liberal arts; he was discussing with his teachers problems of theology and philosophy; he was succeeding in holding his own in power of argument among his fellow-students. Education among the Franks at this time was not on a very high level, for there was too much confusion and strife in the land. But the Frankish Courts still held their scholars, and the "Dark Ages" were by no means as dark as they have often been painted.

Ouen was at the royal Court of Neustria when King Chlotar died, in 629, and his son, Dagobert, now in his twenties and already, as we have seen, for six years the king of Austrasia, became the ruler of all the Franks. He is remembered as the last Frankish king worthy of the name for over a hundred years to come, until the Frankish monarchy revived in the mid-eighth century. He was a king in power as well as in title. Not only did he carry on a strong government from his Court, but he travelled around his kingdom, his various lands, dispensing justice to the wronged and alms to the poor. Among the nations of the west he held firmly his due place; in the east he was an ally of its Emperor, in league with Constantinople against common barbarian enemies. Men readily obeyed, respected and praised him. Moreover, he united discretion with his power. Once again, as under Chlotar, the nobles of Austrasia, always restless and striving for their own cause, began to show jealous anger at their subjection to a ruler who held his Court in Paris, a Neustrian city. Dagobert quelled their resentment, at least in part, by following his father's example; he sent his own son, then but three years old, to be crowned as king of Austrasia at its chief city, Metz, with the title of Sigebert the Third.

Dagobert, long before his entering upon the rule of Neustria, had recognised a future source of support in Ouen, a young man of about his own age. Now he made him his confidential secretary and the Keeper of his Royal Seal. It was this minister's duty to present to the king the petitions of suppliants, the charters, wills, laws, which required his signature, to deliver these, when duly sealed and signed in royal assent, to those appointed to receive them, bishops, judges, heads of departments. Ouen's work was the easier in that he quickly gained the respect and liking of men, from the king downwards. He had grown up tall and good looking, serious and responsible beyond his years, one to whom many confided their problems. Nor did he think only of his work at Court. On land given him by Dagobert from the royal demesne he built the monastery of Rebais in the woodlands of Brie, between the rivers Grand and Petit Morin, tributaries of the Marne, and brought there one of Columban's followers, a monk of Luxeuil, to be its abbot. For long he thought of entering its life himself; only the strong will of Dagobert and his own colleagues in political matters held him back.

If not in a monastery, then, yet in the world he was held a devout servant of religion. In the year 636-637 Judicael, king of Brittany, came hurrying to Dagobert's Court, then resident at Clichy, near Paris. His Breton people had been rebelling against the Frankish king's suzerainty, and this king had sent them warning to amend their ways and give proof of their loyalty; otherwise, he swore, his army would march upon their lands. Judicael made his peace with Dagobert, and was presented as reward with fair words and many gifts. But he would not eat in the royal hall; instead, he went off to breakfast in Ouen's house. He himself, we are told, was " a religious man who feared God greatly," and he had heard the same of the man whom he chose as his host.

4

For ten years Ouen's working with his king went on in harmony and peace. Then, in 639, when he was only thirty-five, Dagobert died, leaving the kingdom of Austrasia in the hands of his elder son Sigebert as before; his own Neustria came to his younger boy as Clovis the Second. The change was bitter for Neustria and for Ouen. Clovis was but five years old. His mother, Nantchild, was nominally Regent of the government. The mayor of Neustria from 641 onwards was Erchinoald by name, a man who lacked force and determination. He did his best to gain control; but he found himself defeated. Neustria's nobles and bishops quickly took possession of its affairs.

The kingdom's rule in dispute among many men; a little boy upon its throne, already showing signs of the wayward, uncontrolled youth into which he was to grow; over these things Ouen thought until he was sure that for him work at Court was no longer possible. Now again the desire of service as priest of the Church rose up in new strength before his mind. As he talked the matter over with his friends, he found that before he could be ordained priest he must spend a year in some kind of preparation. This started him on his travels, and he preached a mission throughout Aquitaine, as far as the Spanish border, perhaps farther. On his return he received his ordering; and so well did he fulfil his office that shortly afterward, upon the death of its holder, he was consecrated in Reims Cathedral bishop of the diocese of Rouen.

5

Not from Ouen's earliest *Life*, a mass of fervent eulogy compiled in the eighth century, but rather from the history of his time we know that his forty-three years as bishop, from 641 until 684, were full of public disturbance and destruction. Rouen was in Neustria. As the years passed and Neustria's king, the boy Clovis, grew up from child to youth, he became increasingly irresponsible in ways and in character. In due time he married, and for the sake of his queen Ouen frequently took the road from Rouen to the Neustrian Court.

The story of this queen is a striking one. It begins with the Neustrian Mayor Erchinoald. One day, like St. Gregory the Great long before, he walked through the public market-place and caught sight of a captive from England put up for sale as a slave. This time the captive was an English girl, Bathild by name, and she was very beautiful. Erchinoald could not resist the sight of her. He paid her price, took her to his home, proudly showed off her rare loveliness to his friends as his cupbearer, and soon was begging her to be his wife. Always she refused him. She was thinking of the young king, Clovis; he, too, had fallen in love with her and she saw him constantly at Erchinoald's house. At last his will conquered her and Erchinoald alike, and she yielded her consent. After their marriage, while she watched her husband rapidly sinking into feebleness of body and of mind, she gave herself, for her spirit was as brave as her form was beautiful, to the labour of attending those ceremonies, rites, and official appointments which he himself refused to consider or to carry out. In her difficulties with her nobles and her bishops, in the many problems facing her inexperience, she often called Ouen to come from his Cathedral to her aid.

In 656 she called him, when word reached the Neustrian Court that her royal husband's brother, King Sigebert of Austrasia, had died and that the mayor of Austrasia, Grimoald, a man far stronger than her own Mayor Erchinoald had ever been, had seized Austrasia's crown for his own son, a mere boy. He himself was to be the power behind the throne. The rightful heir, another Dagobert, was sent off to Ireland, where he was lost to sight in exile for nearly twenty years.

Again Ouen came to his queen's aid in the following year, 657. Her husband had just died; her eldest son, also a little child, had been acknowledged as Neustria's King Chlotar the Third; and she herself had been appointed Regent for his kingdom. From this day for nearly ten years she was busy with Ouen's help in signing charters, in confirming and debating the measures proposed for Neustrian rule. Above all, she did her best to help the Church of her land, its monks and nuns, its oppressed and unhappy layfolk.

6

This in itself was no light toil. But her greatest labour, the labour which was to end her years at Court, was coming upon her. Soon after the death of Clovis, Erchinoald, mayor of Neustria, also died. His loss, indeed, might have caused little distress. But he was followed as mayor by a man, Ebroin, who was a driving fury, who stands out above all mayors of the Neustrian Franks through his determined battle to win dominion over all the Frankish people. From the beginning Bathild felt compelled to resist him, and her opposition cost her dear. It was not that Ebroin was an enemy of the Church which Bathild loved so well. He gave of his wealth for its work, and the founding of the abbey of Notre-Dame of Soissons was due to him and his family. His ambition to rule brought him into a struggle to the death with nobles and bishops of both Neustria and Austrasia alike. Ouen, too, suffered from his ruthlessness.

There is another side, however, in the story of their relations one with the other. Frankish rumour of the time declared that Ouen the Bishop gave counsel to Ebroin the mayor in his drive for power. If this rumour was true, and we cannot say that it was, then Ouen's counsel might perhaps have been given in some hope that good might come to the distracted lands of the Franks from Ebroin's strong and determined will, that Ouen saw some chance of peace if Neustria and Austrasia were united under one mayor's rule. We do not know enough to judge.

Ebroin steadily advanced in power, and his hostility towards Bathild steadily increased. In 662 Grimoald, the mayor of Austrasia, was delivered into his hands, to die in prison at Neustria's chief city, Paris. Now no more could Grimoald hold his son upon Austrasia's throne, and it was given to another son of Clovis and Bathild, Childeric the Second. By this time Bathild's courage and energy were failing her, and she knew that she could do no more. Before 667 she sought safety and shelter in the abbey of Chelles near Paris, a house which she herself had raised and endowed. There she remained until her death about 680, and in the course of years for her devotion and her charity the Church enrolled her name in the canon of saints.

Ouen lived to look upon still more of tragedy. In 673 he saw Chlotar the Third dead in Neustria. Soon Childeric the Second, king of Austrasia, was ruling all the Franks. Childeric was foolish of mind and quick of temper; and two years later an angry vassal murdered both him and his queen as they rode hunting near Paris in the Forest of Livry. Ouen himself gave them burial.

We need worry no more over Frankish kings. The succession to the rule of all the kingdoms of the Franks rested henceforth on a contest between their rival mayors. From her nun's cell Bathild watched in prayer while her enemy, Ebroin, mayor of

Neustria, fought with all his power against the nobles of Austrasia, led by Leodegar, St. Léger, whom she herself had appointed bishop of Autun. Before the struggle ended, Ebroin had been tonsured and sent to monastic prison at Luxeuil. He had escaped, and in his turn he had seized Leodegar, had put him to torture and to death, and had hidden his body in an unknown grave, lest any should honour him as martyr. Some years later, in 680 or 681, Ebroin also was struck down, by one of his own Frankish officials in revenge for unjust treatment. It was early one Sunday morning and he was on his way to church.

We turn in relief from these records of bloodshed to look at Ouen as traveller: journeying to the border of Spain for the cause of Christianity; journeying across the Alps to worship at the shrines of Rome; journeying to Cologne on a mission of peace between Neustria and Austrasia; as an old man, no longer able to ride his horse, driving around his great diocese in a carriage drawn by mules. Such journeys had filled the days between his workings as bishop, as statesman. His last days found him travelling to the royal house at Clichy, close to Paris, " to serve the needs of king and people." There he died, and in solemn state his body was carried to its burial in Rouen.

His life, then, covered the long time of the struggle for power in France. Three years after his death, in 687, Pippin the Second, of Heristal, mayor of Austrasia and grandson of its first mayor, Pippin of Landen, won at Tertry, near St. Quentin, a decisive battle against Berthar, mayor of Neustria. This victory not only assured the mastery in government of Austrasia and its mayor over all the Franks, but it paved the way for the rising of the Carolingian house in this Pippin the Second's son, Charles Martel.

The fame of St. Ouen spread far and wide. In the tenth century offerings from his relics were received with joy by Oda, Archbishop of Canterbury, and were laid by him to rest in splendid enclosure within his Cathedral. To England also,

The Rise of the Carolingian House

Frankish Kings of the Carolingian Line, beginning with
Pippin III, the Short, in 751

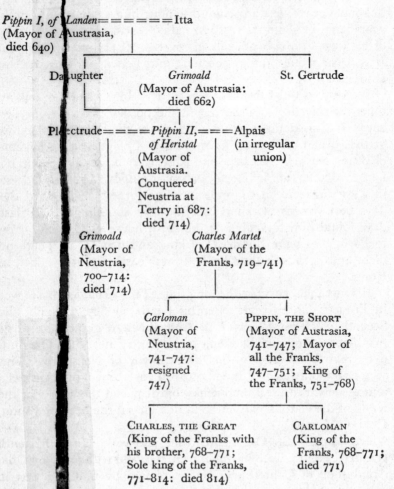

Pippin I, of Landen========Itta
(Mayor of Austrasia,
died 640)

Daughter   *Grimoald*   St. Gertrude
(Mayor of Austrasia:
died 662)

Plectrude=====*Pippin II,*===Alpais
         of Heristal   (in irregular
        (Mayor of   union)
        Austrasia.
        Conquered
        Neustria at
        Tertry in 687:
        died 714)

Grimoald   *Charles Martel*
(Mayor of   (Mayor of the
Neustria,   Franks, 719–741)
700–714:
died 714)

Carloman   PIPPIN, THE SHORT
(Mayor of   (Mayor of Austrasia,
Neustria,   741–747; Mayor of
741–747:   all the Franks,
resigned   747–751; King of
747)   the Franks, 751–768)

CHARLES, THE GREAT   CARLOMAN
(King of the Franks with   (King of the
his brother, 768–771;   Franks, 768–771;
Sole king of the Franks,   died 771)
771–814: died 814)

shortly afterwards, the abbot of St. Ouen's monastery at Rouen wrote his petition, praying the English king Edgar to send aid for its rescue from decay.

7

While Ouen as Frankish bishop and statesman was making his journeys and honouring the memory of Columban of Luxeuil, Irishmen of Columban's Celtic strictness were still during this same seventh century wandering across the sea in search of solitude. We read of Kilian, an Irish hermit who ventured from Ireland to France, was befriended by Faro, bishop of Meaux in the time of St. Ouen, and built his cell at Aubigny, near Arras. To Faro came also another from Ireland, a young man who had left home and family to seek quiet for prayer. Faro answered his petition for some retreat in the woods near Meaux with a smile: " Yes," he said; " I have a bit of land belonging to me, not very far away. It is very lonely, indeed, and if you like, we will go and look at it."

They went, and the place was all that Fiacre—originally Fiachra—could desire, hidden in the forest of Brie. The bishop then and there made him a gift of its title and left him to his solitude and his work. Fiacre made a clearing among the trees, then raised with timber and loose stones a cell and a chapel, which he solemnly dedicated to Our Lady. Here he prayed night and day, lived on next to nothing, had a thoroughly happy time, and regularly passed on the offerings of kindly peasants for his support to wandering pilgrims like himself and to poor men who asked for charity.

His *Life*, on which we are depending, now takes a sudden leap into legend; but the legend makes pleasant reading. There were soon so many who came to seek his help, to stay for a night or two in their own journeys, that it seemed to his eager mind entirely necessary to widen his little home. Permission to build further was readily given by Faro, and once more Fiacre set busily to work. Trees were falling, trenches were gaping, shafts and pillars were being shaped, and all was in a state of upheaval when a traveller passed by. The traveller was a lady of high rank, and she was horrified at this havoc in the midst of a private forest estate. She hurried at once to the bishop's palace and told Faro that some agent of Satan himself was ruining his land. The bishop had better go and see with his own eyes what was going on. The bishop set out and found Fiacre in no saint-like mood. The work was hard enough, he said, without some interfering woman coming to insult him and to wrong the good bishop. He was sitting idle, nursing his anger, upon a rock among his buckets and spades. But his guardian angel came to his rescue just after Faro arrived, for to their immense surprise the flat hard rock on which Fiacre was sitting slowly began to sink into a comfortable, hollowed-out seat. The young man thought this was surely a sign for his encouragement; the bishop knew it was a miracle, and that Fiacre's work was to be blessed by God. He ordered the noble lady to stop her silly talk immediately and vowed that any woman henceforth who came near this house of prayer would be promptly visited with horrid disaster. News of the incident spread abroad and aroused much curiosity. Soon another noble lady came to see what really was happening; but her courage failed her when she was near, for she knew well the bishop's warning. God, however, would not bother to punish her maid, she thought, and she pushed the unwilling girl forward. " Go you and look and tell me what you see," she said. The maid suffered nothing; but sickness came upon the lady and she lost the sight of one of her eyes.

So St. Fiacre's house in the woods of Brie was finished at last, to become not only a haven for poor men and for pilgrims, but a hospital for the sick.

There is another story of this saint, and it is true. In the course of time his fame spread from the old province of Brie and its city of Meaux throughout the land of France. Centuries went by, and still in the seventeenth his image was hanging in Paris, at the doors of a small hostelry, the Hôtel Saint-Fiacre.

Many stayed in this house as they passed through the city, the more readily because close at hand in the Rue Saint-Martin there were stables, and coaches for hire, a necessity for travellers in those days. This convenient location was widely advertised, and eventually the cabs and coaches of Paris won their name of " fiacres " from the saint and his hotel.

Wandering also along the roads of France at this time were other Irishmen, bent on preaching or on visits to holy shrines. Some of them are still remembered. An Irish bishop, named Failbe, took with him on a journey to the sacred places of Rome a young man called Sigiram, or Cyran, who had been cupbearer at the Court of Chlotar the Second and was to be head of a cloister not far from Bourges. There is a description in Frankish record of Sigiram walking from place to place in Italy, lending a hand to labourers in Italian vineyards and telling them of the things of God as they sat resting over their supper after the day's work was done.

More important in the annals of saints is that Richarius whose name was well known in the Middle Ages through his monastery near Abbeville. He, also, was young when, in the days of Queen Brunhild of Austrasia, two Irish priests came wandering through his native Ponthieu of Picardy to preach their faith. Their names were Chaidoc and Fricor. The people of Picardy were still so stoutly pagan that they set upon the two missionaries, threw stones and evil words at them and chased them through the fields. Just then Richarius came in sight, rescued the strangers, and carried them off to his own home. His charity received return; for these Irishmen talked to him all night, answered all his questions, convinced him that they had the right answers, and turned his somewhat unstable and rudderless mind towards a determined road of life. He, too, became priest and monk; he, too, went out on missionary crusade, across the Channel to England. His work at last came to the notice of King Dagobert the First, who invited him to his Court and gave him aid from his wealth. Shortly afterwards Richarius handed over to another's care the little church he had built in his own town and went to the retreat of a hermit's cell ten miles distant, at Forest-Montiers, in the woods around Crécy-en-Ponthieu. A monastery rose there in course of time. But the chief cloister dedicated in his name stood on the site of his former church, at the scene of his conversion by those Irish wandering preachers; a place in that day called Centula, but afterwards crowded by pilgrims who knew it as the great Abbey of Saint-Riquier.

8

Probably the most important Irish wanderer of the seventh century was one who not only lived a monk's life in France, not only converted many men, but inspired there the founding of a religious house which down the course of years was to be for countless pilgrims a haven of Irish tradition. His name is known to all students of medieval record: Fursey of Perrona Scottorum, Péronne of the Irish; and three countries saw his work.

He was born of an aristocratic house in Ireland, was well taught his Catholic religion, learned much in various Irish abbeys, and at last, with his parents' blessing and aid, built a monastery for himself and other kindred souls. There he lived until, one day when he was walking home to see his family, he was seized by a sudden attack of sickness, taken to the nearest cottage, and lay there unconscious and to all appearance dead.

Into his *Life* there is woven another Irish story of vision such as that of Brendan the Voyager. Here Fursey, his life on earth seemingly over, is carried off in the hands of angels to the doors of Heaven; he hears the sound of their wings as they bear him upwards; he catches the song of multitude upon multitude, crying *Holy, holy, holy, Lord God Sabaoth*! Protected by those who hold him, he passes safely through the four fires which burn sinners who break their baptismal vows, by lying, by greed, by strife, and by fraud. He sees as in a black cloud the forms of demons flitting past like shadows, foul and misshapen. His terror deepens as he listens to Satan, greedy for his soul, accusing him of many sins, quoting against him from holy writ the very words of God himself. But stoutly his guardian angel pleads in his defence the mercy of Heaven and the natural frailty of man. The Devil at last is conquered; Fursey is safe. Now he is given a moment of joy, joy so great that in its quest no labour would seem hard, no length of time tedious.

Then alas! at the very entrance to the country of soul's content he meets two of his own Irish people, men well known to him, who stay as they pass, for they have a message to give. He must return for another sojourn among those below in this world of sorrow. " Why fearest thou? " his friends ask. " The labour is but for a day. Do thou go forth and bid thy fellows on earth to flee from the wrath to come; for surely upon their land are marching hunger and distress. Bid teachers and leaders of the Church to hold in awe the anger of the Lord let loose against them. Half-hearted are they in their work, and negligent of the souls in their charge. Half-hearted are they in their lives, doing good with the right hand and evil with the left. Warn, too, those who of their pride and folly fast beyond their strength and fall prey to delusions of the night, to delusions of conscience, and so, all unawares, to grievous sin. Warn the pastors who neglect study of sacred books, absorbed in the doings of man's human interests. Bid each man attend to his own calling; the priest to his holy office for souls, the monk to his prayer in the silence, the workers in the world to their duties in the Church, and all with patience, diligence, and love. And as for thee, Father, do thou deny thyself, live strictly, and minister to thine own Irish folk." With these words ringing in his ears, Fursey awoke to consciousness and to health.

Up and down Ireland he preached for twelve years. Then, about the year 631, facing a breakdown through the crowds of people who constantly gathered around him and hearing that jealousy was stirring up enemies for his harm, with a few of his monks he crossed the sea and came to England, to the men of East Anglia, to Norfolk and Suffolk.

East Anglia at this time was under the rule of a king named Sigebert the First. As a young man he had been banished from England by his stepfather, Raedwald, who had been not only East Anglia's king, but overlord of the English in the south. Raedwald had been baptized, had made a perfunctory gesture of Christian profession, but had quickly fallen back into heathen ways. Sigebert had fled to France, where he, too, received Christian baptism. He, however, remained faithful; and when he came to East Anglia's throne, in 630 or 631, he took energetic steps for the conversion of his people. In this he was fully encouraged by his bishop, Felix.

Felix was himself a wayfaring saint. He had left Burgundy, his own land, and had crossed to England to aid in the work of teaching the English, those men of Germanic race who had taken Britain for their own. Honorius, to whom as Archbishop of Canterbury he presented his credentials and told his desire, sent him to Sigebert and his East Anglians, most of whom were still altogether or largely pagan. The king had been glad to welcome him, and soon his bishop's seat was settled at Dunwich, in Suffolk.

Fursey offered his aid to Felix, the bishop, was readily accepted, and threw himself with all enthusiasm into the mission of preaching, journeying up and down East Anglia. After a while, urged on by yet another vision and exhortation which he again thought to come from on high, he told the king, who was most happy in this help from Ireland, that he had it in mind to build a monastery on English land. Sigebert willingly made over to him a fortress, stoutly enclosed, and Fursey laboured with much zeal to adapt its interior for his purpose. It stood in a pleasant spot " near sea and woods "; Bede gives its name as Cnobheresburg, " Cnobber's Burgh," and many have held the thought, possible but by no means proved, that its memory still dwells in the ruins of Burgh Castle in Suffolk.

That remains uncertain. But we can truthfully look back upon Abbot Fursey on the Anglian coast as he told those of his monks whom he judged worthy to hear it his story of visions in Ireland and in East Anglia. In Bede's monastery of Jarrow, as late as 731, an old monk loved to repeat what he had heard from " a very reliable and religious man." This man had himself been among those in East Anglia who listened to Fursey's marvellous tales. It was winter-time, the man had said, and very, very cold; all was ice and frost out of doors. No doubt it was not much warmer inside. There sat Fursey, in a thin, threadbare habit; but as he spoke the memory of those sights which he had seemed to see, those sounds of fear and joy which he verily believed that he had heard, still sent the sweat pouring down his face. The " religious and reliable " witness remembered the scene vividly. To make the story he told even more lively in its warning, Fursey bore, it was said until the day of his death, a scar upon his face and shoulder. He told those who asked him, not in idle curiosity, but in a genuine desire to learn, that as he was carried through that place of punishment on which those who still dwell on earth may not look, an evil spirit threw at him one of the sinners imprisoned in its sea of flame, and that the force of the heat had caused a deep burn and this permanent mark. Satan's follower, he said, had done this in deliberate malice because Fursey had been a friend of that sinner on earth.

9

The years in East Anglia were difficult for all, for ruler and men and monks, including Fursey. There was always fear that Penda, king of Mercia, hungry for conquest, would fall upon their borders. At last this uncertainty, this terror haunting his people, became too heavy for the king, Sigebert, and he resigned his crown " to fight," as he said, " for a crown that should

MAP FOUR: Journeys of Saint Fursey and Saint Amand

endure to all eternity " among the monks of Bury St. Edmunds
in Suffolk. His rule, which had been shared even during his
reign by his kinsman Ecgric, now came to Ecgric in entirety.
In or about 635 Penda did march out from Mercia, and there
was a fierce battle in East Anglian land. In their hour of crisis
his people dragged Sigebert from his monastery to the field,
but he refused to fight. Both he and Ecgric were killed, and
Anna, a nephew of Raedwald, succeeded to the East Anglian
throne.

Anna held his throne, terror though there always was, for
nearly twenty years. He was devotedly Christian; he gave
women of his royal house willingly to the religious life and
furthered Christian working inside his kingdom and without.
But the shadow of Penda lay dark over all.

Perhaps this shadow helped to make Fursey restless. He
had for long been troubled. There was no peace even for prayer
in this worried country, and yet there were so many heathen
to try to teach. At last he made up his mind. Among the
monks who had come with him from Ireland were two of his
own brothers, Foillan and Ultan. Foillan was with him in his
monastery; Ultan was living a hermit's life in the wilds of
East Anglia. Fursey now placed his community in charge of
Foillan, who was not only monk but priest, and went to join
Ultan in the fens. For a year he tried to find peace there; but
this was really impossible, since rumours of Penda's menace
and his plans for attack were always reaching even this far-off
hermit's cell.

Once again Fursey began to think. He seemed to be doing
no good where he was; he was no soldier, no statesman, and as
a monk he had no quiet. Across the Channel, he thought,
perhaps he might find this peace. For in France the spirit of
Columban was still powerful to hold abbeys and men of
solitude in that very strict discipline beloved of Fursey's own
Irish soul. The *Rule* of St. Benedict of Nursia had not yet
gained dominion on the Continent nor had it settled in
permanence among English monks; and in East Anglia there

was, indeed, a confusing number of monastic patterns of life at this time.

Fursey left for France. There he found a warm welcome from Erchinoald, at that time Mayor of the Palace under Clovis the Second of Neustria; as we have seen, he held his office from 641 onwards, so that Fursey must have arrived in France in or after that year. Erchinoald gave the newcomer land at Lagny on the Marne, between Paris and Meaux, and there Fursey built his third monastery. Not long afterwards he fell seriously ill again, when he was on his way to visit the brothers he had left in East Anglia. It was his last illness; he died in a monastery of Irish monks at Mézerolles on the river Authie, between Abbeville and Arras.

Now begins the story, based on truth and wrapped around by legend, of the world-renowned abbey of the Irish, Peronna Scottorum. Fursey's friend and now also his devout admirer, the Mayor Erchinoald, decided to bestow upon his memory honour which should bring delight and comfort to many men. He had a residence at Péronne on the river Somme in Picardy, and there he, too, had built a monastery. It was beautiful, spacious, and in all respects worthy of its service. But it had no relics, and no abbey of any repute in Erchinoald's days failed to boast with proper pride its holy treasure, a relic of some saint's earthly tabernacle. Here, then, for this abbey at Péronne, was the body of a hermit abbot, a recipient of visions, this Fursey himself, blessed by Heaven with privilege allowed to few. And was not Fursey the godfather of Erchinoald's own son? He determined to lose no time in securing his prize.

10

We pass from history to legend. While Fursey was still on earth, we read, he had raised from death by his prayer the only son of Haimo, a powerful noble of Ponthieu. From that moment, as may well be imagined, Haimo had held Fursey the greatest saint on this earth. When, therefore, he heard of his death, the same thought came to him which had so delighted Erchinoald. Surely it was for him to make a splendid shrine for the relics of this man who had done so much for his joy in life! With all despatch he made for Mézerolles, which lay in his own Ponthieu, and was thrilled beyond words to find that what he was eagerly seeking was there, still unclaimed. When Erchinoald also came hurrying up, a little later, to his intense surprise he saw the precious body of his saint laid in all ceremony upon a bier, surrounded by candles, by clouds of incense, by monks chanting psalms, and by a strong guard of Haimo's men. " Give me back my monk! " he shouted in a rage, " or let God judge between you and me." " Why so angry? " replied Haimo. " If you are willing, God indeed shall settle this matter. To-morrow we will let two bulls which have never yet felt the yoke draw this bier in whatever direction they shall choose, and that shall be to us a sign." It was done, and the bulls pulled off straight on the road to Péronne, followed by all the peasants of the district, and by Erchinoald and his monks, singing praise to God.

The procession was suddenly halted. In the distance appeared the banners of Berchar, Duke of Laon, marching at the head of an army. " I, I myself gave him all that was in my power," said Berchar. " Gladly would he have come to be with me, but you, Erchinoald, you would have none of it. Now, though never did I see him in life, now give it to me to guard his body. Or if you will not, let Heaven decide. Put two children to guide the bier, and let them direct it as they will." Again it was done, and two little boys, seven years old, proudly led the bier as before, towards Péronne. There the sacred treasure was placed in the monastery's church, and all preparations went forward for its solemn enshrining.

So far the legend is a very familiar one. It now takes a rather more individual turn. Leutsinda, wife of Erchinoald, watched this arrival and all its ceremony from her window. She was a jealous lady, and her anger rose. " Look here! " she

rudely burst out when her lord came to tell her the great news.
" You leave me and our sons and daughters without a penny
or an acre of land, and you give it all to a perfect stranger,
sprung from Heaven knows where! " " Darling," said
Erchinoald, " you must not say such things." To which
Leutsinda retorted : " If you don't change your ways, I shall
ask for a divorce." " Stop talking nonsense, Leutsinda," said
her husband sharply. " You can have a divorce if you like.
But you will lose everything that I have given you. And you
have no idea how much we have gained by knowing Fursey.
You had better remember that he is a saint, and if he gets
angry with you, you and yours will go straight to hell."
Leutsinda smiled in contempt. " Now listen," she said.
" What harm can a man do me who has been a month rotting
in his grave? "

The ritual of the enshrining took place with all honour on
the ninth of February. Leutsinda went with a great crowd
following her to see the tomb and ordered the lid to be raised
that she might look inside. No one refused her, and, the tale
ends, she was immediately struck with blindness, which lasted
until, as is usual in these stories, she repented and regained her
sight.

We return once more to history, the history of the two
brothers, Foillan and Ultan, left behind in East Anglia to face
the Mercian power. At last in a particularly savage raid the
monastery of Cnobheresburg was plundered of its possessions
and its monks fled in despair. Its abbot, Foillan, almost lost his
life. When he could pull himself into peace for a moment and
begin to think of the future, he begged for money wherever he
could, used it to buy back at ransom all of his monks whom he
could trace, held prisoners by the enemy here and there,
searched the ruins of his abbey for any treasure left behind or,
in the case of precious books, carelessly thrown aside by Penda's
men as of no earthly value, loaded all—and it was little enough
—into a boat, and with his brother Ultan crossed to refuge
in France. Erchinoald gladly received them as Fursey's

kin at Fursey's shrine of Péronne, and there for a while they stayed.

In course of time, however, we do not know why, feeling seems to have turned against the two brothers as strangers from abroad, perhaps because they had come from England. At last, we are told, they were forced to leave, and wandered into Belgium, where we shall find them in the next chapter. Ultan, it appears, returned some time later to Péronne, for we hear of him as its abbot.

The figure of Fursey, as its narrative pictures it, is full of legend, and many readers may well question the wisdom of repeating these old stories. The answer here is that Fursey, not so much by his life on earth, although that, too, has its worth and interest, but rather by his death gave a heritage of inestimable value to the world. This, at least, is true, however much of legend encircles its fact. Among the Franks of his day his visions had made him a prophet, a soul to whom it had been given to journey beyond this world of time and to come back to tell men of the things which he had seen—things which, they firmly believed, were to be their own destiny for good or for evil after death. These Franks naturally battled for the honour of keeping his relics, and they enshrined them in all reverence.

For the Irish, here was a hero of their own country. Péronne became a centre for Irish pilgrims to the Continent. Constantly, year by year, they travelled there to make their devotions around these holy relics of their own saint. At Péronne they received hospitality and knew that they had an Irish home in their wanderings. There they received the Bread of wayfaring men from priests and monks of their own people.

Nor was this all. Between Péronne and England grew up a correspondence of men who respected the tradition of secular learning. Evidence for this correspondence has been left to us in an appeal, sent in the late seventh century by an abbot of Péronne, an Irishman whose name in Latin form was Cellanus, to Aldhelm, the scholarly abbot of Malmesbury in Wiltshire,

England, the writer of Latin letters and the researcher into the science of Latin metric and verse. Cellanus had read with great joy some of Aldhelm's work, and now he wrote to implore him in the cause of brotherly love to send him more. Had not Malmesbury itself been founded by Maelduib, an Irish wanderer into England's West Country?

For very many years Péronne lived on, faithful to its Irish tradition among the Franks. At last in the ninth century, with so many other monasteries in France, it was destroyed by the pirate Vikings of Scandinavia.

CHAPTER NINE

SAINT AMAND AND SAINT WILLIBRORD

Belgium and the Netherlands in the Seventh Century

IN THE last chapter we looked at a Frankish saint, noble in rank and a dweller at Court, who worked and journeyed for his country and its rulers, for his Church and for Irish monastic life. He laboured in France. Now we turn to look at yet another Frankish saint. He belonged to the same seventh century; he also was noble in rank and dweller at Court, also a Frankish Court; he, too, was a bishop, devoted to his Church and to the Irish-Celtic code of Columban. We shall find, however, in his work four elements which make for interest in their difference.

First, this second Frankish bishop, Amand, is remembered for his work not only in France, but largely also in Belgium. Second, he did not journey on missions of State or on pilgrimage; rather, he was a wanderer in the Irish sense of the word, one who loved solitude, but who loved, too, hastening to distant countries, wherever he heard that there were heathen men, lost without light. Third, whereas Ouen was respected and held in awe in his lifetime, Amand met universal honouring only after his death, for his life on earth was one of constant disappointment. Fourth, although Ouen deeply revered Rome and made pilgrimage to its shrines, Amand so loved the See of St. Peter that he dedicated abbey after abbey in St. Peter's name.

Christianity, of course, was not first planted by Amand in Belgium. Long before his time its teachings had been carried to the very regions where he was to work; in the sixth century by St. Vedast or Vaast, bishop of Arras, and in the first quarter of the seventh, by St. Géry, bishop of Cambrai. But much, very much, remained to be done. There were still many heathen in this land of the eastern Franks.

Amand was born in Aquitaine, of Roman descent, it was said. His early years clearly reflect Irish custom. Like many Irish boys of an earlier time, he left his home and an attractive prospect in the world, against the wish of his parents, and went off to find the training he wanted in a school on the little Île d'Yeu, forty miles from the coast of Vendée in west-central France. Next, Tours drew him through its shrine of St. Martin, the monk of the fourth century. There he prayed the prayer of the Irish, that he might spend his life *in peregrinatione*, as a stranger in exile; there he was received as monk. Then he went farther east to Bourges, where Austregisel, or Outril, who himself has a day, May the twentieth, in the calendar of saints and a medieval narrative of his *Life* and *Miracles*, was at that time bishop. With this bishop's permission and aid the young monk built a cell near the Cathedral and against the upper wall of the city, where, so at least his *Life* tells us, he lived as a hermit for fifteen years.

There now remained, it seemed to him, one last stage of preparation. He must visit Rome and gain some knowledge in that Holy City concerning his future. To Rome, if we may believe the same *Life*, he went, and decided there to offer his energy for the teaching of pagans in far Frankish regions.

2

On his return he travelled to the Frankish Court to talk with the king himself, probably Chlotar the Second, as the time seems to have been some years before 629, the date of Chlotar's death. He wanted, he told the king and the royal counsellors, to preach Christianity to the people who lived in the lowlands about the rivers Scheldt and Scarpe, north of Cambrai to Tournai and Ghent. His petition was approved; yet there was a general agreement in the Court that he ought to receive consecration as bishop before starting out. This he did receive, after the early Irish manner, as a bishop without a fixed see; he was to be truly a wanderer, in search of heathen. We do not know exactly the year in which he began this work; it was probably in or soon after 625.

For some fifty years he journeyed here and there near or in Belgian land, and the years were full of trouble. Together with his work of preaching he always kept his monastic rule, and his movements are marked for us by the abbeys which he founded as centres of support for his labour. Between the Scheldt and the Lys, on the rising ground of the Mont-Blandin, he built in about 630 a monastery of St. Peter, which was to live for centuries. Its land is now part of the city of Ghent. The people who lived around it then were not only heathen, but barbarous; and Amand fought long and hard to win a hearing, to turn them from their ritual worship of the spirits of Nature and of idols enthroned in their temples. He asked the aid of Aicharius, bishop of Noyon-Tournai; he worked under the authority of Dagobert, since 629 king over Frankish lands; but each availed him little. As he stood in the midst of the crowd, preaching with all the force of his mission, both men and women hurled sticks and stones at him, and not seldom with a rush seized and threw him into the river. Men who had come from France to help him in the work soon grew weary of that effort which seemed so futile and vain, went back to their own lands, and left him without support. As other missioners in these hard days had done and were to do, he, too, bought slaves, who in gratitude for their ransoming listened to his words, understood what they could, and received baptism at his hands.

It would be pleasant if we could believe in the turn for the better, the coming of encouragement, of which Amand's biographer tells; but, of course, the medieval biographer has no uneasy scruple in facing miracle. He tells that Amand, struck by pity, restored to life a criminal hanged on the public gallows by sentence of Frankish law—it might be, possibly, that the wretched man through the rough and ready manner of dealing justice in that day, was not quite dead—and that by this marvel Amand at last awed the people of Ghent into silence. From very curiosity they listened to a man who by his magic, they believed, could wake the dead.

Amand's chief tradition, however, rests not in modern Belgium, so far as geography goes, but just across its border, in France; not in St. Peter's abbey on the Mont-Blandin, but in another monastery of the same dedication, known as the abbey of Elnone, built by him in 630 or shortly afterwards on a site given by King Dagobert amid the marshland between the Scarpe and its tributary, the little Elnon. Around that site now hurries the busy life of the town of Saint-Amand-les-Eaux, much frequented for its mineral waters and mud baths. For three years, from 639 until 642, his work in this region was shared by a monk of Columban's monastery of Bobbio, named Jonas. This Jonas wrote a *Life* of Columban, in the preface of which he mentions his years with Amand and tells of laborious journeys around Elnone, up and down sluggish streams through sticky, oozing mud.

3

A third abbey, not actually founded by Amand but built at his urging and under his guidance, is of interest for its connection with both Frankish and Irish history. In 640 Pippin the First, of Landen, that first mayor of Austrasia, died, leaving his wife, Itta, and two children: a son, Grimoald, whom we have seen as Pippin's successor in office, and a daughter, Gertrude. Both mother and daughter were of intense religious conviction. The story goes that when Gertrude was a little girl,

King Dagobert, king of all the Franks, had come to visit her father in his home among the people of Belgium. As they sat at dinner in his hall, the king told Pippin that a young noble of Austrasia, also a guest at the table, was eager to marry this daughter of his. The mayor, himself very willing, readily sent word to Itta, his wife, to bring the child into their presence. They came, and he told his small daughter, then about eight years old, of the great honour offered her. Gertrude gave one look at her suitor, gorgeously arrayed in tunic of silk and in mantle glistening with gold, spat at him, and in her clear, child's voice said that in Heaven's name she would have no bridegroom but the Lord Christ. Such a story, as we all know, occurs frequently in the annals of saints; it is mentioned here because it is entirely in keeping with other pictures of Gertrude's character.

She was fourteen when her father died; and Itta asked advice of Amand, then working near Pippin's castle, concerning the future of this girl, now of age for betrothal. " Give her to religion," answered Amand, " and with your wealth build for her a monastery." So rose the abbey of Nivelles, a house holding both monks and nuns, as did a number of monasteries in the early Middle Ages, with an abbess at the head.

As the walls of this new abbey slowly came into shape, Itta grew increasingly impatient. Bids for the hand of her young heiress were arriving one after another. At last the abbey was almost finished, though it still lacked much of its furnishing, even its necessities. But Itta could not wait. One day on a sudden impulse she seized her scissors and cut short her daughter's long, flowing hair into a nun's cropped head. Gertrude was delighted; now, she hoped, young men would leave her in peace. Prayer and study became her twin passions; she gave every spare moment to books, and even sent messengers to Rome in search of manuscripts which she could not find in Belgium or France. Both mother and daughter entered the new abbey, and, though Gertrude was not yet twenty, because of her determined mind, her following of strict life, and her

169

pursuit of knowledge, Itta won consent from Amand that she be installed as abbess.

In this abbey of the seventh century Gertrude as abbess and Amand as director welcomed those homeless brothers of Fursey, Foillan and Ultan, driven from Péronne as aliens and strangers. Nivelles, they knew, would be friendly to the Irish; and, indeed, when they came to its gates, Grimoald, brother of the Lady Abbess and mayor of the land, promised them his protection. He did more. He built for them in Belgium another monastery of the Irish, at a place called Fosses, not far from Namur; and Itta's enthusiasm provided it with all necessary properties. Here Foillan, its abbot, laboured with Amand in his mission to the heathen of the district, and from here he often went to talk of the things of God and man with Gertrude at Nivelles. Here, in 652, he heard of Itta's death. From here, on October the thirteenth, some three years later, he started out on one of his journeys for the aiding of those in need.

On the morning of his departure he had, it seems, a strange foreboding of evil to come; and when after Solemn Mass he said good-bye to his brethren, he asked them to make search for him if he did not return, to bring home his body if death befell him on the way. Three of the monks of Fosses went with him, all on foot, but they took with them a horse in case of accident. They walked all day, and when darkness was coming on, as the road was unfamiliar to them and very lonely, they were glad to meet a man who in friendly fashion, as it seemed, gave them good night. They asked him if he knew of any cottage where they could find a lodging. At once he told them to follow him and led them by winding trails through the forest of Seneffe. Hidden in its depths was a peasant home where they were greeted with a heartiness that somehow did not ring true. They did not like the look of the men they saw, and they decided that they would do well to keep awake all night. There was nothing to be gained, they thought, by moving then and there, because they were now out of their way and because one of these men had promised to guide them in the morning.

All kept watch until after the Night Office. Then, shortly before dawn, as nothing had happened and everything seemed peaceful, Foillan told the other three to forget their fears; they had a hard day's march ahead of them, and they had better get some sleep. All four thankfully lay down. After a little while the cottage door silently opened; men came creeping in; there was a sudden rush; the monks were helpless and all were killed. The murderers hurriedly dug a rough trench in a pigsty near the house and buried the four bodies in that one grave. Then they made off as fast as they could from this place of their crime, taking with them the horse and any things carried by the monks which would not be recognised when offered for sale at a safe distance. Seventy-seven days, according to the story, until the middle of January, the monks of Fosses and of Nivelles searched far and wide. At last the bodies were found and carried reverently through the night to Nivelles and thence to Fosses for burial.

In 659 Gertrude knew that her own last days were approaching, although she was only thirty-three. For long she had left the practical business of her abbey to monks appointed by her and had given her hours entirely to prayer, to reading, and to the spiritual and intellectual problems of the monks and nuns of Nivelles. Now she declared her wish that Wulftrude, her niece, one of those nuns, should succeed her as abbess, and sent one of her monks to ask Ultan, who after Foillan's death had been elected abbot of Fosses, if he could tell her the day of her departing hence. Ultan, seemingly as gifted with Celtic foresight as his brothers, did not hesitate a moment. " To-morrow," he said, " the seventeenth of March, Gertrude, maid of the Lord Christ, shall go upon her way. And bid her, my son, that she fear not nor be anxious in her going, but depart in joy. The blessed bishop Patrick will be waiting to bring her to the company of Heaven." The messenger hesitated, evidently worried, for he was not accustomed to visions and prophecies.

After a moment he plucked up his courage and said to the reverend abbot of Fosses: " Did Heaven *tell* you this? " Ultan gave him short answer. " Don't stop to ask questions. Go quickly and tell her. To-morrow you will find out." The morrow came, St. Patrick's Day; Gertrude received viaticum, and died as she was giving thanks.

4

Other monasteries which were held in tradition as marking the scenes of Amand's labours, built by him in honour of St. Peter and St. Paul, stood at Marchiennes, on the Scarpe; at Renaix and at Leuze, between the Scheldt and the Dendre; and a little house at Barisis, near Laon. One brief chapter in his *Life* describes him at work on the Scheldt near Antwerp. He did not stay there long; but record says that he left a church, also dedicated to St. Peter and St. Paul, in the region where Antwerp now stands and that this church remained to cheer the hearts of those who came after him.

From the founding of monasteries we come to Amand's wider work as bishop. We saw that, when he was consecrated bishop, he was given no definite see as the centre of his administration. This lack of settlement remained with him during all the years of his episcopal working, except during three, probably from 646 to 649, when we may picture him as bishop of Maastricht in the Netherlands. It is easy to think that even this brief settling into the care of one Cathedral, one diocese, was not brought about by his own wish, for he loved too much to be on the move from place to place. There is some reason to suppose that it may have been caused by the request of the ruler of its land, Sigebert the Third, who was king of Austrasia from 632 until 656, and whom, tradition tells, Amand had baptized as a little child.

During these years in Maastricht Amand again knew failure and bitter disappointment. At last he poured out his misery in a letter to the man lately elected as Pope, Martin the First. The clergy of Maastricht, he wrote, simply would not obey him. They were notorious, too, for open and deliberate sin against their calling. Might he, then, depart from his seat of rule, to live in silence and peace, far from a bishop's never-ending troubles and perplexities? He was doing no good where he was.

We have the Pope's answer, a letter of sympathy with a sharp bite of exhortation. A Christian bishop, to his mind, would do better to punish his erring clergy than to retreat before them. Did not the Lord of Heaven himself fight his own battle with Satan for the sake of men's souls? And disobedient clergy were not the only problem for rulers of the Church in this year of 649. Heretics were busily spreading their lies, and bishops must be brave and bold to deal effectively with both!

The letter, whether it arrived in time for Amand's meditation, or, as is more probable, arrived too late, did not keep the bishop from leaving his see. Unwilling heathen, he decided, were easier to work with than unwilling men of God, and a martyr's death at pagan hands would be pure joy to him.

There remain two other narratives about Amand's travels, neither of them true beyond doubt; yet, true or not, they reveal Amand's repute among men of a later time. They thought of him, and truly, as dashing off with all the speed he could command to any place in any country still dark through heathen ignorance, with no thought of how he would reach it or what its people would do to him, if only he could teach them of better things. One of these stories concerns the Slavs of Austria, to whom he is said to have hurried from Belgium, through Germany and across the Danube, and from whom he won little success, not even a martyr's witness. The other story shows him on a long and dangerous journey to the Pyrenees in search of the Basque people, ferociously pagan, fiercely cruel, rejoicing in sudden descent from their mountains to plunder the Frankish lands below. Once again Amand escaped with his life; but the Basques remained savage, and blind to all better things.

5

Here, then, in contrast with Ouen, so definite in aim, so successful, we have a man who wanders ceaselessly, driven by missionary desire, who is constantly failing and as constantly beginning anew elsewhere. As we try to find possible reasons for his failures, we come upon some details which may be only straws, but, nevertheless, straws blowing in the wind of reality. It was said that, by a stern rebuking of Dagobert for some carelessness in his work, Amand so offended the king that for a while he was banished from the royal Court. When at length Dagobert sought a reconciliation, it took all the persuasion and skill of Amand's friend, Ouen, then a layman in the palace, to induce him to baptize Dagobert's baby son, Sigebert. It was also said that Amand asked and gained permission from Dagobert to force baptism by political duress upon unwilling pagans, a story which reminds us too much of the eighth century and its conqueror, Charles the Great. These stories, again, may not be true, but one detail, also relating to Amand's character and of the same colour, is certainly true. The abbots of his various monasteries were allowed no independence, save in very minor matters, in their ruling; instead, all were required to consult and to obey Amand as their head. It may, then, have been some element of autocracy, some pressure of his own will in his mission, which prevented him from gaining the heathen he longed to win.

Yet he broke ground for those who followed him, and broke it so memorably that they called him the Apostle of Belgium. His monasteries of Elnone and of the Mont-Blandin at Ghent were famous in the ninth and tenth centuries. For Elnone, Alcuin wrote his verse; at St. Peter's on the Mont-Blandin, St. Dunstan of Glastonbury spent months of refuge from a hostile English Court. The name of St. Amand still is found in many a church and in many a town or village of French or Belgian land.

In his *Testament*, a little letter of his old age, composed at a time shortly before his death about 676, he wrote to Frankish powers, spiritual and secular, these words: " To all of you it is not unknown how I have journeyed to and fro, far and wide, among all provinces and peoples, for love of Christ to teach and to baptize; and how through His goodness God has snatched me from many perils and brought me to this day. Now I am tired and wearied by many labours, and very, very old, near the hour of my death. Soon I hope to pass from this world. And so I beg and beseech that no man, neither bishop nor abbot nor layman of any rank whatsoever forbid my body to lie at Elnone, among the brethren to whose prayers I commend myself, body and soul."

There he was laid to rest.

6

From the Celts, from the Franks, we come now to the English who went abroad. The English settlers in Britain, now divided into their various kingdoms, were advancing steadily out of heathen ignorance. In the last quarter of the seventh century we find monasteries both in the south and in the north.

In the sixth century the Irish had been crossing the sea to learn from Scotland, from Wales, at Whithorn, at Llancarfan and Menevia. Now the English were journeying to Ireland, to learn in Irish monasteries. " Every one of them the Irish welcomed most gladly, lodged and fed them day by day, provided them with books and teachers, all without a penny of payment," records an Englishman, none other than the Venerable Bede.

This zeal of Englishmen to learn from Ireland, and the harmony of practice established between the English and the Celts of Ireland, were to give life to one of the most important movements in journeying abroad during this seventh century. As the monks of Wales in the sixth century thought of their kinsmen who had crossed the Channel to Brittany, and followed them there to nurture Church life among them, so now the English, whose fathers had been Saxon and pagan, remembered those of their own Germanic race, still heathen on the Continent. The problem was, when and how to begin work among them?

It began, in all appearance, through an accident of politics. In the north of England in the year 678, Wilfrid, abbot of Ripon and bishop of York, started out from his diocese of Northumbria for the Continent. He had achieved wealth and high distinction in his forty-four years of life. He had restored to newness of beauty his Cathedral after long neglect; he had built two of the most magnificent abbeys of his time, at Ripon in Yorkshire and at Hexham in Northumberland. He was a fervent follower of Rome in ritual, usage and faith, and he had been a leader in the closing of the lasting rift between the Celts and Rome.

But now he was a very angry man. Theodore, Archbishop of Canterbury, Primate in England by Papal authority, had judged this northern diocese of Wilfrid to be too vast for administration by one bishop, and, in Wilfrid's absence, had consecrated other men to share its charge. Promptly Wilfrid decided to travel to Rome to appeal against this action to the Pope. He did not dare to go by the usual route, by Étaples, for this would bring him to Neustria, where Ebroin, Mayor of Neustria, was his enemy. Ebroin, in his ambition to rule, hated the rival Frankish land of Austrasia; and his wrath had mounted high when Wilfrid, as one possessed of influence and power, had listened to the appeal of Austrasian nobles and had brought back that exiled heir to the Austrasian throne, Dagobert, to his Frankish crown and kingdom. For the past two years this exile of nearly twenty years had been enthroned in Austrasia as Dagobert the Second, and Ebroin was longing to lay hands on Wilfrid for revenge.

Now, therefore, in 678 Wilfrid took ship and crossed the Channel by another, less known route, which brought him to shore in Frisia. Medieval Frisia extended much farther than the modern Friesland, a province of the Netherlands. The Frisians of the early Middle Ages dwelt in the country stretching from the mouth of the Scheldt, at a point just north of Antwerp, along the coast of the North Sea and a little distance inland, to the mouth of the Weser in West Germany.

Christian mission had already reached them through the Franks. Very early in the seventh century a church had been built, enclosed within a fortress, at Trajectum, where now stands Utrecht. It was built by Frankish power, which had captured the city. The Franks knew the Frisians through exchange in trade, and Frankish ambition was always seeking to conquer and to add territory to its own. Dagobert the First, king of the Franks, in an attempt to justify the conquest of Utrecht, had handed over this fortress with its little church to the bishop of Cologne in Austrasia, bidding him work for the conversion of Frisian men. The bishop did nothing. Later on, in the reign of Dagobert's son, Clovis the Second, we have seen St. Amand working at Antwerp, and, as bishop of Maastricht, in charge of lands stretching out to Frisia. He, too, anxious as he was, left the Frisians as heathen as he found them.

A third bishop, in Amand's own day, laboured among the Frisians with some success. This was Eligius, now known as St. Eloi, born near Limoges in France, the friend of St. Ouen since they were boys together at the Courts of Chlotar and Dagobert. Their later years divided them widely in their secular work. Ouen, as we know, became Keeper of the Great Seal and secretary to his king; Eligius was Master of the Mint under Dagobert, and won such renown as a worker in precious metals and gems that he became the Patron Saint of goldsmiths and jewellers. Both men were consecrated bishop side by side in the Cathedral of Reims in 641, when Eligius received a double see, of Noyon and of Tournai. From Tournai, as his *Life* tells us, he worked among the men of Flanders and of

Frisia, around Ghent, around Antwerp, and among the barbarians living along the shore of the North Sea. Some of them listened to his words.

7

Wilfrid, once in Frisia, had intended to travel on through Austrasia to Italy; but on his arrival he encountered two things which delighted him. The first was " a multitude of heathen," and Wilfrid was happy about this because he had a missionary soul, as well as a mind for architecture. The second, a very necessary accompaniment to the first, was a friendly welcome from Aldgisl, the Frisian king. Promptly he forgot his wrath against Archbishop Theodore and his errand to Rome. He stayed in Frisia all the winter of 678-679, teaching his pagans and baptizing his converts. When Wilfrid was not angry (and this was seldom enough!), he was a man of magnetic charm; and here in Frisia he found an ally in Nature herself. The Frisians were fishermen, as dwellers along the North Sea. Of late their harvest had been poor and scant, but after Wilfrid's coming it grew into enormous hauls. Surely, thought the Frisians, Christianity must hold power through the deeds and the character of this miracle worker.

News of Wilfrid's success excited Ebroin to fury. He wrote to King Aldgisl: " I will send you, I swear it, a bushel of gold coins if you will hand over this bishop to me alive, or kill him and send me his head." Aldgisl tore up the letter before the eyes of Ebroin's messengers and threw it on the hearth of his great hall.

When spring came to open the roads and men began again to travel freely, Wilfrid remembered his grievance, forsook his fishermen, and went on his way to Rome. Soon the new Christian life of Frisia, left untended, died away.

8

Some eight years went by. Then the thought of the northern heathen across the Channel came to a new birth; and here we begin the main story of the Frisian mission. In Ireland, about 687, an Englishman named Egbert was studying in an Irish monastery—we are not sure just where it was. He was a priest and a monk, possibly a bishop, one of the many English who had gone to Ireland to gain inspiration from its keen spirit of life and learning. By this time, in 687, he had known Ireland for over twenty years, because we hear of him there in 664, in that year at the point of death as a victim of the Yellow Plague. Then and there he had solemnly vowed that if the Lord would spare his life, he would pass the years that remained to him in exile from his native England, working as " a stranger in a foreign land."

For a long time, then, until 687, he had obviously thought Ireland to be sufficient exile from his own country; but when he heard of the pagan peoples on the Continent, he immediately felt it his business to go and minister somewhere among them. The Lord, however, to whom he prayed with immense fervour on this matter, had different plans for him. He was first detained in Ireland by business of his monastery which he could not refuse, and long afterwards, when Ireland had wholly conformed to Roman usage, was sent to Iona to urge the same yielding there upon its monks.

Egbert was disappointed, but he cheerfully found another monk of his abbey to take his place, one Witbert, also an Englishman who had lived long among the Irish. Witbert went deliberately to Frisia. The English, as well as the Franks, had dealings with men who traded with the northern seaports; probably, also, Witbert had heard of Wilfrid's work there. Things in Frisia, however, had changed much since Wilfrid's stay eight years before. The ruler of the Frisians was now a

King Radbod, of fierce and war-loving spirit, passionately devoted to his country's political progress and to the heathen faith of his fathers. He had gathered his forces and had driven the Franks from Frisia; he was triumphant in its regained independence and was entirely hostile to any attempt of foreigners to introduce Christian teaching. After two most unhappy years Witbert gave up and returned to his Irish cell.

This was a second misfortune for Egbert, but his energy did not fail him even now. He talked and worked without cease until he found yet a third volunteer, once again a monk of English birth, a priest named Willibrord. He had lived in Ireland for twelve years, and all men held him in respect. In 690, with eleven other men, Willibrord started for the Netherlands.

He was now in his early thirties. Northumbria was his home, and there his father, a strict Christian, had given him, still only a little boy, to the care of the monks of Wilfrid's abbey of Ripon. Under Wilfrid as abbot and director of his life he had grown up; he had been novice in religion and was now a professed monk; from Ripon in 678 he had gone to Ireland. This was the year in which Wilfrid, now bishop of York, had left England for Rome; indeed, his leaving may have sharpened Willibrord's desire to seek new study in Ireland.

Now, as Willibrord journeys with his eleven followers across the North Sea, we may stop a moment before we come to his adventures abroad to think of three factors which will mould his work. First, we are now dealing with Englishmen, although they have been taught by the Irish. Their motive in travel will be what is usually described as practical. They will go forth with a definite, carefully thought-out plan, so far as their knowledge and the circumstances allow. Like the Irish, they will journey from place to place; they will love solitude; they will found churches and abbeys; they will await the revealing of God. Yet in increasing measure they will debate, they will take counsel with authority, they will organise, they will use the powers that can aid, both of Church and of State. In other words, the wayfaring English saints of the eighth century will be missionaries rather than hermits of island, forest, or lake.

Second, we shall find the work of these English missionaries carried on in close contact with Rome, under the direction of the Papal See. There will not be found among them the arguments, the pleadings of Columban for his own Irish use and custom. In his abbot, Wilfrid, Willibrord had known a passionate devotion to the Holy Father and his see. Willibrord was to show a like loyalty, as were those who followed him from England to work on the Continent.

Third, this devotion to Rome will include the monastic life according to the Benedictine *Rule*. In the first half of the sixth century, before Columban established his Irish abbeys in France, this *Rule* was born of the genius of St. Benedict of Nursia, now Norcia, a town among the Umbrian Apennines. As a young man he threw off the training in rhetoric and philosophy which, as convention commanded, he had been sent to follow in Rome. For a while he lived in a cave at Subiaco, on the course of the Anio, and eventually he gathered in its region a number of communities living under regular religious routine. When he judged that the fullness of time had come, he founded at Monte Cassino in southern Italy the house which was to mother monastic life of the future in the West.

Its *Rule* conquered all previous disciplines because its founder knew two truths of basic importance. In his own words, his was *hanc minimam inchoationis Regulam*; "a very *little Rule* with which to make a start towards higher things." The young men who turned their feet towards monasteries in the sixth century were, in great measure, ignorant of what lay before them, unaccustomed to a regular pattern of prayer, manual labour, and reading. Obedience, too, sat uneasily upon their minds. Columban therefore, as we have seen, bound upon his monks far too heavy a burden. Further, Columban's *Rule*—a name far too precise—had been vague, defined in general terms, and, where it descended to detail, largely concerned with punishments. St. Benedict described and drew his pattern in full and clearly shown detail, not only in regard to prayer, of the day and of the night, of Sundays and week days, of summer and winter, but in regard to daily and nightly living, to prescription of food and drink, of clothing for warm and for cold weather, of sleep, of speaking, by word or by sign, and of silence; in regard to household and personal articles for use; in regard to guests, to letters and gifts, to journeys made outside the monastery; in regard to work in the garden and in the fields, in the kitchen and the bakery; in regard to reading of books and to skilled practice of arts and crafts; in regard to rest at midday as well as at night; in regard to the duties of each dweller of the community, child, youth, and old man, priest and lay, from the Father Abbot himself down to the stranger who knocked for admittance at the outer doors. Punishments were levied only when all other means of remedy had failed; and all was thought out and devised in a spirit of firm but kindly reason, by one who understood both the possibility and the frailty of his fellow-men.

Finally, the *Rule* was the result of long and scrupulously planned labour. In preparation St. Benedict had not only studied the wisdom of Western authorities, such as Ambrose, Jerome, Leo, Augustine, among others, and *Rules* and *Lives* of Fathers of the East. He had carefully read canon law; and very probably also civil law, so far as it concerned his purpose. His code, so definitely thus prepared and planned, was intended by its author, as Dom John Chapman in his work on the sources and aim of this *Rule* has made clear, not only for his own monastery, not only for his own country, but for general use in the abbeys of the West, those abbeys which were so soon to follow its direction.

The sixth century, then, had seen the discipline of Columban in France, of Benedict in Italy; the late sixth and the early seventh century had seen Columban practice still persisting in France and in Belgium. Gradually, however, a union of the two codes was even then coming about, and in the late seventh and the eighth century the Benedictine *Rule* won the victory and became the prevailing pattern in Frankish religious houses of stricter life.

In England, also, in the seventh century this *Rule* was winning its way, in the south and in the north. It was Willibrord's Abbot Wilfrid of Ripon who first introduced it to the north. After this pattern, therefore, Willibrord himself had been trained. But to his training at Ripon he had now added his twelve years of Irish experience, and he was also bringing from Ireland his eleven companions.

9

The little band of twelve landed in Holland at the mouth of the Oude Rijn, the Old Rhine, near Katwijk, and all made their way by boat along its course to Utrecht. When they arrived they found new change in Frisia. Utrecht was now once again in the hands of the Franks; under their mayor, Pippin the Second, Pippin of Heristal, they had won back a goodly portion of Frisian land south of the Rhine. Much nevertheless remained to the Frisian king, Radbod, who was still ruler of many people. His anger against the Franks as his conquerors extended to anger against the Franks as Christian men, and thence to Christian missionaries of any race. Christian creed was now linked in his mind with Christian seizure of his territory.

Willibrord saw quickly that he had no hope of success, in Utrecht or elsewhere, unless he gained authority and promise of support from Pippin. He therefore set out without delay to place before this mayor his petition. As Pippin talked with him, the thought in the mayor's mind was just the contrary to that of the heathen Radbod: Christian conversion would, he hoped, widen the secular holding of the Franks. Readily he gave his good will to the mission and promised to stand behind it for its defence. Temporal support thus won, Willibrord next turned to think of spiritual. Soon, probably in 692, he was venturing on the journey across the Alps to Rome, to ask from the Head of the Catholic Church formal authority and sanction for this work which he planned to do in Frisia. The Pope, Sergius the First, was as eager as Willibrord himself. He listened to his ideas, approved them, and sent the young priest on his way back with the Papal blessing, with relics of the saints for the honouring of the churches to be built in Frisia, with a definite " dismissal " from Rome as its representative in that far-off land, and with an injunction to keep him, the Pope, regularly informed of all that was being done.

Much, however, had happened in Frisia while Willibrord had been absent. His fellow-workers, certain that a bishop was badly needed for their mission, had elected one of their number, Suidbert, for this office. We do not know whether some feeling against Willibrord brought about this election in his absence, and caused the election of another rather than himself, the leader of the little band in this foreign country. On the other hand, it is possible that Willibrord wanted to devote himself to the office of abbot (and in the Ireland where he had lived so long an abbot was still of major importance); perhaps Suidbert as bishop was intended to work under the guidance of Willibrord as head of the community in Frisia.

Two more surprising events followed the election. Suidbert did not seek consecration on the Continent from a Frankish bishop, but from Bishop Wilfrid in England. Secondly, " not long afterwards " this newly consecrated bishop for Frisia left Frisia and his work there and travelled east to try to convert the people who lived between the rivers Ems and Lippe in West Germany. This, of course, may have been only a temporary mission; and Willibrord himself was eager to reach out to the heathen as far as could be. Perhaps, however, hostility on Pippin's part to the election of Suidbert had its influence on Suidbert's going, first to England, and then to Germany.

At any rate, his work soon came to an end when the people for whom he was working were conquered by other Germans and scattered. He did not return to Frisia. Perhaps this pleased Pippin, for at the petition of his wife, Plectrude, he gave Suidbert a gift of land at Kaiserswerth on the Rhine, near Düsseldorf. There Suidbert built a monastery, and there he remained until in 713 he died. He left, it must be said, a firm impression of faithful work behind him; and both Holland and Germany revered him as saint.

On Willibrord's return we find him for a time at Antwerp, near the Frisian border, rejoicing in the church of St. Peter and St. Paul which Amand had built. Then he turned all his energy upon Utrecht and the villages round about, with most encouraging results. King Radbod's feeling against Frankish conquerors and English missionaries had relaxed something of its bitterness. It may have been about this time that he saw his daughter, Theutsinda, married to Grimoald, a son of Pippin and Plectrude. Pippin himself rejoiced when at last Willibrord gave consent to his own election as bishop. As we are told by Bede in his *History*, " with the approval of the brethren in Frisia, Pippin sent Willibrord to Rome, where Sergius still held the Papal See, asking the Pope to appoint him Archbishop for the Frisian people."

The petition was granted. On November the twenty-first, 695, in the church of St. Cecilia in Trastevere, Willibrord received his consecration. It was the eve of St. Cecilia's Day. It was also two days before the Feast of St. Clement of Rome, held in tradition as another man who had lived in exile for his faith. The Pope, as he laid his hands upon Willibrord, remembered this and gave him a new name of " Clement," a name which Willibrord always delighted to use.

He made his Archbishop's home among the Frisians in the ancient castle of Utrecht. It was Pippin's gift to him, and with it Pippin gave one tenth of the revenue from the city's public treasury. The little church inside the walls was now in ruins, but Willibrord rebuilt it and gave it a dedication to St. Martin. In Utrecht he also founded another church, that of St. Saviour, to serve as his Cathedral.

Many friends helped the mission as it fought its way. About 698 Irmina, abbess of Oeren near Trier, Germany, gave Willibrord a little monastery standing on her own abbey's estate; and some years later Pippin and Plectrude greatly enlarged its bounds. Thus Willibrord became abbot of a well-endowed religious house some hundred and sixty miles from Utrecht, a house which in the course of years was to become the famous abbey of Echternach. During Willibrord's hard work it gave him a beloved place of retreat, of peace and solitude, far from the problems of his see.

Friends from home, also, visited him now and then. In the winter of 703-704 he had the happiness of welcoming Wilfrid of York, his abbot of so many years past. This is the Wilfrid whom we saw in 678 as a man of forty-four, bishop of York, starting out for Rome in passionate resentment at the loss of what he held to be just and due to himself. Now he was old; but the same anger and the same insistence upon his rights were driving him a second time to plead his case before a Papal court at Rome. In the years that had passed between these two journeys he had moved constantly and miserably from place to place in his struggle against archbishop after archbishop and king after king in his English land; from prison to prison in the north of England and in Scotland, to long exile in the midland kingdom of Mercia and the southern kingdom of Sussex. Peace was finally to come to him in 706 as bishop of Hexham in Northumberland and abbot of Ripon in Yorkshire; three years later he died, on a journey, at his monastery of Oundle in Northamptonshire.

His name may fittingly be remembered here, for he was indeed a wayfaring man, and the Church remembers him as saint upon the twelfth of October every year. He worked in his exile, here and there, with zeal for the teaching of souls; he did very much to enhance the glory of the Church in art and architecture in England, in the fostering of the practice of the Benedictine *Rule*. But his spirit was not that of the early wayfarers who forsook all for love of God and their fellow-men.

10

Sometimes, both before and after he became Archbishop, the determined indifference of King Radbod of Frisia so discouraged Willibrord that he went off to find relief in other fields of work. Once we find him travelling by boat to the Danes, who lived north of Saxony, beyond the estuary of the Elbe. Here, however, he could make no impression upon either the natives or their king, whose name was Ongendus, for all were convinced and devoted heathen. The king, to be sure, received these strangers with fitting ceremony; and when after a short stay they left his unfruitful land, he allowed them to take away thirty Danish boys. Probably he thought this only a kindly gesture and in no way expected them to absorb Christian doctrine. But Willibrord nurtured the hope that some day they might return to convert their own tribesmen. On the way back to Utrecht, after careful effort of instruction, he baptized them all. His own language was akin to theirs, and with some trouble he managed to make himself understood.

Adventure befell the party before it reached its journey's end. A storm came on, so violent that Willibrord's boats were driven to take shelter on an island, now thought to be Heligoland, off the coast of West Germany. Men of Frisia, strange to say, were living on this island, subjects of the same King Radbod, although they had not been conquered by Pippin and his Franks. Like Radbod and his friends they were fiercely pagan. They especially worshipped a god whom they called Fosite, and their island they called Fositesland. Fosite may have been originally a tribal deity. Perhaps in later days his cult was mingled with that of Forseti, of whom Old Norse Eddic poetry tells, sitting ever in Glitnir, the great hall of judgment that gleamed bright with gold and silver, to settle and put to rest disputes between men.

So deep was the reverence of the islanders for this god that not one of them, from warrior to little child, would dare to touch any creature, beast or bird, that browsed or settled or flew near his sacred shrine; they even dared not call aloud when they came to draw water from his holy spring. Death was the inevitable penalty for such sacrilege, if not from the wrath of the god, from the men who honoured him. They were then more alarmed even than angry when one day word ran round among them that Willibrord, this stranger of alien worship, was not only baptizing into Christianity three of their own men, doubtless bewitched by his Christian magic, in their own god's stream, not only breaking the silence by his clearly spoken words, but that he was actually allowing his hungry monks to kill for their dinner one or two of the oxen grazing near by. As it happened, King Radbod himself was at the moment visiting the island, and news of the insult, for so the islanders held it, was at once carried to him.

Radbod arrived to investigate, learned all that had been heard and seen, renewed all his rage, and ordered penalty, the most severe he knew. As Frisian justice decreed, he commanded that lots be cast among the offenders, and that any one of them on whom a lot descended should at once be put to death. Three times a day the lot was thrown, for three days, while Willibrord and his followers expected their end. All escaped until sunset on the third day, when, at the last casting, the lot caught one of the monks. While all the others were horrified at his fate, Radbod decided that atonement had now been made and allowed his unwelcome guests to depart without delay.

Another time we find Willibrord in the province of Zeeland, on the island of Walcheren, the south coast of which faces the estuary of the western Scheldt. Here he boldly knocked into pieces an idol, revered from time immemorial, and received in return a sharp blow on the head from its guardian. But he survived.

As often as he could spare the time, he went for brief retreat at Echternach. There we find him called to minister to the nuns of a convent in Trier, the city nearby. Many of them were sick, for an epidemic was raging in the district, and Willibrord's ministry brought comfort, we are told, and even power of healing.

II

Meanwhile he was thinking of the future. Some of his most able followers he consecrated as bishops who should carry on the work after his death. We do not, however, read that they were assigned any see, and Utrecht remained the centre of this mission to Frisia. Priests, too, were ordained, including men native to the land. Churches and monasteries were built, largely through the generosity of Pippin and his wife. One of these cloisters stood on land given by Plectrude at Susteren, in the Dutch province of Limburg, near the river Maas, built " for a community of strangers from afar, and of other men who fear God."

But always, under a thin veneer of harmony, Frisian resentment against the Frankish occupation of so much of their land was still simmering. For the later years of his life Pippin was glad to leave the burden of part of his responsibility, as Mayor of the Franks in charge of Neustria, to his son Grimoald, described in Frankish chronicle as " temperate, mild and just." In April, 714, as Grimoald was on his way to visit his father, ill in bed, and had stayed a moment to pray in the church of St. Lambert of Liège, he was struck down while he knelt by a pagan, probably of Frisia, named Rantgar; " son of Belial," the chronicle calls him. Eight months later Pippin himself died, and the tumult of civil war broke out among the Franks.

Pippin's two legitimate sons were dead; there remained only a third, Charles, borne to him by a mistress. History knows him as Charles Martel, " the Hammer of the Saracens." His father at his death had left to his widow, Plectrude, the regency in Frankish government for his three grandsons, all of lawful title. They were only children now, but eventually, so he directed and willed, they were to hold office as mayors of Austrasia and Neustria. Charles Martel, as illegitimate, was left without political rank. He was, however, a man of adult years and exceedingly ambitious. Battle at once flared up between him and Plectrude, now officially in control of Frankland, east and west.

This disruption among the Franks was exactly the chance for which the Frisians had longed. Under their king, Radbod, they rose to recover their lost lands, overran Utrecht and the surrounding country, drove out Willibrord and his monks, wrecked the hated Christian churches, and triumphantly restored the worship of their heathen ancestors. Willibrord fled to his abbey of Echternach. Now, in 715, all that he had done in Frisia seemed to lie in ruins, hopeless and dead.

12

Yet when four years had passed, he was back again. The revolt of the Frisians was over; the rule of Frankish power was again firmly established in Frisian land. During these four years Plectrude had thrown Charles Martel into prison; but he had escaped to meet her forces in a great struggle and to crush them. In the end he had made himself supreme ruler among the Franks, and, with them, among the Frisians. Moreover, most important for the Frisian mission, Charles Martel was its friend and ally. In 719 Radbod died; his successor was now ready to work with the Church in Utrecht. Willibrord returned, looked upon havoc and confusion everywhere, and started courageously to build again. Charles aided him with funds from his own resources, for he liked and trusted Willibrord and had already seen his little son baptized by him. This son was to play a leading part in Frankish history as Pippin the Third, or Pippin the Short.

For two years, from 719 until 721, we see Willibrord busy

and happy in this work of restoration. He was now well on in his sixties, and he had had a hard life. A letter sent long afterwards, in 753, by St. Boniface to the Pope, then Stephen the Second, tells of the courage of this fellow-countryman of his: " Willibrord remained preaching in his see and in its church of St. Saviour," he wrote, " until his strength failed him in old age." We do not know when this forced him to retreat; we read of him in 728, and we believe that he died at Echternach on the seventh of November, 739. There his relics rested for the reverence of pilgrims, and there his Feast was kept with all solemnity year by year.

We know little, indeed, of Willibrord's inner life. None of his letters is left us to speak of his longing to see his friends in England, of his loyalty to the Holy See, of his respect for Pippin and his sons, Grimoald and Charles Martel, of his discouragement in the struggle against Radbod. His *Life* was written by Alcuin in the late eighth century, but it holds more praise than information. All in all, we may perhaps think of him as of St. Amand. They tore away briars and weeds from the ground, they sowed, they watered; but neither their time nor their character allowed the full harvest. Amand had not the tact, and Willibrord lacked power of organisation; both needed the genius of Boniface for their work's continuance.

We have, however, the interesting record called the *Calendar of St. Willibrord*. This belonged to him; he himself wrote (in Latin) on the margin of the page for November: " In 690 Clement-Willibrord came overseas to the land of the Franks; in 695, although unworthy, he was ordained bishop at Rome by the Apostolic Lord, Pope Sergius. It is now the year of our Lord 728." The Calendar was written by an Englishman, it would seem; its script is English, and it holds the names of many English saints. Its date falls in the early years of the eighth century.

The names which it commemorates point to its use by Willibrord. Cecilia, Clement, and Pope Sergius mark his connection with his own experience in Rome; Patrick and

Brigid with Ireland, where he lived so long; Paulinus, Edwin, Oswald, Oswine and Cuthbert with Northumbria, his own land; Amand and Suidbert with Frisia, the scene of his work.

Down the years, from the Middle Ages to modern times, men have reverenced Willibrord at Echternach. There in that little town they have gathered every spring on the Tuesday of Pentecost, Whit Tuesday, to offer their prayer in the symbol of the dance. This " Dance of St. Willibrord " is famous, nor is the custom strange. From the time of the women of Israel, who went out after Miriam, the sister of Aaron, with timbrels and with dances; of David who danced before the Lord with all his might; of the Psalmist who called to men to praise the name of their King in the dance; from the days of Greek drama to our own days, which still endeavour to express in the body's motion truth which cannot be given in words, men have turned to this outlet of their feeling, their need, their desire.

So at Echternach the people gather in thousands, with bishops, with priests, for the ritual of their saint; the chanting of the *Veni Creator*; the exhortation of the preacher; the reverent dancing through the streets of the town, between dense crowds of spectators, up the steps of the church, up and down its aisles, and around the shrine of Willibrord. Four or five abreast they dance, three steps forward, two steps back, and as they go they sing a litany, with its constant refrain, *Heiliger Willibrord, Bitte für uns!*

CHAPTER TEN

SAINT BONIFACE;
SAINT LULL; SAINT LEOBA

Germany in the Eighth Century

THERE IS no wanderer of these early Middle Ages who journeyed across the sea and across mountains, through forest and wilderness, in perils of waters, in perils of robbers, in perils by the heathen and among false brethren, more bravely than did Wynfrid, known to all by the name of Boniface. There is no bishop who carried more faithfully the burden which came upon him daily, the care of all the churches of his mission to the Netherlands and to Germany. There is no man who loved more his own country and his friends, his monastery and his books, or who, with greater fortitude, left them all to organise the rising Christian life of Germany, to build there church and school and cloister, to tell of the Christian faith to unnumbered heathen of barbarian tribes, and finally to die at their hands.

It was the need of Frisia after the destruction of Christian work by Radbod's fury that called Wynfrid from the West Country of England in 716. He had been only a child when his father had placed him for training at the monastery of Exeter, in Devonshire. From there he had gone on to study at the abbey of Nursling, near Southampton, Hampshire, where its abbot, Winbert, had encouraged him greatly in his love of books. Of course, he read those which a monk should know. He grappled also with problems of the analysis of words, with grammar and the science of metre; he wrote and rewrote his own Latin prose and verse until at last he became recognised as a master of Latin style. Many came to Nursling to win from him the enlightening of their minds, or begged by letter the gift of his knowledge. All his spare time he read and wrote; yet always he kept in due round the *Rule* of St. Benedict. When he had passed his thirtieth year he was known to the English world as scholar and teacher, monk and priest.

Not only, moreover, was he a man of learning and of religion. He was wise in debate, firm in decision, quick to disentangle the needless from the needful, ready in time of crisis. It was he whom Ine, king of Wessex, sent to Bertwald, Archbishop of Canterbury, to represent his realm in matters of high importance to the Church of the West of England.

And, lastly, he was friend to his brother-monks, his fellow-clergy, to a multitude of men and women who found in his cheerful vitality the encouragement they lacked. His abbot, Winbert, now growing old, thought with joy that Wynfrid would surely be elected his successor at Nursling.

Then, in 716, when Wynfrid was about forty, he came one day to this abbot with a petition. Might he go to do what he could to help the Church in Frisia? Willibrord had fled; Christians were scattered or dead throughout the country; the heathen were working havoc in Utrecht.

Abbot Winbert pleaded with him long and earnestly; yet in the end, of course, he yielded his community's need to the far greater one of Frisia. The year was still young when Wynfrid set out for London, with two or three of his brethren who had asked to share the work. From London they crossed to the coast of the Netherlands, then went by boat on the river Lek to Wijk-bij-Duurstede, and so by the Kromme Rijn, the "Crooked Rhine," to Utrecht.

Deep disappointment awaited them. It seemed that there was nothing they could do, work as they would. The churches lay in ruins or were given over to pagan ritual. King and people were united in hatred or in indifference towards the Christian mission. In the autumn of 716 Wynfrid and his companions were forced to return home, and Nursling dutifully tried to crush its delight.

For eighteen months Wynfrid waited. The good Winbert died, and election as abbot fell on him himself. He pleaded his unwillingness, and all knew the reason. In the spring of 718 he talked with his bishop, Daniel of Winchester. The bishop shortly afterwards appointed a monk of adequate ability as head of Nursling, and Wynfrid, he declared, was free to go abroad to try once more his fate.

Again he journeyed to London with other men of adventure, and again he crossed the sea, but this time to France, to a point near Étaples. He was on his way to Rome. In him we shall find the final fastening of the bond between the Papal Chair and the English mission sent to the heathen of the Continent. His failure in 716 had given him to think. Now he was determined to start his work anew under the direction, under the authority, of the Holy See.

2

Summer was closing in as he crossed the Alps, and the cold was bitter. In northern Italy he dreaded attack from savage soldiers of the Lombard king, but Rome at last was reached in safety. All that winter he stayed in the City, visiting its holy places, talking with the Pope, since 715 Gregory the Second. In May, 719, Gregory gave him farewell: " In the Name of the Indivisible Trinity and by the authority of blessed Peter we bid you go forth, bearing word of God's grace to the peoples who wander bound in their unbelief. And may God go with you."

For thirty-five years Wynfrid carried these words in his mind. He worked under four Popes: Gregory the Second, Gregory the Third, Zacharias, Stephen the Second. Three times in all these years he was in Rome to seek the Pope's blessing; now, in 718-719, when he first received his commission, and in token of this a new name of Boniface, the name of a martyr whose Feast fell on the day before the ceremony; in 722, when Pope Gregory the Second consecrated him bishop on St. Andrew's Day, the thirtieth of November, a bishop for German lands, with no fixed see; and in 738-739, when he needed further authority and more workers for his now widely organised fields.

In 732 there came to him new responsibility, clothed in further conferring of honour, when Pope Gregory the Third raised him to the dignity of Archbishop in Germany. He still, however, had no see of his own. Not until 745 did the Frankish rulers of State decide, with the Pope's approval, to appoint him Archbishop of Cologne. Frankish bishops, however, jealous of his power and of his standing as Papal Legate in Germany, resisted the plan. It fell through, and shortly afterwards he was given a seat as bishop of Mainz. He was never Archbishop of its cathedral, for Mainz did not become a metropolitan see until long after his death.

From the day when, before his consecration in 722, he took the oath prescribed for bishops and promised entire obedience to the Catholic Church and to its rulers, the successors of St. Peter, until the day in 752, only two years before his death, when he wrote to a Pope lately elected, Stephen the Second, praying " that I may be able to remain your faithful and devoted servant, as I have served the Apostolic See under three of your predecessors," Boniface, as we shall now call him, kept his word with fullness of loyalty. In this faith he led his clergy and his people. To Cuthbert, Archbishop of Canterbury, he wrote in 747: " We have decreed and declared in our Synod our will to hold fast the Catholic Faith and Unity, to yield submission to the Church of Rome as long as life shall last for us." To Rome, as Pope succeeded Pope, he constantly referred his problems, asking for counsel and decision. In return there came unceasingly from Rome to Boniface enheartening, detailed answers to his problems, considered one by one; and, to those with whom he was working, bishops, nobles, clergy and layfolk, the voice of Papal power, standing firm behind his labours.

To the secular powers from whom he, and the Pope for him, asked aid and protection, Boniface tried hard to give the co-operation, the respect, which he desired to give; to the mayors of the Frankish people: to Charles Martel, who was ruling when he began his work in 719; to the sons of Charles Martel, Carloman and Pippin the Short, who, after the death of Charles in 741, shared with one another the rule of Mayor of the Franks until Carloman retired to a monastery in 747. This same co-operation he gave to Pippin as sole mayor from 747 until 751; and to this same Pippin under a changed title from 751 onwards, when the Franks, having asked counsel of the Pope, decided to replace a puppet king by a real one. The last of the worthless sovereigns of the Frankish royal house, Childeric the Third, was deposed; and Boniface himself anointed, as king, Pippin the Short, first of the Carolingian line and father of Charles the Great.

3

These years in all their course were filled with conflict, as Boniface struggled with unceasing perplexities. When he returned in 719 from his first visit to Rome he began the difficult work of trying to convert the Thuringians, a wild people of the north-east, no doubt sent among them by the Pope himself as a trial of his power of endurance. He soon discovered that the time was too early for this attempt, and in this same year we find him a fellow-labourer of Archbishop Willibrord in Frisia. So successful was their partnership that Willibrord, now weakened by old age, began to hope that Boniface might follow him as bishop there. Boniface, however, was eager for his own field of battle in Germany; and in 721 he went on his separate road.

In 721 and 722 he was in Hesse, land of the Eder, the Rhine, and the Main, and there he returned in 723, after his journey to Rome and his consecration as bishop. About 725 he turned eastwards to Thuringia, the land which already in 719 he had briefly penetrated, a land of dense forest extending mile after mile; about 735 southwards into Bavaria. Christian teaching had been brought to Thuringia earlier, we may think by the Irish St. Kilian of Würzburg; tradition declared him murdered there. We have seen Eustasius, successor of Columban in the abbot's chair at Luxeuil, working among the Bavarians. But neither in Thuringia nor in Bavaria nor in Hesse had the work progressed far. As to the Saxons, the bitter struggle between them and the Christian profession was to come half a century later in the time of the grandson of Charles Martel, Charles the Great.

In this earlier century of Boniface, pagan ritual and worship were found everywhere in Germany. Not only did heathen men banquet on meats offered in sacrifice at the shrines of idols; men professing and calling themselves Christians did the same, content merely to mark the sign of the Cross over the luscious feast. Boniface did not dare to allow in Christian homes food from various wild animals and birds—horse, wild and domestic, beaver, hare, jackdaw, crow and stork. Who knew whether such meat had not been offered previously in pagan ritual? Christian people who should be offering through their priests requiem Mass were taking part in pagan rites for their dead. Christian profession was penetrated and mingled inextricably, it seemed, with heathen practice. The carrying of charms and amulets on one's person, the use of augury, the working of magic spells, were common to many, heathen and Christian alike. Boniface even felt obliged to write to Rome for instruction regarding the ritual of the Paschal candle, blessed in church on Easter Eve, so confused had this become with the pagan ceremony of the fire kindled in spring-time to honour the rising sun. Among the faithful who came to church were some who sold their own slaves to the heathen as offerings to unknown gods in human sacrifice and never thought this wrong; " murder," the Pope called it, when he wrote to Boniface. Numberless were the wells, springs, streams and trees revered in worship as the dwelling places of some Power which must be propitiated. Every one who has read of Boniface knows the story of the famous oak of Geismar in Hesse, the " oak of Jupiter," which the wind, after the first light stroke of his axe, blew down in miracle to the panic of heathen men, the oak which in his hands yielded its wood for the building of a little monastery and church of St. Peter.

Nor were the heathen active in barbarous worship alone. Towards the end of his years in Germany Boniface wrote to Pope Stephen: " Please forgive me that this letter comes so late. I have been so busy in rebuilding churches burned by the pagans. More than thirty have been plundered and set on fire."

4

Among the converts and Christians, also, there rose other problems, problems of practice, hard to decide. To the mind of Boniface all must be done decently and in order. He wrote to ask the Pope question after question regarding the proper administration of sacraments in this far-off mission field. What do I do, he asked, about those baptized by pagans, or by Christian priests who have taken part in heathen rites? About those baptized by heretics, and not in the Name of the Father, the Son, and the Holy Spirit? About those duly baptized in the Name of the Holy Trinity, but in barbarous words of native dialect?

At one time, in Bavaria, Boniface ran into trouble in this matter of baptism in uncouth language. Among the many Irish priests working in Germany was one named Virgil, Ferghil in his native land. Like so many of his countrymen he, too, had come *pro amore Christi* to the Continent from Ireland, where he had been abbot of the monastery of Aghaboe which, as we saw, had been founded by St. Kenneth in Ossory. In Bavaria he was working hard to convert heathen souls, but, like Columba and Columban, with little thought of the Archbishop in charge. Then the horrid report reached Boniface that, in spite of a reputation for learning, Virgil was baptizing babies and converts in a Latin which lacked all sense of grammar: *Baptizo te in Nomine Patria et Filia et Spiritus Sancti.* This to a disciplined mind was so irregular that Boniface ordered Virgil to repeat the rite anew, and, as usual, he reported what he had done in a letter to the Pope, then Zacharias.

The Pope was shocked at the order. Heresy indeed, and omission to baptize with water in the proper words with right intention, yes, that would make repetition necessary. But mistakes in form of grammar, No!

Marriage, too, presented its difficulties, especially in regard to the rules of kinship between the parties. Only remote cousinship could be permitted, Pope Gregory the Second wrote in 726, and that only as a concession to " barbarous people." Fifteen years later Boniface was writing to Pope Zacharias to ask what he was to do with a man of noble rank who wanted to marry a widowed lady who was his cousin, his aunt by marriage, and a religious who had broken her vow of chastity? He would not, of course, have troubled the Holy Father with such a question, but the man was declaring that the Papal See itself had given permission for the wedding. To which Zacharias promptly replied: " God forbid the accursed lie and scandal! "

In the matter of ordination Boniface pleaded, and won his plea, that this be advanced for priests from the canonical age of thirty to that of twenty-five. Priests, he said, were so badly wanted in Germany. Was he to blame, he asked Zacharias, for ordaining at times and seasons other than those prescribed? The same letter asked that he be told exactly where in the Canon of the Mass he and his priests ought to make the sign of the Cross.

This same Boniface, so careful and anxious that all things be done aright, with magnificent skill ordered and organised for the Church the lands in which he worked. Bavaria in 739 he divided into four dioceses: one, centred at Passau, which he found already existing and possessed by a bishop, and three which he carved out, placing their bishop's seats respectively at Regensburg, at Freising, and at Salzburg. In 741 he made yet another see for Bavarian land, at Eichstätt, then the home of a monastery, where he placed as bishop one Willibald of English birth whom we shall meet again in our story. In the same year he created for Hesse a diocese with its see at Buraburg, near Fritzlar; for the Thuringians he made two: one governed from Würzburg, the other from Erfurt. The new bishops of Buraburg and of Würzburg had also come from England.

From 742 until 747, under the sons of Charles Martel, Carloman and Pippin who shared office as mayors of the Franks, synods were assembled regularly through the determined will of Boniface to put in order the discipline of the Church. By them not only were pagan practices forbidden and condemned, but also the many evils which abounded among bishops, priests, and deacons in German towns and villages. The letters of Boniface to Rome, to England, tell again and again of these latter troubles. " For the greater part," he wrote to Pope Zacharias, " the sees of bishops in our cities here have been handed over to grasping laymen or adulterous clergy for secular enjoyment. What do I do if I find deacons who from the time they were boys have spent their lives in foul, filthy, immoral pursuits of every kind; who, ordained ministers of the Church, sleep with four or five mistresses, yet neither blush nor fear to read the Gospel at Mass, to proceed to the priesthood, declaring themselves fit to make intercession for the people and to offer the Holy Sacrifice, worthy, indeed, to be elected and consecrated bishops? Their children, born to them illegally, even to bishops and priests, cry aloud their guilt. May I have your authority, Holy Father, to deal properly with such? "

Definite instruction came in answer from the Pope: " You

have informed me, my brother, that you have found far more false priests than true: men who pretend to the name of their sacred calling but have never been called to it by Catholic bishops, men who delude the layfolk, who confuse and disturb the ministry of the Church; roamers without title, men effeminate, homosexual, murderous, sacrilegious and hypocritical; many runaway slaves, falsely wearing monastic tonsure; servants of the Devil arraying themselves as priests of Christ, living under no authority of a diocese but doing as they choose, looking to the people for protection from their Fathers in God; men who call together the peasants of the countryside, and these come willingly enough, to " minister " to them in their loathsome falsity, not openly in the churches, but hidden in village gatherings, in cottages, where their folly and ignorance will escape notice by their bishops; who neither preach the Catholic faith to the heathen nor themselves know and understand that faith aright; who neither teach nor require from their hearers that renouncing of Satan, that belief in the One God and Holy Trinity, which any candidate for baptism old enough to understand what it means must profess. These men, my brother, are ministers, not of God, but of Satan. You are to forbid them every priestly act. You are to send them to a monastery, there to do penance for the rest of their lives."

This instruction could well be understood; but how was Boniface to capture these sinners? And there was always that other problem eternally present. What, if he forbade priests truly and rightly ordained, but guilty of mortal sin, to exercise their office, what about the *lack* of priests? To Egbert, Archbishop of York, he wrote concerning a priest who had fallen into immoral living: " If I remove him from his work, as in strict obedience to canon law I ought to do, babies will die unbaptized, for there are so few priests to carry out what must be done. Is it better, or, shall I say, less evil, to have a man like this ministering at the altar, if I cannot find one more worthy, than to let a multitude of heathen die in darkness? Besides, he has amended his ways; both priests and layfolk who do not know of this man's past wickedness respect him; they all would be shocked if I told them the truth. Is not the risk of keeping him less than the serious loss to so many of my people here?"

It was very hard, also, to decide whether one should, or should not, exchange friendly talk with priests and bishops of notoriously evil ways when one met them at social functions. At his consecration as bishop in 722 Boniface had solemnly sworn to have no dealings with such men unless he could hope to help them towards better things. In the last years of his life he wrote to Zacharias: " In the spirit I have kept my oath, for my soul has not consented to their devising. But in body I have not been able to stay altogether aloof, when I have been at the Frankish Court, called by the necessity of the churches, and have found there priests of this kind. I have had to speak with them. Yet I have not held fellowship with them in the communion of the Body of Christ."

5

Some of the most fruitful and permanent work of Boniface was done in the founding of monasteries, built for the strengthening of new Christian life in the regions around their walls. There were, indeed, monks and monasteries in Germany before he arrived, but he found them badly in need of direction, discipline, and reform. Synods in 742 and 743, held under the guidance of Boniface as Archbishop, ordered that monks and nuns guilty of immorality should be cast into prison, there to do penance on bread and water; that monks should not bear arms or fight as laymen in the army; that they should not hunt or wander through the woods with hounds, or keep hawks and falcons for sport. A letter written in 747 to Archbishop Cuthbert of Canterbury referred in words of the strongest condemnation to that evil, prevalent both in England and among the Franks, the possession and rule of a dedicated house of religion by a " lay " abbot. " The layman," Boniface wrote, " whosoever he may be, emperor or king or governor or count, the layman who through trust in his secular power wrests a monastery from the control of bishop or abbot or abbess, who takes it upon himself to rule it as ' abbot,' to hold monks under his obedience, to hold in his hands its revenues, that ' abbot ' the Fathers of the Church declared to be a robber, sacrilegious, a murderer of the poor, the wolf of Satan entering the sheepfold of the Lord, a man to be condemned and banned with the uttermost anathema before the judgment seat of Christ."

Another difficulty turned up in the matter of Irish wandering bishops, of no see, attached, as in Ireland of the sixth century, to various monasteries for the fulfilling of their functions under the direction of their abbots. This was contrary to the sense of churchly constitutional order held both by Rome and by Boniface himself.

In Hesse Boniface established monasteries, one at Amöneburg near Marburg, of St. Michael, and another at Fritzlar, close to the river Eder, in honour of St. Peter. Thuringia held the abbey of Ohrdruf, not far from Erfurt. Three cloisters for women were placed near the river Main, at Kitzingen, at Ochsenfurt, at Tauberbischofsheim. All these followed strictly the *Rule* of St. Benedict.

Although these abbeys are well known to history, it is the name of Fulda which lives on most vividly in our minds. The story of its founding is told in the *Life* of Sturm, written in the ninth century by his pupil, Eigil. Sturm, a son of Bavarians of noble rank and Christian profession, had come as a lad under the instruction of Boniface. The Archbishop had met him, it seems, when he first went to survey the conditions of Church and people in Bavaria about 735. Young though Sturm was at that time, he gladly welcomed an invitation to join in work under this scholar and leader of missionary enterprise. The abbot of Fritzlar, already a growing centre of religion, gave him thorough training. There Sturm was ordained priest; and there, after three years of teaching and preaching on the banks of the Eder, he began to long for a stricter monastic life, enclosed in study and contemplation.

Boniface understood his longing only too well. When Sturm at last ventured to ask that he might go forth to find some place in which to build a cloister more remote from the noise and conflicts of the world, " Go out," Boniface said to him, " into the wilderness, and try to find a place meet for the dwelling of servants of God; for God is able to raise up for His servants a place in the desert." With two companions Sturm started out, travelling on foot through land wild and lonely, " seeing scarcely anything but sky and earth and trees, spreading far and high." Along the valley of the Fulda they walked until they reached Hersfeld, now Bad Hersfeld, known for its mineral springs. They looked around; it seemed a likely spot. They built some rude huts of branches, covered them with bark, and remained there some time to explore.

At length they felt satisfied, and Sturm returned to report to his Archbishop. Boniface listened, asked many questions, and decided that Hersfeld was not far enough from the fear of barbarian attack. Sturm, he said, had better push on still farther into the wilds. The three adventurers, therefore, embarked upon the river Fulda, presumably in some kind of roughly constructed canoe or raft. Along its banks they searched, landing to fight their way over hills and through the forest, and found no retreat which Boniface might approve. In deep discouragement Sturm once more went back to the Archbishop, then at the abbey of Fritzlar. He was given a good meal and rest, allowed to pour out the story of his wanderings, assured that he would find in the end what he was looking for, and sent back to try again.

Riding on a donkey, he set out alone, once more over hill and valley, stopping now and again in mingled amazement and despair to gaze at roaring waterfalls and rushing streams. By day as he tramped, picking his trail, he sang psalms aloud, trying to forget his fear; towards nightfall he built a fence of branches, for his protection while he slept from the wild animals which he could hear moving, screaming, howling in the forest around. One day he came upon a crowd of Slavs swimming in the Fulda, near the highway to Mainz. His donkey was terrified, and Sturm himself did not at all like the sound of their barbarian voices, jeering at him and his beast; but they did not touch him. Four days he rode through the woods, seeing nothing but their dwellers, bird and beast, in the tangle of tree and bush and briar. Then suddenly he came out into a rough clearing, and somehow there he knew that he had found his journey's end.

Fulda, of Hesse, lies on its river in the midst of hills, between the Vogels-Berg and the Rhön-Gebirge. It was 744 when the monastery was built, under the direction of Sturm, its first abbot. To Boniface it was what Echternach had been to Willibrord, a beloved retreat of rest and quiet. There he used to climb one of its hills, a special favourite of his, that he might be entirely alone for a while, and he did this so often that the monks called it " Bishop's Mount." In 751, three years before he died, he wrote to Pope Zacharias: " There is a place in the depths of the lonely forest, among the people whom we are labouring to teach. There we have built a monastery; its brethren are living under the *Rule* of St. Benedict, practising strict abstinence from meat and wine and fermented drink. They have no servants, content in the toil of their own hands. I obtained it by honest effort, and by the gift of devout and God-fearing men, especially of Carloman, once ruler of the Franks; and I have dedicated it in honour of the Holy Saviour. If your kindness will allow, in that place I hope soon to rest for a space of time, for I am now old and weary; there, too, I would lie after my death. Four different peoples, to whom with God's help we have declared the word of Christ, are known to dwell around it. As long as my body and mind allow and I have you to help me, I can still serve their need."

6

From thinking of monks, both bad and good, Boniface turned to grapple with the heretics who were sowing error in every direction. There were many sorts and kinds of these, and all of them deadly. The most interesting were two men called Aldebert and Clement, who gave the Archbishop a struggle long and fierce.

Aldebert was a Frank, who had beguiled many simple folk by declaring that an angel of God in the form of a man had brought him sacred relics from the world's farthest bounds. The peasants to whom he talked believed that he was as holy as the Apostles themselves and that he was working constant signs and wonders among them. His accusers swore that he had won consecration as bishop by bribery. He disdained, they said, to dedicate a church in honour of any one of the Apostles or Martyrs and saw no point in pilgrimage to Rome. In his own honour he set apart places of prayer, " befouled " them, as the orthodox said. He put up, they went on to say, crosses and little shrines in fields and at springs of water, wherever it seemed good to him, and bade men gather there for worship. Multitudes did. They would have nothing to do with other bishops, would never go inside the churches of God, but would come to these unholy places declaring, " The merits of holy Aldebert will help us." To his most eager followers he distributed filings from his nails and hairs from his head for their veneration, telling them to carry these together with the relics of St. Peter, Prince of the Apostles. Worst of all, in uttermost wickedness and blasphemy against God, when people threw themselves at his feet as penitents, he would say: " I know all you have done; all your secret thoughts are open to me. There is no need for you to confess, for all your sin is put away and forgiven. Go home in peace."

Clement was an Irishman. He would have nothing to do

with the rulings of the Church or with the writings of the Fathers, Jerome or Augustine or Gregory. Synods, too, meant nothing to him. He was lawfully a bishop, he said, in good and proper standing, although he had two sons, born since he declared his consecration. He followed Jewish ordinance in maintaining that a Christian might properly marry his deceased brother's wife. Against the faith of the Fathers he taught that Christ, Son of God, when He went down to the world of those departed hence, freed all who were held in prison there, believers and unbelievers, worshippers of God and of idols alike.

In 743 Boniface tried, condemned, deposed from their ministry and imprisoned both these men; and in 745 he sent a careful account of the charges against them to Rome for judgment before a Papal Synod, which also found them guilty. Nevertheless, they persisted in their evil ways. In 747 Zacharias wrote to the Archbishop that in the next Synod to be assembled in Germany they were again to undergo investigation of the most thorough kind. If, after a third condemnation, they refused to repent, their case was a last time to be referred to Rome, for final decision. With this letter, however, all evidence which we can trust concerning these rascals comes to an end.

One more accusation of heresy is also of interest. It concerned that Virgil who in 746 had been worrying Boniface by baptizing babies in bad Latin. Two years later he was again troubling the Archbishop by teaching that there was another world, that there were other men, another sun, another moon, beneath our earth. " The only thing to do with this man," Zacharias wrote to Boniface, " and I do not know whether he is truly a priest or not, is to find out if he is indeed spreading such absurd and hurtful doctrine, against God and his own soul. If this shall be proved a fact, you must bring him before a council, forbid him to function as priest, and expel him from the Church."

But once again the Irish Virgil triumphed over Boniface. Already by his wit and his learning he had won the friendship of Odilo, Duke of Bavaria, and now since about 747 under

Odilo's protection he had been sitting in the Bavarian see of Salzburg. The bishop placed there by Boniface had died, and Virgil, a simple priest, had as abbot of Salzburg's monastery been administering its diocese in the manner which we have noted as prevalent in Ireland as early as the sixth century, with a bishop to function in episcopal rites under his jurisdiction. There he stayed, until, in 767 according to the annals of Salzburg but, in any case, after the death of Boniface, he was consecrated bishop of the see by orthodox Catholic authority, to which he had undoubtedly proved that he was no heretic. He worked with all zeal for many years more to promote Catholic faith and practice among his own people, among the heathen far and wide; he died in 784, and in 1233 his name was added by Rome to the roll of saints.

Lastly, after the spiritual problems of his people had been dealt with, there remained for Boniface the physical and the legal. What did one do with lepers? If they were cast out into solitude, they would die of starvation. Might they come to church for Holy Communion? Were monks and nuns to flee from their monasteries to escape infection in time of plague? Was a man who has murdered his father, or mother, or brother, or sister, ever again to receive the sacred Host? Should he fast from meat and wine all the rest of his life?

7

Passionately as Boniface loved his work, splendidly as he ordered and organised it, it is his human side as man and friend which especially attracts us as we read the many letters written by and to him. Men and women in number he drew, especially from his own England, to share with him his work abroad; and we find among them those whom he appointed abbots, abbesses, and bishops. For each he had work prepared; to all he gave in delight his hospitality, his guidance, his support, his companionship. A priest, who in a company of workers came to him from the abbey of Glastonbury in Wessex, wrote to his fellow-monks at home: " God has prospered and kept safe our journey to these lands of heathen Hessians and Saxons, thanks to your prayers. I want you to know that when our Archbishop, Boniface, heard of our arrival, he actually came a long distance to meet us and welcomed us most kindly."

One of the last letters of Boniface, sent to Fulrad, abbot of the monastery of St. Denis near Paris, showed the same spirit of care for his own. Would Fulrad, it asked, help him in a matter which he was laying before Pippin, lately crowned king of the Franks? " I pray you," he writes, " convey to the King this thought on behalf of my friends and myself. This life of mine on earth, this course of my days, through my frailty and sickness must soon see its end. And so I pray his Royal Highness in the Name of Christ, that he of his generosity will show me while I still live what provision for the future he is willing to make for my disciples." Then comes a passage taken from a letter which Boniface had written to Pippin himself, describing these followers of his: " They are nearly all strangers in the land. Some are priests, stationed in many places for the service of the Church and the people; some are monks, vowed to their cells; and some are children, busy in their lessons. Some, too, are growing old, for they have toiled long with me and have helped me in the work. For all I am anxious, lest they be lost in this land after my death; lest, if they do not have support in your provision and in the protection of your Highness, they be scattered like sheep without a shepherd; lest, too, the Christian folk who dwell near the pagan borders lose the faith of Christ."

The letter holds a note of warning for the reader. In the enthusiasm which Boniface compels upon us for his work and the spirit in which he worked, it is easy to exaggerate his success. Here we see clearly that much was still at stake, that very much remained to be done, that Boniface could not surely count upon the Frankish authorities to uphold and to support his mission after his death. No doubt the very number of bishops, priests, abbots and abbesses of English birth whom he had promoted in Germany, with whom he had worked in deep affection and loyalty, caused ill-will and lack of co-operation between him and both Franks and Irishmen of Church and State. Nor are we to forget that Boniface could not have succeeded as he did had he not possessed and firmly at times asserted a strong and determined will, a will which also at times came into collision with authority. On occasion, loyal and faithful as he was, he dared to differ from the Papal See in questions of administration or of wisdom of policy, constrained by his view of Frankish powers. As need compelled him, he boldly took his own way amid the tangle of Frankish politics. In Germany rival powers resented his turning in a direction that did not march with their own; bishops and priests, abbots and monks, resented the discipline of his reforming decrees, resented, too, the scrupulous conscience which would not allow their Papal Legate even to talk at ease with those whom he suspected as heretics, whom he knew as evil doers. The words which Boniface wrote in his last ten years do not bear the mark of one who wrote in peace, without fear of what the future was to hold.

Letters continually went back and forth between Germany and England, to and from Boniface and a multitude of friends. Often a gift went with them, " with my love, that you may keep me in mind "; a cloak of wool and goats' hair; thick towels for drying the feet after the ritual of the Maundy washing; napkins, bed coverings, incense. To King Ethelbald of Mercia went a hawk and two falcons; to Archbishop Egbert of York two casks of wine " that you may make merry with your brethren."

In return Boniface gladly welcomed warm clothing; cinnamon and pepper, much valued as seasoning; a silver cup inlaid with gold, to be given to the altar as a chalice; two heavy capes to throw over the shoulders in a storm of rain. These capes arrived from King Ethelbert of Kent, who begged in return a pair of German falcons, so excellently keen for hunting, so rare in his own country. Above all, Boniface asked his English friends to send him books. And the books came. From Archbishop Egbert and from Hwaetbert, abbot of Bede's own monastery of Wearmouth-Jarrow, there arrived Biblical commentaries of Bede, " who shone in the house of the Lord as a candle to light men to knowledge of the Scriptures "; from Archbishop Nothelm of Canterbury and from Gemmulus, deacon of the Church at Rome, precious letters of Pope Gregory the Great, to lighten problems in Germany. From these letters sent by Gemmulus from Rome some went again from Germany across the Channel to Britain, directed by the thoughtful mind of Boniface to Egbert of York. " I think," he wrote, " that you have not yet seen these. I will send more, if you will let me know, for I have received many of them myself."

Fellowship in prayer was constantly sought and given. King Aelbwald of East Anglia wrote that the name of Boniface was remembered in the abbeys of his realm at every Hour of Office, seven times in the round of night and day. Nor was counsel wanting, both mild and sharp, on the part of Boniface. Together with his words of deep affection, so often written, he was not afraid to send keen rebuke, and to the highest in the land; to Archbishop Cuthbert of Canterbury, for the sins of the English Church; to King Ethelbald of Mercia, for the sins of his own wicked indulgence.

Sometimes in these letters we catch a sense of labour and weariness. " Toil as great, and danger greater than that of other bishops is laid on me," Boniface writes to Archbishop Cuthbert. " An Archbishop, as the ancient canons declare, carries the burden of the charge of a whole Province. I am afraid, if I may put it so, that I have undertaken once and for all to steer a ship through the waves of a raging sea, a ship which I can neither guide securely nor abandon without sin." To an English abbot he writes the same: " Have pity upon an old man, tried and tossed on all sides by the waves of a German sea." To Archbishop Egbert he declares: "One letter could not possibly tell you all the evils which come upon us, from without and from within."

The evils from without we have seen; here at least Boniface brought discipline out of disorder; gave knowledge for ignorance, and left in Germany not only a firmer Christian faith but the constitutional framework on which the future was to build in spite of all his fear. The sorrows of within were never conquered. It is noteworthy how often the word *peregrinatio* occurs in his letters. He writes to Abbess Eadburg in Thanet, the isle of Kent: "Please pray for me. I ask you because my life here in exile is so stormy. Everywhere is hard work, everywhere depression." The same thought goes to one of the hierarchy in Rome: "One of the hardest things about living in exile is that, when one is sad and gloomy, one's friends are far away; and one's enemies are close by, to worry and vex the soul. How I wish, my brother, that I had you here to comfort my loneliness!" In a letter to the abbot of Wearmouth-Jarrow, he asks: "If it would not be any trouble, could you send me a cloak? It would be such a comfort in my travels."

From Rome came stern words to spur him on, in a letter from Pope Gregory the Third: "My brother, you will not be permitted to stay on in one place when your work there has ended. Wheresoever the Lord shall open to you the way of saving souls, there cease not to preach. And, beloved, do not let the journeys vex you, rough and devious as they are. By your toil the Christian faith will spread far and wide."

And often the joy came back to lighten his way. To another English abbess he told of his *amor peregrinationis*, his love of this foreign land. Even here, was he not working among people akin to his own English race? A letter addressed by him "To all bishops, priests, deacons, clergy, abbots, abbesses, to all Catholics among the Anglo-Saxons who fear God," prayed them all: "Keep in mind the Saxons of Germany, for they themselves often say, 'We are of the same blood as the English, of the same bone.'" Torhthelm, bishop of Leicester, wrote to him: " I know from your letter that you are thinking day and night on the conversion of pagan Saxons. Who would not rejoice in these works, that men of our own race are beginning to believe in Christ, God of all power and might? "

Yet Boniface was entirely honest with the English and with himself concerning them. " You must know," he wrote, " how I rejoice in the good actions, in the praises of our nation of the English, and how I mourn and am sad in their sins and the censure they receive."

8

In 753 he knew that but little time was left him for his work, unfinished as it was. The year before he had consecrated as assistant bishop, without see, one of his English priests, Lull by name, taught and trained by him; he had gained his hope that after his death Lull would carry on his mission, established then as bishop of Mainz in his place. He was nearly eighty years old. But trouble had developed in Frisia, the land of his early labour on the Continent, and he was determined, if it were at all possible, to see peace restored there before he died. After the retirement of Willibrord, Archbishop of Utrecht, to the abbey of Echternach, another bishop, appointed and consecrated by him, had carried on the work in Frisia. He was not bishop of Utrecht; that see remained vacant. Then Carloman, mayor of the Franks, had asked Boniface to consecrate for Utrecht a bishop of its own. This he had done, but not until after 741, some years after Willibrord had died. Utrecht once again had a bishop; but its Archbishopric upon Willibrord's death had ceased to exist.

In this year of 753 not only was its see again vacant, but it was in dispute; and we find Boniface writing with all his energy of old to Pope Stephen the Second. The bishop of Cologne, one Hildegar, was laying claim to it, on the ground that, as we have seen, in the seventh century Dagobert the First, king of the Franks, had given the fortress of Utrecht, with the little church enclosed within it, to the diocese of Cologne, bidding its bishop work for the conversion of Frisia. This former bishop of Cologne had done nothing; and later on, Pope Sergius had entrusted Utrecht to Willibrord. These facts, argued Boniface, made a far more convincing claim for possession of its own see by Frisia than its possession by Cologne on the ground of that gift of a little ruined church, neglected by the indifference of Cologne's bishop, amid a people, too, still very largely heathen. Mission work was badly needed in Frisia in this very year; and he was ready to do all in his power to further it. His plea prevailed, and almost at once one of the English workers with Boniface, Eoba by name, one, who like Lull, had already been an assistant bishop without see for the aiding of the mission in Germany, was duly appointed bishop of Utrecht.

Whether this appointing took place in Germany or in Frisia itself, we do not know. We do know that in 753 Boniface travelled to the Netherlands, to Utrecht. From that city as centre, once again, as long before, Boniface, with Eoba this time to assist him, began a campaign of preaching and baptizing. The work was carried on in the coastlands north-east of the Ijssel Meer, where movement was difficult as the roads were so often interrupted by stretches of water. For the winter of 753-754 Boniface probably returned to Utrecht, his head-quarters. The following spring, however, found him again journeying up and down in the north-east. One morning—it was the fifth of June—he was near Dokkum, which we know as north of Leeuwarden, the chief town of Friesland. The sun had just risen, and Frisian converts were gathering around the Archbishop's encampment that he might lay his hands upon them in confirmation. Suddenly a band of armed men rushed down. The followers of Boniface ran to the defence, but the noise reached his tent. He came out, saw the tumult, raised his hand and forbade battle. " Let us not give evil for evil," he called. " The day so long desired is here, and the time of

our departure is at hand." To the priests and other minor
clerics who were pressing forward to protect him he cried aloud
the same in English, for many of them from England knew
little of the native tongue. In but a moment he was dead.

Around him, it is said, fell fifty-two of these companions of
his, Eoba, the bishop, among them. Tradition, probably of the
ninth century, ascribes to an eye-witness a story that, as his
murderer came upon him, Boniface instinctively tried to shield
his head with the Book of the Gospels which he was holding,
" that this Book which he had loved to read in life might be
his safety in face of death." The raiders ransacked the mission
camp, seized and broke open all the boxes they could find, in
search of gold and silver. To their disgust they found books,
and in their fury they threw these away in the fields and
marshes, or, in the case of the more shrewd and calculating,
hid them in hope of future sale. The priest Willibald, who
wrote our best *Life* of Boniface shortly after 754, said that some
of these precious books were recovered. The body of Boniface
was carried to Utrecht and from there to Mainz. Finally it
was laid to rest at Fulda, as long before he himself had asked.

Many wrote from England to tell of their grief, among them
Milret, bishop of Worcester, who summed up what Boniface
had done for men of Germanic race in a letter to Lull, the pupil,
friend, and successor of Boniface at Mainz: " He crowned his
long toil," wrote Milret, " in a foreign land by a glorious death;
and now he stands in joy with Christ and the dwellers of the
City of Heaven, a faithful intercessor, God willing, for our sins.
It will surely be for our souls' exceeding good to try to follow
out the lessons which he taught so well."

9

No story of Boniface, however brief, should lack something of the life of Lull, and of the cousin of Boniface, Leobgytha or Leoba, abbess of a convent founded by him near the river Main.

Both Lull and Leoba were born in England, and both, it would seem, in the land of the West Saxons, Wessex, from which Boniface had come. We find Lull as a boy at the house of Malmesbury in Wiltshire, taught by its abbot Eaba, who with affection called him " Lytel," " the little one." Here Lull read Latin as he found it in the works of Aldhelm, once abbot of this same monastery, from about 675, and bishop of Sherborne in Dorset from 705 until 709. Here he was trained in Aldhelm's Latin style. We now read with pain its swollen, artificial pages; but Lull was immensely proud of his own Latin prose written in imitation of his model. He tried his hand, also, at Latin verse, of which Aldhelm had left so much for so many Englishmen to study, and he found great delight in absorbing Aldhelm's acrostic schemes, arranged in figured form, grotesque in their elaboration.

We come upon him next in Rome, a pilgrim accompanied by " a whole crowd of relatives." His visits to shrine after shrine soon came to an untimely end, for an epidemic of plague, the scourge of Europe in these centuries, brought death or flight for his kinsfolk and left him not only alone but struggling up from sickness slowly back to health. At this time, about 738, when he was in his late twenties, he wrote from Rome a letter to an abbess and a nun in England, we do not know of what convent. To them he pours out his tale of loss, of illness, of homesickness. How badly he misses now those days, some two years before in England, when these kindly Sisters had nursed him through a similar attack! He has been whiling away the long days of convalescence, he writes, in composing an acrostic

" figure-poem " of his own. It holds their names, and he is sending it to them in the hope that they will like it. The letter, especially in its opening address, drips with the fatness of alliteration, of far-fetched words and mannered periods.

But there was something better at hand. In 738-739, as we have seen, Boniface was in Rome, and we may think of a meeting of these two, soon to be master and pupil. In Boniface Lull saw an ideal vocation. In him he found, too, a scholar like the Aldhelm of Malmesbury whom he had never known in life, one who could teach him more of verse and prose concoctions, a happiness for leisure hours.

If he did not return with Boniface to Germany in 739, he followed him very speedily. He, with other young men of his own England—Denehard, who so often served Boniface as messenger to and fro across the Channel, and Burchard, whom Boniface was to consecrate as the first bishop of Würzburg— then wrote to Cuniburg, an abbess in his English land, that they " had been received under monastic rule of life by Archbishop Boniface and were helping him in his work." Lull's first efforts were directed by Boniface to study in Thuringia, probably in preparation for his admission to the diaconate, which took place about 740. Here sickness troubled him again; we find him asking leave to stay on a little longer in Thuringia, because weakness of his eyes and persistent headaches had hindered his reading.

Like Boniface, he was three times in Rome. The second visit took place in 746-747, the third in 751, when he was now a priest; and both times he was carrying letters of importance. In 751 Boniface entrusted also to him many problems for debate in personal talk with the Pope.

Long before this Boniface had been thinking of Lull as his successor. In 742, when he was nearly seventy, he had written to Pope Zacharias to ask whether a successor might be appointed, and the Pope had answered: " By no means, unless you should be in danger of death. In that case, you may name the man whom you judge most suited to follow you," a concession, Zacharias declared, which he would give to no other prelate. Six years later, in 748, when Boniface at last possessed a see, in Mainz, the same Pope urged him never to forsake this see, old and frail as he was. " But," Zacharias added, " if in answer to your prayer God shall give you a perfect man, one who is eager and keen for souls, you will consecrate him bishop to act as your representative." In 752, then, Boniface ordained Lull as an assistant bishop without see, acting under him for his aid. In the same year he wrote to beg Pippin, king of the Franks, that Lull might indeed follow him at Mainz when he died.

In 753 Boniface commended this lately consecrated bishop to those in power among the Franks, in Germany and in Thuringia, before he left for Frisia. Already he had a feeling that he might not return. Would Lull, he asked, carry on the building of churches in Thuringia and finish work on the abbey of Fulda? Then he told him of his wish to be buried at Fulda, gave him his last blessing as his " dear son," and went on his way.

This desire of Boniface was fulfilled, and Lull was bishop of Mainz from 754 until 781, when he was made its Archbishop by the Pope. We do not know very much about his life during these nearly thirty years. As he had not the gaiety which illumined the many dark days for Boniface, so, also, he had neither his strength, his gift for making many friends of every class and kind, his genius for organisation. Neither did he have the same opportunity as Boniface. The menace of Greeks from the East, of Lombards from the North, battles against Saxons and against Saracens, took the energy of the Pope and the king of the Franks until Pippin's death in 768. Then, when in 771 his brother Carloman's death made Charles the Great sole ruler of the Franks, the firm hold of Charles upon administration, upon matters of Church as well as of State, his determined " crusade " to conquer and then to bring under the Church the heathen Saxons, gave little scope for Lull in either initiation or accomplishment.

There are, to be sure, letters; but we miss the interest of the constant discussion of problems between Boniface and Rome and Canterbury, York and Winchester. King Pippin wrote to Lull to bid a general thanksgiving for a most fruitful harvest after fearful cold and hunger, endured for months in the winter just past. The letter contains a sentence of high importance in the history of tithing: " See, and order in Our name, that each man, whether he will or not, give his tenth in alms for the support of the Church and the poor." Tithing had already been prescribed in a Council of Frankish bishops long before, but this order of Pippin pointed the way to the enactments of Charles the Great in his Capitularies. At another time, we read, fasting and prayer were imposed by Lull as bishop upon his clergy and his people in Thuringia because of the danger of flooding rain.

Private letters came, of course, from fellow-bishops and from priests in need of counsel. There are three from Megingoz, bishop of Würzburg after the death of the English Burchard. The first tells that his sister, an abbess, is at the point of death and he is afraid lest one of her two nieces, both of them nuns under her rule, may be elected to her office. Neither, in the judgment of Megingoz, is old or wise enough for this responsibility. Her abbey, we see clearly, was one of the many Frankish houses of religion regarded as reserved for keeping in one family's hands. Megingoz's second letter deals with a matter even more difficult: a seeming conflict of view with regard to the permanence of marriage relations in the writings of St. Jerome, St. Augustine of Hippo, and Pope Leo the Great. His third asks Lull to join him in warning one of his relations, firmly bound by secular tie, of the folly of a rash attempt to enter monastic life.

A priest named Wigbert, one of Lull's workers, who has returned for a visit to his native England, writes to Lull in trouble. His family want him to stay in England; in fact, they are threatening to will the family land and property to another if he persists in going back to the mission field in Germany.

" I confess to you in the Name of the Lord," he writes miserably, for he was a much divided and, it would seem, a rather weak soul, " that against your desire no power of this world, no secular friendship, can in any way hold me here, for I love and revere you above all other men. Please, will you, my master, think and decide what seems good to you in this matter, and write to tell me your advice? Much of my life has been spent in wavering and negligence. I don't seem to have any anchorage within me to cling to, and it is high time that I had one and used it."

An abbess named Suitha, we learn from another letter, is excommunicated by the bishop for her sin in allowing two of her nuns to wander freely in the world outside their cloister for their own pleasure and their undoing. They are to be rigidly excluded, she is told, and she herself is to fast and pray, until all three prove true repentance.

From across the Channel, Alchred, king of Northumbria, and his queen, Osgeofu, ask the help of Lull in assuring for them peace and friendship with King Charles of the Franks. Archbishop Cuthbert of Canterbury informs Lull that a General Synod in England has decreed yearly remembrance of the day of the martyrdom of Boniface; his Feast is to be honoured as those of Pope Gregory the Great and Canterbury's own Augustine. Cuthbert's successor at Canterbury, Bregowine, reminds Lull of the days spent by them in friendly talk at Rome. As in the case of Boniface, gifts accompany the letters; Alchred and Osgeofu send twelve cloaks and a ring of gold; Bregowine offers a reliquary, made of bone. Again and again books are asked for by Lull and sent to him. Albert, the master of Alcuin in York and Archbishop of its Cathedral, writes to Lull some time between 767 and 778: " The information into which you are inquiring, in regard to tides of the sea flowing on the coast, is not to be had, and what we hear is probably false. The books on cosmography have not yet reached us, and those others which we do possess have very bad illustrations and script. I have often meant to get my own copies made, but I could not find a copyist; perhaps your very asking will help on things here." From this Albert of York Lull asks for books of Bede: the Commentaries on Samuel, on Ezra and Nehemiah, on the Gospel of St. Mark. In the same letter he writes that " the Church day by day is beaten, oppressed, and vexed, because the princes of our time make new customs, new laws, after their own desires." Bishop Cyneheard of Winchester, on the other hand, begs Lull of his kindness to send from Germany any books on secular science not yet known in England, especially on medicine. With this petition he sends clothing as a present, tunics of wool and linen, made in the English manner, shoes and coat of leather and hide.

A letter to Lull from another Cuthbert, abbot of Wearmouth-Jarrow, Bede's twin monasteries in the north of England, is lively and of real charm. He writes: " I was so glad to receive your gifts and, above all, that pall of pure silk which you sent for the honouring of the relics of Bede, our master. It was good of you, too, to send me that covering of varied colour to keep the cold away from me myself. But, indeed, I gave it with a great thrill to Almighty God and his blessed apostle Paul, for the adorning of Paul's altar in this church of his! I have now lived here in this monastery under his protection these six and forty years. You asked me to send you something of the works of Bede. I have been busy with my boys in making copies, so far as we could manage this, and I am sending you the *Life* of St. Cuthbert, in verse and in prose. I would so gladly have done more. But the winter just now over has caused the most horrible suffering in this island, through bitter cold and ice and storms of wind and rain. The hands of our copyists were so numbed that they could not get many books ready.

" Would you mind my asking you a favour? If you have a man in your diocese skilled in making vessels of glass, could you get him over here to me in England when the weather is not so bad? Or even someone outside your diocese, if only he would come? We are quite helpless here, quite ignorant of this art. He would receive a most friendly welcome from me, if I am still around. I do, also, very badly need someone who can play the harp. I have a harp, but no one to use it. Would it be too much for you to try to send him as well? Now I hope you won't despise me or laugh at me for asking. You shall have those other works of Bede, I promise, if I live long enough to get them copied."

Many letters still asked for a fellowship of prayer between England and Germany. Among them was one from the king of Lull's own Wessex, Cynewulf, and his bishops.

About 781 the pallium which marked his new rank of Archbishop of Mainz arrived for Lull from Rome. As was regularly required, before his promotion to metropolitan dignity he had forwarded to the Pope in writing his Profession of Faith. We still have its words.

Lull, like Boniface, followed regularly the ordering of the Benedictine *Rule* and watched over the monasteries in his charge, with a special affection for Fulda, the happy house of peace. Nevertheless, in connection with this same Fulda a shadow lies over his name. Tradition tells of a struggle between Sturm, the first abbot of Fulda, and Lull, the bishop of Mainz. The *Life* of Sturm, written by Eigil, himself Fulda's abbot in the early ninth century, states that Lull for a long time entirely refused to allow the body of Boniface to be taken from Mainz for burial in " that wilderness " where Fulda lay and that he was only induced to yield by a deacon's solemn statement on oath that Boniface himself had desired it, as the deacon had learned from a vision of the night. Besides this, we may believe that strife also continued long and intense between Sturm, jealously guarding the independence of Fulda from diocesan control, an independence declared by decree of the Pope himself, and Lull, who as bishop wanted to exercise his own supervision over it. Eigil, at any rate, records the following words as spoken by Sturm to his monks of Fulda just before his death: " Pray for me to the Most High God, and if I have done aught of grievous sort among you, or have unjustly offended anyone, forgive me; and I, too, forgive from my heart all insults and affronts against myself. I even forgive Lull, who has always been against me." It was perhaps in rivalry with Fulda that Lull devoted so much time and energy to the building and honouring of the abbey of Hersfeld in Hesse. Sturm had first, as we saw, noted its site as one which might well hold a monastery; but the actual founding has always been connected with Lull's name.

Lull's last letters tell of that haunting ill-health which had clung to him all his life. Like Alcuin, he wrote: " I am being driven by continual sickness of body from this passing light of time towards my departure hence, to render account to the Judge, just but stern." He died in 786, when Alcuin was in his first years as Master of the Palace School under Charles the Great at his Court of Aachen, and two years after the birth of Raban Maur, the learned abbot of Fulda and energetic Archbishop of Mainz. His greatest gift to the life of books, so dear to him, was his legacy to the world of the letters of Boniface.

10

It is always pleasant to turn to those pages in which Rudolf, a monk of Fulda under Raban Maur, told of the life of Leoba, nearly sixty years after his abbey had received her body for burial beside the grave of Boniface, her kinsman. Boniface knew many women whom he called his friends. Abbesses in number poured out their troubles to him, asked his advice and sent him gifts. The wise ruler of the abbey of Minster on Thanet, the Lady Eadburg, gave him books and copied for him in letters of gold the Epistles of St. Peter, at his own request, " that I may always have before me the words of him who sent me on my way hither to Germany."

But Leoba—Leobgytha, as Boniface thought of her—was especially his comfort and joy, from the time when as a young

novice under the rule, it would seem, of that same Abbess
Eadburg, she had written him a letter in her best Latin:

" To the Most Reverend Archbishop Boniface: Leobgytha,
his kinswoman, least of the servants who bear the light yoke of
Christ, sends her prayer for his abiding health and happiness.

" I ask your Clemency that you deign to remember the
friendship which long ago made a bond between you and my
father, Dynne, in our West Country. He died now eight years
since. Would you offer to God your prayers for his soul? My
mother, Aebbe, too, I commend to your thought, for she is of
your family, as you know better than I. She is still living, but
much vexed by illness. I am their only daughter, and, unworthy as I am, I should be so happy if you would be to me
as a brother. No man of our kindred gives me the confidence
and hope which I find in you. I am sending you a little present,
not because it is good enough, but that you may not forget
me while you are far away.

" Would you of your kindness correct this letter, so crudely
composed, and send me some words of your own as a model?
I do so badly want to hear from you. I send, too, some verses
which I have tried to make in proper poetic style. They, also,
need your help. I learned writing of verse under Eadburg's
direction. She never stops searching into the mysteries of Holy
Scripture." There follow four Latin hexameters, largely made
up from those of Aldhelm, that master of learning in the West
of England.

Rudolf had found out much of what he knew about Leoba
from a priest named Mago and from four nuns who had lived
under her as Reverend Mother in Germany. She had been the
delight of her parents' middle age, born when they were losing
hope of children, and it was they who had shortened her
baptismal name to " Leoba," " the loved one." They were both
English, of aristocratic family on both sides, and apparently of
Wessex. Their devout Christian following had led them to give
their only child for teaching and training, first, if conjecture is
correct, to Thanet, then to the abbey of Wimborne in Hamp-

shire. It may be, of course, that it was from Wimborne that Leoba wrote to Boniface the letter we have just noticed, and that the Eadburg of whom she speaks in it was another of that name, one of Wimborne's nuns.

Wimborne was a double monastery, holding one house for men, another for women, both united for ruling under an abbess, at this time Tetta, of royal birth, an able and energetic head. Its code was strict. No communicating, of course, was allowed between the two houses. For the women there was perpetual enclosure, unless very special need arose for travelling outside. When the abbess had reason to address her community as a whole, she did so from a window overlooking the courtyard and buildings.

Leoba had a gay young spirit. Long afterwards she used to tell with a wry smile how horrified the Reverend Mother had been when some of her novices had trodden down the earth piled over the grave of an extremely unpopular senior nun, dour and forbidding to her humbler sisters until the day of her death. The abbess ordered them to fast and pray three whole days for the repose of this nun's soul and the forgiveness of their own wickedness. Leoba was sure, however, that the Lord at least understood their feeling! Another time, she relates, the Sister in charge of the nuns' church locked it after Compline and then lost the keys. Matins and Lauds had to be said elsewhere. Reverend Mother knew that this loss was due to the malice of Satan and she ordered a general appeal to Heaven. It availed, of course, Leoba said in serene conviction. Office, indeed, had not yet come to an end when the night watchman found a dead fox lying outside the church doors. The lost keys were in its mouth, and everyone gave thanks to God.

In time Leoba became Novice Mistress. Then a letter was written from Boniface in Germany to Abbess Tetta. Could she possibly allow Leoba to come over to work in his mission? She did, and Leoba crossed the sea. Boniface made her abbess of the convent of nuns at Tauberbischofsheim, on the river Tauber, near the Main. With the same blithe heart and enthusiasm she trained there a large community of Sisters, not a few of whom themselves became abbesses in German lands. She kept the *Rule*, she ordered her convent's life, she cared with all affection for the wants of her nuns; but she also found time for study. Boniface always encouraged her in this, both by his visits and his letters.

She had, blessedly, the courage which the adventures of those days in early medieval Germany demanded. We read, in her *Life*, of the new-born baby found at the edge of the river which flowed through her convent's grounds. Neighbours declared it was the child of one of Leoba's own nuns, fallen under temptation. Leoba called all the Sisters to prayer. Three times a day a procession chanting litany circled the abbey, beseeching the Lord for light and aid. At length a poor wretched outcast, whom the nuns had fed and clothed as she lay at their doors, sick in mind and in body, cried aloud her guilt. Another story tells how people who lived near suddenly found fire shooting up from their wattled cottages, blown in the direction of the convent by the strong wind. Leoba saw their panic, and with complete calm called to them to bring, every one of them, water from the river to throw upon the flames. Perhaps, however, most vivid of all is the picture of her nuns cowering in terror at their prayers in church during a fearful storm of thunder, rain, and quaking of the earth beneath their feet; of her cousin, Tecla, crying to Leoba, " Call, call upon the Holy Mother of God to help us! "; of Leoba rising from her knees and walking quietly to the outer door of the convent, throwing it wide open and raising her right hand to make the sign of the Cross against the lightning and the thunder's roar.

The death of Boniface took from her unmeasured resource and support. Before he left on his last journey to Frisia, he came to see her at Tauberbischofsheim. " Do not forsake this land of your pilgrimage in exile," he bade her. " Hold bravely to your course, carry on the good work day by day, and heed not this body's weakness. Time is not long, suffering is not hard, if your eyes are set upon eternity." To Lull and the older monks of Fulda he especially commended her, to their reverence and their thought. " I pray you all," he said to them, " that when her time comes to die, you lay her, too, in my grave here, that we who in this life together have served Christ with the same devotion and love, may together await the day of resurrection." As a last gift he gave her his monk's cowl for remembrance.

She worked on steadily in her loneliness, and all, high and low, honoured her and loved her. King Pippin and his sons aided her convent; and, after he had succeeded to the crown of the Franks, Charles the Great and his queen Hildegard gave her warm friendship and affection. Now and again she went to Court to see Hildegard. She would never stay there, much as the queen wished it, for " she hated the noise and turmoil of the Palace as a bowl of deadly poison." When old age at last came and her strength failed, Lull made her retire to a little house of nuns at Schornsheim, four miles south of Mainz. Sometimes she went to Fulda, to pray before the shrine of her beloved master and friend, the only woman to whom such a privilege was allowed. Shortly before she died, Queen Hildegard sent to beg her to come again to the Palace at Aachen. Leoba was weary and it was hard to travel; but she still kept her old spirit of courage, and now she journeyed along the Rhine and talked a little while at the Court. Then, " Farewell, my Lady and dear sister," she said, " a very part of my own soul! Christ who created and redeemed us grant that without dismay and terror we may meet in the hour of Judgment. For never again in this life shall we enjoy the sight, each of the other's face."

She died in 780, three years before her royal friend, that woman of gracious charm and beauty who cheered the heart of Alcuin in his Palace School. She was buried at Fulda, but not in the grave of Boniface, for the monks feared to open it. They laid her near, on the north side of the High Altar which he had dedicated in honour of Our Lord Saviour and the Twelve Apostles.

CHAPTER ELEVEN

SAINT GREGORY OF UTRECHT;
SAINT LIUDGER; SAINT LEBUIN

The Netherlands in the Eighth Century

THE REGION of the Netherlands, now the scene of our story, is still that Frisia in which Boniface worked. On a modern map it stretches from Utrecht up along the coast of the Ijssel Meer and the Waddenzee, to Dokkum and the Lauwerszee in the north.

We are now to deal with the experiences of two of our wandering saints in medieval Frisia during the time after the death of Boniface; that is, during the second half of the eighth century. Before we look at these, however, we should remind ourselves of certain things. First, we have already noted in the chapter on Lull the growth of the power of the Frankish throne, in matters of Church as of State, during the rule of Charles the Great, sole king from 771. This will affect Frisia, under Frankish supremacy. Second, the Benedictine monastic life, so dear to Bede, to Wilfrid, to Boniface, will still continue; but it will increasingly be faced by the freer condition of communities largely controlling their own routine under very relaxed discipline. Third, we have now seriously to reckon with the Saxons, living outside the eastern border of Frisia; for the history of this people will be vitally connected in the late eighth century both with the Franks and with the Frisians. It is always to be remembered that there were very many among the Frisians who still hated Christianity and were ready to rebel against the Frankish Christian power which had conquered so much of their land. These joined the Saxons on their border in rising against the Franks. For the Saxons, a wild, ferocious warrior people, were still for a time independent of the Frankish power and determined, if necessary, to fight for their freedom with their lives. They were utterly heathen, and nothing pleased them more than to swoop down upon Christian settlements in Frisia across the border, to incite heathen Frisians to aid them in robbing and destroying Christian churches, in forcing Christian workers, English and Frankish, with Frisian converts, to flee for safety from their homes. And finally, as the ambition of Charles the Great grows stronger, we shall trace the oncoming and the progress of the great and terrible war carried on by him against these independent Saxons, until they were subdued under his political rule and forced to Christian baptism.

2

The first of our two men working in Frisia after 754, the year in which Boniface died, was a devoted abbot of Utrecht. Eoba, bishop of Utrecht, had been struck down with Boniface, as we have seen, and for fourteen years there was no bishop working in its city. This misfortune was due to the character of Gregory of Utrecht, the intimate friend of both Boniface and Lull, whose life we shall now follow.

It was probably in 721, after Boniface had left Archbishop Willibrord in distress of loneliness at Utrecht, that he was travelling along the Moselle near Trier and came to a convent of nuns at Pfalzel. He was weary and in need of food and sleep. Its abbess, whose name was Addula, welcomed the stranger, gave him all hospitality, and with her nuns heard Mass said by him in their church. At breakfast afterwards, no doubt with secret pride, she called her grandson, Gregory, a boy about fourteen, to read at the lectern from the Scriptures. Gregory's father was of high rank among the Frankish people, and the boy was now enjoying, with his grandmother, who had turned to monastic life in her widowhood, a holiday from his lessons under the care of Charles Martel, a mayor of the Franks at this time for a king ruling only in name. Young Gregory was one of the boys of the Palace School; and at the Court of the Frankish king he was studying his books, learning skill in military art, in hunting and other noble pastimes, that he might grow up a loyal and able supporter of the Frankish government.

Now, then, after he had knelt to receive the blessing of Boniface, he read the Latin words of the Lesson from the Bible with all the voice, all the correctness, he could manage. At the end he recited the prescribed prayer and waited in expectation of a word of approval. It came, though not just as he had hoped. " You read well, my son," said Boniface. " But do you understand what you are reading? " " At least," thought the boy, " he speaks my own German, Englishman though he is. But I don't quite know what he means by understanding." He started to read the Latin once more. " No, no, son," said Boniface, " tell me in your own German what it is all about." There was a long silence; Gregory had nothing to say. At last Boniface asked, with a friendly smile, " Would you like me to tell you? " " Please," the boy said. In easy, simple German Boniface explained the meaning and the moral of the passage.

By the time he had finished, Gregory was hanging on his words. Presently he went to find his grandmother, the abbess, and told her that he wanted to go with this man who loved books and understood them. He would learn far more from him, he said, than he was learning at the Court. Addula, naturally enough, was horrified at the idea. Was not the boy already at the best school, the Royal School of the land? Was he not the son of a noble Frankish lord? " How do I know," she cried, " who this wandering priest really is, and where he would take you? " Her grandson in his eagerness forgot his manners. " If you won't give me a horse to ride with him," he rudely told the Reverend Abbess, " I shall go on foot. But certainly I shall go." After a long struggle and much wise and enlightening talk on the part of Boniface, Addula gave way. With dour and grim face she stood to look on as her impetuous grandson rode off with the English stranger.

With Boniface he grew up and learned all that he could, from words spoken, from books, from his own experience. He was with his bishop in Hesse, in Thuringia, in Bavaria; he went with him on that third visit of Boniface to Rome in 738-739. There he passed days of delight, busily carrying off all the books he could afford to buy. There, too, with Boniface, he induced others to join the mission to Germany; he persuaded two Englishmen, Markholm and Markwine, to cross the sea. Now also in Rome, it seems, Gregory must have learned to know Lull, a young man about his own age.

When he was perhaps in his fortieth year, somewhere about 747, he was given the charge, as abbot, of St. Martin's in Utrecht, the monastery once ruled by Willibrord. We have a letter written to him at this time by Lull, still working with Boniface in Germany. It is a message of congratulation on this new appointment, mingled with warning. " Please, I beg of you, don't resent my words, however stupid and unnecessary they may seem," wrote Lull. " They come from the love I bear you, and I send them at my peril. But now that you have gained as abbot temporal power and earthly rule, beware of luxury, of costly clothing, sleek horses, hawks and falcons with curving talons, hounds alert for the hunt, delicious food and drink, fragrant to the connoisseur, tables radiant with service of silver and gold, comfortable beds and soft pillows. And, because we have been friends so long, I would like just to mention that discussion, that resolve, so often spoken of between us. I know, of course, that there is no need to remind one like you of this. But it has lately been brought back to my mind by a priest, impious and disloyal to our faith. He always used to swear that he would accept no earthly honour. And now suddenly, all unexpectedly, he has given us a shock; he has come forth a bishop! "

These words are of interest for their concurrence with the rebukes of Aldhelm in England, of Boniface in Germany, of Councils of the Church in the seventh and eighth centuries, in regard to the unseemly living of the clergy of their time. Here, in Lull's letter, we see the thought of a serious young man about 747. To him a bishopric was something to be avoided if possible, in God's name, as holding out temptations from the Devil. Lull, as we know, afterwards changed his mind, and Boniface died in peace, knowing that he was at hand to carry on the work as bishop in Germany.

In this decision Lull was doubtless wise. When a like call came to Gregory, however, after the death of Utrecht's bishop, Eoba, he would not, could not, assume a bishop's honour and position in matters temporal. This aversion remained true for the rest of his life. At the time, no substitute was found; and from 754 until 768 it was he who as priest and abbot ruled not only his monastery of St. Martin but the great and difficult diocese of Utrecht. What the lack of a bishop of the diocese may have meant during these thirteen years we cannot tell. The ending of the lack was due, not to any change of mind on Gregory's part, but rather to a man who came in 767 from Northumbria's city of York in England, to follow, after a while, in Willibrord's steps and to act as bishop for Utrecht's need. His name was Alubert, and he was a simple priest when he arrived in the Netherlands. Soon, realising the situation, he went home to obtain in England from its Archbishop of York consecration as bishop, and returned in 768 to carry out the rites and ceremonies proper to a bishop's office.

Gregory, then, in one sense hardly fulfilled the promise of his boyhood. He was a gentle soul, no bold adventurer save where learning and books were concerned. Story tells that when Frankish robbers had murdered two of his brothers while they were travelling through dense forest in Germany, when Frankish law had caught the assassins and asked Gregory himself to confirm for them the sentence of death, he petitioned that they might go their way, free and unharmed, warning them to be on their guard against others of his family, less charitably inclined than he. His joy was always to teach. In St. Martin's at Utrecht he fostered a school of learning, and gave it renown. Not only Frisians and Franks gathered there, but lads from Saxony, from Bavaria, from England, from that famous School itself of York, which was then drawing men from far and wide to study under Alcuin. Of course, as Gregory knew and readily admitted, the School at Utrecht could not compare with that of York, and for that very reason the coming of Alubert had delighted him. Nevertheless Utrecht's school did prepare men to encounter the heathen of Frisia, as well as teach them something of the liberal arts.

3

Alubert, bishop in Utrecht, appears but dimly in our picture of the Netherlands mission of this time. He is only of interest to us as supplying what Gregory could not give. Far more important to our narrative is a man of Christian risk and daring, a pupil of Gregory called Liudger, who in his life and work reflects the history of the mission from the time of Gregory's death to the end of the eighth century.

He was not a Frank; instead, he had the advantage of native Frisian birth, dated about 742. His parents were of the Christians in Frisia, and his father a man of wealth and standing. They were very proud of his early promise. Even as a little boy, they said, he would play at binding together bits of hide and bark of trees into " books " and " writing " on these with a reed dipped in mud. They sent him to school at St. Martin's, possibly when he was very young, before the death of Boniface in 754. At some time, at all events, as he himself relates, he " saw Boniface with his own eyes, an old man, bowed by weakness and white of hair, but full of the goodness of life."

Liudger was certainly in Utrecht in 767, when Alubert

arrived from Northumbria to work under Gregory. Now Liudger heard of the learning, of the famous library, of York's School. Soon he was begging Gregory, his abbot and teacher, to allow him to go there to study under Alcuin. And he did go, twice, the first time for a year, the second time for three years and six months, from about 769 until 773. At York he received ordering as priest. He would not have returned in 773 if he had been able to choose, but an incident forced his return. Pirates from his own Frisia made a sudden raid upon the Northumbrian coast. A young Englishman was killed by a Frisian trader, and English anger flared up so fiercely that all Frisians in the north of England fled for home across the sea. Alcuin, then, ordered the unwilling Liudger to go also. For his comfort he carried away with him an " abundance of books."

Upon his return Liudger found Abbot Gregory ill and failing fast. He had had a stroke of paralysis and was helpless, unable to move. But he could still speak, and he carried on his teaching as long as he could. When he could work no more, he gave away his collection of books, the books which he had brought back with him from Rome, dividing them out among his students. Liudger received as his share the *Enchiridion* of St. Augustine, described by its writer as " a book on faith, hope and charity, a book to hold constantly in one's hands, a book in which I think I have covered rather thoroughly what Holy Scripture calls man's true wisdom, his understanding of the due and right adoration of God."

Then, as the Father lay dying, everyone within the monastery waited in suspense for the coming of his nephew, Alberic, for all expected him to be the next abbot of St. Martin's. " Do not fear," said Gregory. " I shall not die before he comes." He came, just four days before Gregory departed in peace. It was, we may think, the year 775. Alberic did succeed Gregory in his abbot's chair. Some years later, perhaps in 778, he was consecrated bishop of Utrecht. The ceremony is said to have taken place at Cologne; at any rate, from this time the diocese of Utrecht was enrolled as part of the metropolitan charge of Cologne's Archbishopric.

How long Alubert, bishop in Utrecht since 768, actually worked in its diocese we do not know. It may be that he had been intended merely to act there for the time being, until a permanent successor to Eoba should be elected. We may now leave him and think of Liudger, who stayed in Utrecht, his monastic home, until Gregory died, and then settled down to work under Abbot Alberic. He did not, however, stay long. Word arrived at St. Martin's of the death of a priest who had been working at Deventer on the river Ijssel, in the modern Dutch province of Overijssel. His name was Lebuin. At Deventer he had died. Very soon afterwards heathen Saxons of the neighbourhood had destroyed his church, and now no trace of his grave was to be seen. More important, however, than finding his grave was the necessity of building a new church for the Christians of Deventer. Alberic, therefore, as abbot ordered Liudger to go to Deventer and with the help of its faithful to raise a new place of worship, if possible on the spot where Lebuin's body had been buried.

While he travels to Deventer we may look at the story of this Lebuin, a story which has long held the interest of scholars.

4

Lebuin was of English birth. His name in his own England was Liafwine, Lebuin being a Latinised form and given him on the Continent. About 770, while Liudger was on his second visit to York, he had arrived in Utrecht and asked to see Abbot Gregory. Gregory was ill, but he could not refuse. The young man, already in priest's ordering, had a petition to offer. He wanted Gregory, and the bishop, then Alubert, to give him permission, authority, and facilities for work. Moreover, and this was more unusual, he knew where he wanted to work. The Lord himself, he declared, in a vision of the night, full of terror, had commanded him not once but three times to get him speedily to the region lying along the river Ijssel, on the border of Frankland and Saxony. Gregory warned him that the Saxons were ready to strike and quick to kill. It made no difference to Lebuin. Out he went to that land of Overijssel, to labour among its heathen, to make friends with its few Christians; to build churches on the Ijssel's west bank at Wilp and on its eastern side at Deventer; to see pagans swoop down upon Deventer's church and set it on fire; to build again patiently after they had gone; even to venture across the border and to face the Saxons themselves in their own still free and independent homes.

Here Lebuin's story throws some light on these Saxon barbarians and their ways. They might and did rejoice in attacking the Christians who lived near their country, but they kept due order in their own heathen land. " The Saxons on the Continent," we are told by the Venerable Bede in this same eighth century, " have no king, but they have chieftains of high rank. In face of war these chieftains cast lots among themselves; that one on whom the lot falls they follow as leader, and they obey him as long as the war lasts. At its ending this leader again returns to his usual rank among them, their equal but no longer their commander-in-chief." Here is the primitive German custom, which reminds us of the Roman naming of a dictator to guide Roman soldiers in time of crisis.

The earliest *Life* of Lebuin, written in Latin about the mid-ninth century, also speaks of chieftains. It tells us more, however, for it describes the custom of these Saxons of the early Middle Ages to gather in general assembly once a year in central Saxony at a place, Marklo, on the bank of the river Weser. To this place came both nobles and simple men in great numbers. Above all, there came elected delegates, chosen previously from the districts of the land to represent their dwellers in this council. For each of these districts twelve men of noble birth, twelve men of free though humbler family, twelve serfs, men bound by right of their masters to work for them upon the soil, were chosen as representatives. By them, now meeting in council to act for their fellows, the business of making, amending, and amplifying the laws of their land was carried out; of deciding the cases of dispute and of crime brought before them; of preparing for war or for peace in the year to come. Debate on every point lasted until all voices rose in consent.

This description of formal law-making, remarkable in itself amid a people so given to piracy, slaughter, and ravage, is our first account of representative government in the Middle Ages on the part of a barbarian nation. To Lebuin, however, its interest was entirely different. Here to him there seemed to be an opportunity heaven-sent to try by his words to win this people to Christian good will and peace. He decided to attend the gathering and to seize his chance. His friends on the Frankish side of the border warned him of the danger. " You will not escape," they said. " God, who sent me there, will take care of me," answered Lebuin. " I shall escape all right."

On the day appointed the Saxon people came flocking in their multitude to Marklo, to the great Field of Council. The Chief Priest offered prayer to the gods of his country, that all things on this day might be well-pleasing in their sight and of profit to the Saxon life and cause. The elected delegates were in their places, sitting in a wide circle. The first speaker rose. Suddenly, from the crowd behind, Lebuin ran out into the centre of the circle and faced the assembly, wearing his priestly vestments, the Cross and the Book of the Gospels held high in his hands. " Hear ye all! " he cried aloud. " I am the messenger of the Lord God All-powerful. From Him I bear command to the Saxon people one and all! " Then, in the sudden hush of astonished silence, he continued: " O Saxon people, the Lord of heaven and earth, if you will become His men, will give you such prosperity as you have never known. No king to this day have you had; no king shall have power to prevail against you. But if you will not swear loyalty to this One God, terror will come upon you, even now prepared. A king there is who shall march into your fields for plunder and ravage, who shall weary you in war after war, who shall drive you into exile, who shall take your lands and your lives. To him and to his sons you shall be in subjection bound."

By this time the Saxons had recovered from their surprise. A great shout of anger rose from the field: " Seize him! Kill him! " It was their custom to put to death notorious offenders by pressing around them in a close circle and hurling at them sharpened stakes of wood. Now, then, every man of quickness and strength of body among the crowd, eager to do his share, ran hither and thither, fought to reach and to tear out a stake from the field's boundary fence that he might hurl its pointed end at this man who had thus cast shame upon his ancestral gods. Alas! in the rage and hurry not one of them thought to keep guard over the victim. When they turned round to do the deed, Lebuin was no longer in sight. The angel of the Lord, probably appearing in the form of some sturdy Christian among the heathen multitude, had promptly hustled him off into hiding within the forest near the Field of Council.

Howls of anger and disappointment filled the air. Then a Saxon chieftain, whose name was Buto, sprang upon the stump of a tree cut down by some forager seeking timber for his home, and raised his hand for silence. " Hear you all! " he called in his turn, " and judge my words. From whatsoever nation envoys come to us, Frisians or Northmen or Slavs, we, the Saxon people, receive them in peace and hear patiently their words. Now the messenger of some god unknown has come to us, this god worshipped by Christian men, and how have we treated him? Well may you believe these things to be true which this man foretold, seeing how easily he has escaped our hands. Surely these things of evil shall speedily come to pass! "

At once, some of those present, in fear or through Christian influence, shouted their assent. Much murmuring, much talk followed. But there seemed now nothing to be done except to start once again the business of this interrupted meeting. Lebuin meanwhile reached Deventer, breathless but safe and sound.

The story, true in its description of Saxon custom, seems to prophesy too pointedly the coming Saxon War to be true in all its detail. One may say, of course, that the lust for conquest in the mind of Charles the Great was already well known and that Saxony lay right upon his path. At least, we may suppose that there must have been some ground for the tradition of Lebuin's courage. No further attack was made upon his church at Deventer as long as he lived. Then, as we have seen, after his death the pagan Saxons destroyed it.

5

Liudger duly arrived in the town to search for Lebuin's grave. Since he could find nothing, he turned to the building of the new church. Its foundations were already laid when, so the story goes, a vision came to him in a dream. He seemed to see Lebuin himself and to hear his voice. " Dear brother Liudger," the vision declared, " good is your work in the Lord. Those relics of mine for which you are searching you will find buried under the wall which you are raising on the south."

Liudger obediently dug again, found this time the grave without any difficulty, and there at last, with the help of men of Deventer, brought into being, if not into beauty, the church he had been sent to build. By the mid-ninth century this holy place was renowned for many miracles. At that time a house of canons was serving in the church instead of Benedictine monks, in accordance with the less austere, less monastic life put forward by St. Chrodegang of Metz.

St. Chrodegang held high place and repute among the bishops of Germany in the middle years of the eighth century. He belonged to a family of noble rank in the Rhineland; in his younger days he lived long at the Frankish Palace and was head of the diplomatic and legal corps of secretaries in the service of the Frankish mayors, Charles Martel and his son, Pippin the Third. Pippin named him bishop of Metz, capital city of Austrasia. As its bishop, from 742 until his death in 766, he did many things and set on foot many reforms. But the most famous was that which brought his Cathedral clergy at Metz into a community which shared house and refectory and sleeping quarters under his own charge and in direct communication with his own residence.

His purpose was to restore order and discipline to the idle, dissolute, and even immoral life of many Frankish priests of his time. It was, of course, the same purpose which was driving Boniface, his contemporary. Like Boniface, Chrodegang was entirely loyal to the See of Rome and to the Frankish authority of State. Like him, he was devoted to the Benedictine *Rule*; he founded near Metz a Benedictine monastery at Gorze which was to be famous in later days. In drawing up a *Rule* of his own for his own Cathedral clergy, for his " canons "— *canonici*, as he called them—he drew not only from the older example of St. Augustine of Hippo but very much from the code of St. Benedict himself. His clergy observed the regular round of monastic Office, received sacraments, order, and counsel from their bishop somewhat as from an abbot, and instruction from constant reading.

Yet in certain respects the *Rule* of Chrodegang differed essentially from that of Benedict. His " canons " were not aloof from the world, not secluded within monastic enclosure. They worked with and under a bishop appointed by a Frankish mayor; they were part of a Church united to the power of the Frankish secular authority which presided over its Synods, named its bishops, and sent its missionaries where it would. They were, it is true, subject to the bishop under whose eye they lived in the precincts of his Cathedral; but they made no vow of monastic obedience, of obedience without hesitation, without question. And, lastly, they made no vow of monastic poverty; they were free to use and to enjoy the property, the moneys which had fallen to them by inheritance or had been earned by them through service rendered outside their community.

This *Rule* of St. Chrodegang was to carry its influence and its pattern throughout the Frankish kingdoms and across the Channel to England; countless monasteries were to adopt its example or to receive it in exchange for their Benedictine discipline of old. And in it there lay seeds of evil for the future, of another harvest of laxity entirely unforeseen by its founder. After his death these seeds of evil were to ripen in houses of religion where Benedictine regularity was no longer observed and monastic life had fallen into decay.

Liudger's mission was now fulfilled. For a brief while we may probably think of him as working again in Utrecht under Alberic, abbot of its monastery of St. Martin, and after 778 bishop of its diocese. In 780, however, we find him stationed as mission priest in the northern Netherlands at Dokkum, where Boniface had died twenty-six years before and where a church now stood in his memory. His continued story will reflect the grim events of the Saxon War from 772 to 785.

6

This Saxon War had begun almost as soon as Charles found himself in 771 sole possessor of the Frankish throne. At first his intention was to tame and to impress by his power these Saxons who were continually making raids upon the lands ruled by him, both Frankish and Frisian. He seized Saxon fortresses and he built new ones; all of them he garrisoned for the guarding of the country around. Then he went further in his determination to subdue this free people. As Boniface had destroyed the oak of Geismar in Hesse, sacred to the lord of heathendom, so in 772 Charles overthrew the holy shrine of the Saxons, the pillar of wood revered by them as symbol of their supreme god's power to uphold and support all things that are. This insult the Saxons never forgot. Again and again they rose to ravage; again and again Charles defeated them, here and there. Readily the defeated barbarians swore submission for the future; as readily they broke their oath, rallied their forces, and hurried to plunder again.

As the years went by, Charles decided on new measures. Now, he determined, not only, not merely, would he fight to punish the past in order to keep under control the future doings of these stubborn, defiant men. He would fight to conquer them entirely. And more: like Clovis, first king of the Franks, he would march out to force this heathen Saxon people into the Christian Church, to " compel them to enter," as had written that great Augustine of Hippo whom Charles loved to read. He kept his resolution. Again and again we read of Saxons driven to baptism in their multitude, only to return from this christening to the ritual of the gods whom their fathers had known and worshipped in awe. In 780, as the Frankish annals tell, Charles took a further step on the road to this Christian conquest. He marched to the river Elbe and there divided Saxon lands among his bishops, his priests, and his abbots, for their care and pastoral charge of conversion and administration. Soon, to his thought, Saxony would be not only a Frankish but a Christian land, and completely under his control.

Two years later, in 782, the Saxons themselves immeasurably sharpened the edge of this resolution of Charles. They fell upon and slaughtered one of the king's armies under the Süntel range of hills, on the right bank of the river Weser. Two nobles, high in the royal service, lost their lives. From the moment he heard of this disaster, Charles stopped at nothing in his desire. Year after year he returned to battle; murder and massacre pushed forward his advance. Year by year the Saxons fought back in desperation, led by a Saxon noble, Widukind by name. In the end, in 785, they were forced to own themselves beaten. Widukind submitted, and received the sacrament of baptism from the Church in the presence of Charles as godfather. Charles wrote of his joy to the Pope, then Hadrian the First;

and the Pope ordered three days of thanksgiving in solemn chant and litany.

But this joyful end was only an end for a time, not for fullness or for permanence. And it was largely the Christian nature of the crusade of this Frankish king which kept the minds and hearts of these newly-baptized Saxons still in ferment, if not of resistance by arms, yet of secret rebellion. Some time between 775 and 790, to give the broadest range of theory, in 780, it may be, or in 782 or 785 or 788, according to various calculations, Charles brought down upon the Saxons the force of a General Edict, a code of law, by which in the future their lives were to be controlled.

Among its provisions this Edict decreed death for the man who broke into or robbed with violence a Christian church; who, without necessary cause, approved by a Christian priest, dared to eat meat on the fast-days of Lent; who called upon a pagan god as he stood by the funeral pyre of kinsman or friend; who deliberately refused Christian baptism. This penalty of death, it is true, might be remitted if the sinner's Christian priest solemnly declared that of his own will he had made confession of his guilt and had done the penance given him. Fines were imposed upon those who, without excuse approved by the priest, neglected to bring their children to baptism until they were more than a year old; upon those who practised heathen ritual; upon those who buried their dead in places sacred to heathen deities.

The yearly assemblies, imbedded in the old Saxon tradition, were no longer to be held; no general gathering of the Saxons might take place except by express command of King Charles or his representative. All Saxon men, whether noble or free-born or serf, were to pay every year to the Christian churches and clergy one-tenth of their substance and their earnings.

It was this last order which held the Saxons in continual unrest, which brought them to open revolt during the latter years of the eighth century. Even Alcuin, now a fervent worker at the Court and an equally fervent admirer of its king, wrote bitter words to his friends, to Charles himself, about this impossible burden pressed down upon those so lately heathen in name as well as in conviction and still so largely ignorant of the Christian faith.

7

With these happenings in mind we can return to Liudger, now beginning his work at Dokkum in northern Frisia in 780, the eighth year of the Saxon War. Frisian rebellion soon rose in sympathy, in union of resistance against Christian control. In 784 Liudger was driven out. Nearly two years he spent in Italy, in Rome and in the Benedictine monastery of Monte Cassino. After the victory of Charles in 785 he returned to the Netherlands. Here he himself was to know in his own life the determination of Charles the Great to direct and to organise matters of Church as well as of secular life in the lands of his dominion. The king had heard of this young, energetic priest, and now he directed him by his own express command to lead a mission to the country east of Dokkum, in the north of Frisia between the Lauwerszee and the mouth of the river Ems. Liudger obeyed.

While he laboured there, busy in journeys on the mainland, to islands off the coast, he came by boat one day to Heligoland, that little isle off Schleswig-Holstein, north-east from the Ems. There, we remember, Willibrord had landed, and in the casting of lots had faced death. But now the fear of the great Frankish king seemed nearer to the islanders than even Fosite, the island's Spirit of Power. Liudger, with none to stop him, destroyed the pagan shrines and received into Christianity, the great king's religion, even an island chieftain's son.

Once again, however, and from this land east of Dokkum, this newer field of work, Saxon and Frisian unrest drove him out. A pleasant story is given in tradition concerning this second time of exile. Among Liudger's most zealous followers here in north-east Frisia was a man named Bernlef, who told everyone that he owed his recovery from blindness to the prayers of this Christian priest. An earnest Christian himself, he was loved by all, Christian and heathen alike, for his gay and friendly spirit and for the love he bore his own Frisian land. He had a gift of music and often would sing to his fellows songs of the heroic deeds done by their warriors of old. When Liudger knew that he and his companions must again leave their work for a while or most probably lose their lives, he asked this Bernlef to do what he could in their absence, which, he hoped, would not be long. Would Bernlef, for instance, layman though he was, try to baptize babies who were sick and likely to die? Very simply and quietly Bernlef carried out the trust; and sixteen little Frisian children received baptism at his hands just before they died.

It was not very long before Liudger returned to his mission; but again King Charles had a fresh purpose for him. When the ninth century opened, he decided to create at Münster in Saxony a new diocese to serve Saxons and Frisians both, to care for the people of the land extending southwards from the mouth of the Ems. He asked Liudger to be the first bishop of Münster. For some time Liudger hesitated, reluctant to assume this high office, with all the publicity, the social life, which it entailed. Perhaps he remembered the solemn words of Pope Gregory the Great in his *Pastoral Rule*, about bishops worthy and unworthy, about the high qualities, and so many of them, which a good bishop must possess. Perhaps he thought back over the past, unable to decide which man had been wiser: that other Gregory, his own master in Utrecht, who had refused a bishop's see, or his own contemporary and friend, Lull, who had dared even to follow Boniface at Mainz. In the end he yielded to the arguments of men whom he could trust and was consecrated about 804. Some five years remained for him in this final labour. He died in 809, on the twenty-sixth of March, at Billerbeck, a little town near Münster, where that same morning he had said Mass and preached for the last time.

He lived, as he had felt it given him to live, a threefold life: of a zealous mission priest and bishop amid the confusion and tumult of his day; of a teacher, who trained his Cathedral clergy in daily lessons, and a writer, who found time to put into words the *Lives* of Gregory and Alberic, his two abbots of St. Martin's, Utrecht; of a soul devoted to the regular life of prayer. In northern Frisia he had learned to fear that raiders from yet farther north might some day descend upon lands lying south and west of them. He had begged King Charles to let him go out on a mission to these Northmen, but Charles had held him firmly at home. He was not a monk under Benedictine vow. It may be that his years in York and the canonical rather than monastic life of the clergy of its Cathedral in those years had left their influence upon him. Certainly, as we have noted, not a few Frankish monasteries of his time were following that same canonical order.

.And yet Liudger lived under no easy discipline. As bishop, we are told, he wore no monk's cowl, but he wore a shirt of sackcloth, to the day of his death. We have two narratives of his life. The second one, ascribed to the late ninth century, tells that he refused to interrupt one of his hours of prayer even at the call of King Charles himself and that when the king rebuked him he answered: " I thought, my king, that the Lord our God took precedence over all men of earth, and that this was in your mind for me when you gave me a bishop's charge." In Münster he established a house of clergy who lived as he did, following the *Rule* of St. Chrodegang.

Among the abbeys which he served he especially loved and visited two. King Charles entrusted to him for his aid in Münster the service of a community at Lotusa, a place held to be in Belgium, perhaps near Liège, perhaps near Tournai, or, again, perhaps at Zele. This was to him a great joy. The greater joy of his heart, however—to him an Echternach, a Fulda—was the monastery which he himself had built, before he became a bishop, in forest land at Werden on the Ruhr. There, so his second *Life* declares, the Lord of heaven sent a mighty wind to uproot the trees which were filling the ground with obstacles and Liudger's heart with despair. There its monks followed the Benedictine *Rule* which Liudger himself for two years had known in Monte Cassino. There, in the outer porch of its church, on an April day of 809, they made his grave.

CHAPTER TWELVE

SAINT ANSKAR

Denmark and Sweden in the Ninth Century

NOT ONLY did Charles the Great establish among the conquered Saxons a bishopric at Münster. Some time after a meeting in 799 with Pope Leo the Third at Paderborn, also in Saxon land, he placed there a bishop as head of a new diocese to carry on his Christian crusade.

More interesting, however, to us is the bishop's seat already established by Charles among the Saxons in 787 at Bremen, near the point where the river Weser meets the North Sea. An Englishman, Willehad, first held its rule. He, too, had been eager to work in Frisia. In Northumbria, his own country, as it was that of Willibrord and of Alubert, he had been approved by a council of bishops, nobles, and clergy, called together by Alchred, king of Northumbria from 765 to 774, and then he left for the Netherlands. At first he worked in the region around Dokkum; then, about 780, after Liudger arrived at Dokkum to replace him, he was sent by Charles to try to convert the Saxons dwelling between the mouths of the Weser and the Elbe. For some years he did his best and gained some reward, even though, like Liudger, the Saxon resistance and rising under Widukind had forced him, also, to leave his work. He spent his two years of exile at Willibrord's abbey of Echternach in Luxembourg. Finally, as bishop at Bremen from 787 until his death in 789, he had under his charge the same people of the tidal waters of the Weser and the Elbe whom he had served as mission priest.

MAP FIVE: Journeys of Saint Anskar

Our story, then, is travelling northwards; and the fore-bodings of Liudger, his fears of menace from the Northmen, are now to prove no dream, no illusion. The conquest, first of Frisia, and then of Saxony, had brought the Franks and their king, Charles the Great, to the edge of danger. North of Bremen, north of the river Elbe, in the land we now call Schleswig-Holstein, and in the lands extending still farther northwards, lived the Danes, unconquered by the Frankish power; and the Danes, those raiders, pirates, Vikings, who were to make the ninth century a horror to Western Europe, were already at its beginning alert to vex the mind of Charles. To a Danish king, Sigfrid, the Saxon rebel Widukind had fled from the march of Frankish armies. Against Godfred, successor of Sigfrid as king, Charles had anxiously fortified and garrisoned the harbours and landing-places on his shores. On the Danish side, Godfred had built his own long line of defence, the *Danewerk*, stretching from the Baltic Sea near Schleswig as far as Hollingstedt.

But Charles committed one great error. In his eagerness to hold subject the Frisian people he destroyed their sea-power, their control as daring and skilful sailors of the coastal waters of the North Sea. Soon the Danes, eager for adventure, for plunder, for the possession of land, were descending upon the Frisians and, a little later, were boldly advancing to attack the Franks. Charles himself, it is true, suffered little but anxiety. It was after his death in 814, in the reign of his son and successor as king and emperor, Louis the Pious, that the Frankish annals tell again and again of Viking raids upon Frisian and Frankish shores alike.

This Louis " the Pious " in one way earned his name. His mind was constantly dwelling on the souls of men, Christian and heathen, clergy, monks and layfolk. His skill and strength in matters political were tragically wanting; but the Danes as heathen weighed heavily on his mind. Some effort, he thought, must be made to lighten their darkness. In this, of course, he had the sympathy and support of the Papal See, which had been so anxious for the conversion of Germany a hundred years before his time.

The feeling for the North was not new-born with this ninth century. Early in the eighth Willibrord had left Utrecht, as we have seen, on a journey north of the Elbe to Denmark. He had won nothing except that permission from the Danish king Ongendus to take back with him thirty Danish boys to the Netherlands. Many years later, in 789, Alcuin was writing to a friend in Saxony: " Is there any hope of Christian faith among the Danes? " Charles the Great had sent to the Danes a priest—we even have his name, Heridac—with the thought that after some years of experience with this unknown and barbarous people Heridac might become bishop in their midst. For this very reason Charles had been unwilling to place the work among them under the care of any see already established.

His death had ended this thought of Heridac's consecration; and Louis the Pious did just what his father had not done. He gave the oversight of this land north of the Elbe to the bishops of the two sees nearest its borders on the south, both in Saxon territory: that of Bremen, founded by his father, and that of Verden, south-east of Bremen, founded by himself. Moreover, in 823 he sent Ebbo, Archbishop of Reims, on a mission approved by the Pope, then Paschal the First, to this people of the North " who know not God, nor rebirth in the waters of baptism, who dwell in the shadow of death." Ebbo preached during the summer of 823, baptized some converts, and returned home. By this time the name of Christian was known among the Danes; but that is all we can say.

The real beginning of Christianity among them was brought into action three years later, and by a Danish prince. The death of the Danish king Godfred had been followed by a long and bitter struggle in Denmark between his sons and other rival claimants for power. At last, in 826, one of these claimants, known to us as Harald the Second, driven from the land in Denmark which he had actually held as king, decided to appeal to the Frankish ruler. With his appeal Harald offered to Louis an inducement which he knew well would give it sure support, his decision to ask for Christian baptism for himself and for the train of followers which he brought with him to the Frankish Palace of Ingelheim, near Mainz.

A glowing description has been left us of this ceremony, celebrated with high splendour and solemnity either at Ingelheim itself or, more probably, in St. Alban's Church at Mainz. Latin verses of the time leave nothing to the imagination. Even the bare record of the Frankish annals states that " Harald and his wife and a great multitude of Danes were baptized, and many gifts were given him by the Emperor, who received him from the font as his son in the Lord." Louis, indeed, was happy; at least part of this Danish land, he thought, by his aid would have a Christian king. Now came the question: Who was to teach the Danes when, by the help of God and the Franks, Harald had won back his crown? What able and experienced priest would be willing to go to Denmark for this work?

2

With this question starts the story of a pioneer and his adventures in the North. His name was Anskar, and most fortunately we have his *Life*, written by a contemporary, Rimbert, the man who directly succeeded him in office. Rimbert wrote the *Life* very shortly after Anskar's death; and therefore it contains much that we may trust as true.

Anskar was a Frank, born in 801 in north-west France, near Amiens. His mother, a woman devoted to the Christian faith, died when he was five years old. In that same year his father sent him to be brought up by the monks of the neighbouring abbey of Corbie, founded in the seventh century by Bathild, then the widowed queen of the Frankish king, Clovis the Second. The loss of one so near to him, the loneliness of a little boy taken so early from his home, the surroundings in which he found himself, among crowded brethren chanting psalms, amid long hours of silence broken only by words which told the joys of heaven and the terrors of hell, seem to have made a deep impression on the child's mind, still dwelling on a pious mother's teaching.

Many years afterwards Anskar told Rimbert of a dream which had come to him in those first days at Corbie. It had been difficult for him, he remembered, when he was only five, to settle down to its round of prayer and lessons. It was easier to play with other boys of the abbey school, to try to forget. Then one night, as he lay asleep in the common dormitory, it seemed to him that he was stumbling through a muddy field which caught his feet at every step. He kept on looking towards the fence at its end, but that, he felt in his dream, he would never reach. On its other side ran a broad and pleasant path, along which there walked a Lady, radiant in face and clothing. With her were many women clad in white, and among them he caught sight of his own mother. With a cry he started towards her, but he could not reach the fence because of the mud in the field which held him fast. Just then the Lady looked up and saw him struggling. " Son," she called to him, " do you want your mother? Some day you shall have her again, if you work hard, as we do here. We who dwell here have no time to be lazy."

Young Anskar, haunted by this dream, now threw himself into his lessons under the master of Corbie's school. In its earlier days Corbie had lived its life according to the manner of Columban's practice in Luxeuil; and, since it had now turned to austere Benedictine ordering, it was still one of the stricter communities in France. In 814, when Anskar was thirteen years old, word came to the monastery that King Charles the Great was dead, the king and emperor whose conquests, power, and magnificence were to make him a hero of legend in future days. Anskar himself had seen him in all his pride. Once more Anskar felt that life was a struggle to reach an end, that reaching this end was uncertain, and that all he could do about it was to press on through its swamp of fear.

Then, so Rimbert tells, he had yet another dream. This time it was a happy one, a vision of heaven, of a passing from darkness and pain into light beyond the power of words to describe, full of colour, full of joy and gladness; of souls real as they had never been on earth; and in their midst a Voice, clearer than all sound, which seemed to him to fill all time that ever was or was to be, saying to him: " Go forth to thy labour and return here to Me with a martyr's crown."

In course of time, after many years of study in St. Peter's School at Corbie, his abbot made Anskar a teacher there. Before very long he was its head, together with a fellow-monk named Witmar. In 822, when he was only twenty-one, he was transferred, together with Witmar and others of Corbie's community, to a daughter house, New Corbie, or Corvey, recently founded in Saxony. Here also he became master of the monastic school.

Four years of teaching in New Corbie brought him, now a professed monk and a priest, to that time of 826 when the exiled King Harald of the Danes came seeking aid from the Frankish Court. Not one of the priests familiar with the Court offered to return to Denmark with Harald to teach his pagan people. Not one knew any other who might be willing, for the reputation of the Northmen was full of terror. Already in 819 the repeated assaults of their ships upon the island of Noirmoutier at the mouth of the river Loire had been driving the monks of its abbey to work anxiously for its fortifying in defence. In 820 thirteen of these ships had landed pirates on the coast of Flanders and had carried them on to attempt a like landing at the mouth of the Seine. At this moment of 826, it is true, there was peace; but no one knew how long it would last, and surely no one was eager to dwell among these barbarians in their homelands. Louis put the question to the council he had called to debate this matter, and there was long silence. At length the voice of Wala, abbot of Corbie, was heard. " I have a monk in my monastery," he said, " who would be exactly the right man to send. Whether he will go to Denmark I do not know. His name is Anskar." Anskar was at once summoned to the Palace. Without any hesitation he declared that he was willing, and Abbot Wala gave him leave to depart.

Mere quickness of decision did not make decision easy for Anskar. Many, both within and outside his abbey, thought him either conceited or a fool. Not a few of his friends begged him to change his mind. Many hours he spent alone, thinking, reading, praying, worried by doubt, uncertain whether, indeed, he could carry out what he had promised, this adventure which no one else seemed willing to share. Then one day, as he was sitting, full of these thoughts, in a little orchard, a favourite retreat of his near the monastery wall, one of his brother monks, Autbert, came to sit beside him. " Do you really mean to go on this journey to the Northmen? " he asked. Anskar, sure that he had enough to bear without being annoyed by friends tiresome and inquisitive, spoke up sharply: " What is that to you? Don't worry me." " I don't mean to be curious," replied Autbert. " I only want to say that, if you really are going, I could not let you go alone. For the love of God I shall go, too, if Father Abbot will let me."

The abbot did, and the two set out, carrying in their packs the vessels, vestments and missals, with personal belongings, which they needed for the work. They rode to Cologne, then travelled with King Harald by boat along the Rhine to Wijk-bij-Duurstede, the river port near Utrecht so familiar to Willibrord and Boniface, then continued their journey northwards across Frisian territory to the country of the Danes. There they settled at Schleswig, on a long inlet of the sea called the Schlei, running far inward from the eastern coast of the present Schleswig-Holstein. In those days this was Danish land.

Nearly two years they toiled, with scant return for their efforts except in the building-up of a little school of about twelve boys. Then trouble upset even this hope. King Harald was again driven from his throne; Brother Autbert fell ill, so ill that he had to go back to New Corbie, where he died. Anskar in great discouragement decided to go home himself, to consult King Louis and other friends among the Franks about his own future.

3

But neither could his friends at home tell him what he ought to do. They were merely giving him the usual advice to " wait in hope " when suddenly that hope appeared from another quarter, a new chance to try elsewhere. In 829 important delegates arrived from Sweden, bringing a petition to the Frankish king. Would Louis send to Sweden Christian men to teach its people the lessons of their faith? The king at once saw the opportunity. Promptly he sent for Anskar. Would he come to the Palace? " Tarry not," the message went, as it is reported in Anskar's *Life*, " not even to shave."

Anskar came, ready for anything. He was delighted at the thought of Sweden. He found a priest, one called Gislemar, to await developments in Schleswig and to do whatever could be done for its mission; he asked Witmar, the monk who had shared his life in the cloister of Corbie, Old and New, to share with him this new venture among Swedish folk. Witmar was willing. The two began their journey, first on land, then by sea, travelling in boats chartered by a company of traders. Midway across the water pirates came down upon them. In the first battle the sturdy sailors, aided by Anskar, Witmar, and other passengers, beat off the attack. Then the enemy rallied, won a hold, swarmed on board the Frankish boats, captured them, seized all that they could find, and barely allowed Anskar and his companions to jump overboard and swim for shore. All the gifts of King Louis for the service of the church and school which Anskar hoped to build in Sweden were lost, including forty books.

With immense effort and carrying only the barest necessities,

Anskar and Witmar found passage on another boat bound for the Swedish Lake Mälaren, which stretches near Stockholm to meet the Baltic. In its length there lie over seventy miles of loveliness. Its waters hold a thousand isles; from its bank now rise turreted castles and picturesque houses of humbler sort. On one of these isles, Björkö, they landed, and came to the old town of Birka, built on a site where now a cross of stone still marks its memory. There that Swedish king who had sent his envoys to Louis the Pious gave them welcome to his people. His name was Björn, and once again we must fear that political advantage lay behind a request for Christian teaching. Björn, too, wanted aid from the Franks. He had heard that King Horik of Denmark, known to history as Horik the First, or Horik the Elder, was even then preparing to march against his land.

Anskar and his friend stayed at Birka a year and a half. Nothing very much here, either, came of their toil, except the baptism of Herigar, governor of Birka, who was to be a devoted worker in the mission of future years, and the gratitude of Christians held captive on the island, who were glad to receive the sacraments long lost to them. At last, in 831, it seemed best once more to return to ask counsel from the authorities at home. Björn with real regret saw the two men depart, and gave them for their journey a safeguard, a letter written, it would seem, in runic symbols.

4

In due course they reported to King Louis all they had done, all they had tried to do. The king deliberated, talked things over with his counsellors, and made up his mind. He decided that the time had come to fulfil his father's intention and to establish a mission see from which work might be carried on for the Danish people north of the Elbe. Its ruler, he thought, should be an Archbishop in rank, with authority to organise and to control in matters spiritual all the Frankish endeavour in that far-reaching land, and his Cathedral should be in the Saxon city of Hamburg where the Elbe flows near the sea, north-east of Bremen. A great Synod of Frankish clergy, meeting in 831, confirmed the plan, and Anskar was chosen as the first to hold its charge.

It was probably at the close of the year that many high dignities of the Church gathered to take part in his consecration by Drogo, Archbishop of Metz. Ebbo, Archbishop of Reims, and the bishops of Trier and of Mainz also laid their hands upon him, together with those of Bremen and Verden to whom Louis the Pious had previously given the care of the Danes.

Shortly afterwards Louis sent Anskar to Rome, praying the Pope that he be approved as Archbishop by the bestowal of the pallium. Not only was this granted by Gregory the Fourth, Pope since 827, but also, before the shrine of St. Peter, Gregory invested Anskar with the authority of Papal Legate in these northern lands, for work among the Danes, the Swedish, and all neighbouring people. In this honour of office Anskar was taking over the similar commission once entrusted to Ebbo of Reims.

From 832, then, when he arrived at Hamburg, for thirteen years we are to think of Anskar as now working there, now journeying through the wild and lonely country north of the Elbe. That his work progressed very slowly is shown by the fact that in default of converts of free birth he bought slaves from heathen traders, instructed them, baptized them and trained them for Christian work. So, in his discouragement, had Amand done in Belgium. Anskar, however, was not left to work alone and unaided. Monks from Corbie came to join him. Help also came from a monastery in West Flanders at Torhout, south of Bruges. Louis had given its community into Anskar's charge for this very purpose, as a basis of support, just as Charles the Great had formerly given the monastery of Lotusa in Belgium to Liudger, bishop of Münster.

Yet for some of Anskar's fellow-workers life in the North

was so austere that they went home. Poverty pressed hard
upon the little band in Hamburg. After eleven years of struggle
this poverty pressed harder, aided by the course of events. In
840 Louis the Pious died. In 843 his Frankish Empire was
divided among his three sons, Lothar, Louis the German, and
Charles the Bald. Now the land of the Saxons bordering on
the unconquered country of the Danes, with the Saxon city of
Hamburg, the base of Anskar's mission to those Danes, fell to
Louis the German, as king of the Franks in the east. And this
Louis the German was very different from his father. He was
possessed, not by thought for heathen souls, but by political
ambition. Moreover, Anskar's Belgian base of support, the
monastery of Torhout, lay in the portion of Frankland now
received by Charles the Bald, as king of the Franks in the west,
and he promptly bestowed it upon one of his own friends. In
this transferring of Torhout Anskar lost a revenue which made
for Hamburg and its workers just the difference between a
provision austere but sufficient, and actual want.

In 845, two years later, a far worse blow fell upon the
struggling mission. The Frankish annals give the bare report
that King Horik of the Danes sent a fleet of six hundred ships
along the Elbe to attack land held by Louis the German; that
there was a battle in which the Danes were defeated; that,
however, they attacked again, and this time captured the
Frankish city of Hamburg.

Rimbert in his *Life* of Anskar gives a more detailed picture.
" Suddenly," he writes, " the pirates swooped down to seize.
It all happened so quickly, so unexpectedly, that there was not
a chance for men of the city to get together, especially since
its governor, Count Bernhard, was away just then. The bishop,
when he first heard of what was happening, tried to hold out
until relief could come, and he was well supported by his
people, both those within the city and those on its outskirts.
But he saw soon that resistance was impossible, for the heathen
were driving fast in their assault and the city was beset at every
point. He gave orders that the relics of the saints should be

taken from the Cathedral and that, carrying these in their hands, his clergy should flee for their lives. He himself had not a moment even to pick up a coat. Men and women streamed around the countryside, wandering aimlessly here and there, running for refuge. Some were taken alive and many were killed."

Two nights and a day the Vikings stayed at Hamburg, and then made off, leaving behind them a mass of fragments and ashes. The Cathedral, built by Anskar himself, with its house for his monks hard by, was destroyed by fire. Many books were lost, among them a bible, written in exquisite lettering, which Louis the Pious had given to Anskar. All things which the church had possessed, all its treasures and furnishings, were either ruined or seized as prize. No precaution had occurred to anyone as necessary; nothing had been removed for safe keeping; and at the time of the sudden raiding no one was able to save anything but the little he could lay hands on as he fled.

5

Meanwhile what had been the fortune of Sweden's converts since Anskar and his friend Witmar had left Birka in 831?

Anskar, appointed by the Pope as Papal Legate for the Swedish people as well as for the Danes, had done what he could. He had talked earnestly, before his consecration for Hamburg, with Ebbo of Reims. Could Ebbo, he asked, find time to go north upon another mission? No, Ebbo firmly replied, he could not; he was far too busy with the unending demands of his own Frankish diocese. He thought, however, that his nephew Gauzbert might be willing to go. And, he asked, in his turn, why should not Gauzbert be consecrated as bishop for these Swedish men? Anskar welcomed the suggestion and, since King Louis the German and his clergy approved it, Gauzbert became bishop for the Swedish land. At his consecrating he, like Willibrord and Boniface, received a new name in token of his new office; henceforward the Church knew him as Simeon.

So Simeon-Gauzbert went to Sweden, to Birka, which was still the centre of work. Probably he arrived in 832, about the time when Anskar reached Hamburg, and probably he stayed among the Swedes some thirteen years, until 845. His career, indeed, is similar to that of Anskar in several details. For in 845, the year of Hamburg's seizing, disaster also fell upon Birka. Heathen men among the Swedish people, driven by their hatred for this new faith which Gauzbert was preaching, attacked the house in which he was living at Birka, drove him and his companions from the town, killed one of them, and carried off anything worth the taking from their small property.

Here Rimbert tells a story which may be worth repeating. It reminds one, at any rate, of the story in the Old Testament of Achan, who wrought folly in Israel in that he took for himself, from among the spoils of Jericho, treasure set aside as sacred, as due offering to be made to the Lord of Heaven. Achan, we read, was stoned to death. The end of Rimbert's narrative, on the contrary, shows mercy to the sinner, in that he sinned through another's hand.

He was a man of high standing in Birka, whose son, covetous of beauty, had stolen from Gauzbert and his monks, amid the confusion of the raid, a book, doubtless rich in colour of illustration and lettering, a gift from their Frankish friends at home. Before long the father lost by death not only this son, but all his family, one after another, until one little boy alone was left to him. His harvest failed, his flocks and herds fell sick, his wealth dwindled away to nothing. The ancient gods of his country, he began to fear, for he was of the heathen people, must be angry, for some reason which he could not imagine, think as he might. In his despair he went to consult a man deeply revered, gifted, people said, with inner sight and power of prophecy. Would he, the distracted father asked, would he cast the lots, according to the custom of this Swedish land, and find out for him which of their gods he had offended and what propitiation he might offer? The seer did as he was asked, cast the lots, and the result was negative. All the gods of his pagan heaven were at peace, he declared, with this afflicted soul. Nothing was of their doing. His trouble came, instead, from a source which he had never dreamed had power to hurt him. It was the God of the Christians who was smiting him in vengeance. " Christ," the seer said, " is destroying you and yours. Something sacred to him, stolen from him, must be lying hidden in your house."

Again the father racked his brains. Then suddenly he remembered that his son had brought home that book. He rushed back to his house, searched everywhere, found the book, wrapped it up most carefully, carried it out of doors and tied it to a stake in his fence, offering it to all who passed by. Not one of his friends would touch it. " There is death in the book," they said. At last in pity a man of Christian faith ventured to put his hand upon it, to carry it away in keeping for the church of Birka. Then the curse was lifted and the little son, the only living possession left, suffered no harm. The father was so impressed by the power of this Christ, the Unknown God, that he came forward for baptism and faithfully kept what he promised at the font. " From his own mouth," Rimbert ends, " I heard this tale."

Gauzbert, once in flight, never returned. He fled straight to his own Frankish people, to become in time bishop of a Saxon see, at Osnabrück, between Münster on the south and Bremen on the north.

Now that their bishop has left them, for a long space we must leave the men of Sweden in the neglect which fell upon their Church, while we turn to follow the happier fortune of the Danes.

6

Louis the German, king of eastern Frankland, cared little for missions to the heathen who lay in the northern lands outside his rule; but he did care for those Saxon lands under his dominion, for the city of Hamburg, and for Archbishop Anskar. When, therefore, he heard that both Anskar and Gauzbert, the bishops appointed for work among Scandinavian peoples, had been driven from their sees, he decided that something must be done, and soon. His advisers, moreover, were always bringing up their fear of the Northmen, the Vikings. If he could not conquer these enemies by force, he thought, at least Christian work in their lands might further peace. At present the Vikings were showing no signs of peace. In 845 they were sailing up the Seine, plundering Paris, plundering the banks of the Loire. On Frisia they were landing men year after year. In 847 Louis, with his brothers, sent strong protest and threat of war to the Danish King Horik, so constantly a menace to Christian men.

Twice, then, in 847 and 848, this Louis the German gathered at Mainz the bishops and leaders of his kingdom to discuss and to decide upon remedy for the situation in Hamburg. Anskar laid before these Councils the truth: that even before the raid of 845 churches in Hamburg's diocese had been lamentably few; that now the city of Hamburg was in ruins; that its clergy were in flight, and likely to face famine if they ever returned; that its Christian people were scattered, living in terror of yet another descent upon their land.

With this tragedy before them, the bishops at these meetings debated long. As they well knew, the see of Bremen, the one nearest to Hamburg, was now vacant, had been vacant for two years. Leuderic, who had held it since the time of Willehad, had died in 845. At last some one moved, for the relief of Hamburg, that the see of Bremen should be added to Anskar's see of Hamburg, that the two should for the future be held as one. Much discussion went forward; much rearranging of responsibility and tenure was gradually settled to the satisfaction, or at least the consent, of nearly all the bishops concerned; the delicate matter of archbishop and bishop was adjusted. Finally a decision was made. In 848 Anskar found himself in charge of the united sees of Hamburg and Bremen and of the mission work in the lands farther north. Much time, it is true, was to pass before his title to Bremen was definitely placed beyond question by a bull of Pope Nicholas the First. Only in 864 was this issued, the last year of Anskar's life. One of the chief obstacles had been the bitter opposition of Gunther, Archbishop of Cologne, under whose jurisdiction the see of Bremen lay. Year after year he had refused his consent.

In 848, then, Anskar was once more at Hamburg. The Northmen had left its ruins to solitude. Now he set to work busily in rebuilding, in gathering together his scattered people, in reviving his monastery, in fulfilling the service of the Church in liturgy and office and teaching. Aid in money and equipment had been given him; Bremen, which had not been assaulted as had Hamburg, was a welcome source of supply. Rimbert states that by his persistence Anskar even won the friendship of the Danish king, Horik the Elder, whose ships had raided Hamburg. How far this friendship was real it would be difficult to say. Nor do we have much knowledge of Horik's dealings with the mission campaign of these years. He did not accept Christianity for himself; but he did at least allow Anskar's efforts for the Danes to go on in peace, efforts which seem to have been centred largely in Schleswig, where he had built his little school in his first years among Danish men. A new church was now built there; a clergy house was established; the school was renewed. Many men who had been baptized years before in Hamburg now came to Schleswig and its clergy for their Christian sacraments, and Christian merchants even made the long journey from the busy port of Wijk-bij-Duurstede.

7

For nearly five years, from 848 until 852, Anskar remained in his charge of Hamburg, of Bremen, of the Danes farther north. All was going well; the city of Hamburg was again rising. Then emergency once more called to him, from his other land of labour, from Sweden.

Sweden, of course, had long been causing him intense concern. Its Christian people, few as they were, had had no priest at all from 845 to 851, nearly seven years; its Christian governor, Herigar, had been in despair; Gauzbert, once its bishop, still firmly refused to return. In 851 a priest had arrived. His name was Ardgar; he was devoted to the solitary life and hated to leave it for the world of men; but because he, too, was worried at the neglect of Swedish souls, he came to Birka. Once again Mass was offered there. Then Herigar died; after some months Ardgar could no longer resist his longing and went back to his quiet cell; by 852 all in Sweden was as neglected as before.

Anskar decided that this could not be; that, now matters in Hamburg and among the Danes were improving, he had better go himself on a second mission to Sweden. This same year saw him leaving Schleswig by boat, moving slowly forward for almost twenty days, past the islands of Lolland, of Bornholm, of Öland, and up the east coast of Sweden to reach for the second time Lake Mälaren and the town of Birka on its isle of Björkö.

In Birka trouble was vigorously alive. King Björn, who had been friendly to Anskar in 831, more than twenty years before, was now dead, and a king named Olaf was ruling. When the island people heard that Anskar was on his way to revive Christian teaching among them, resentment flared up, for during those twenty years pagan belief and custom had grown stronger than ever. Anskar was known to be a speaker of power and persuasion, after his long experience at Hamburg and at Schleswig, and heathen priests in Birka feared his influence. In their fear and hatred they resorted to all the cunning which their minds could contrive. They talked continually of the evils of this Christian religion. Word had come to them, they declared, of angry reproaches made by their country's gods. " You, the Swedish people "—so Rimbert gives the lament of these gods of Sweden—" have long enjoyed Our favour; through Our bestowing, your land has long dwelt in peace, in prosperity, in abundance. To Us you have offered your sacrifices, your worship, as was due, and pleasant has your homage been in Our eyes. And now you are withdrawing from Us the wonted offerings; more slowly you make your vows; even, a thing of great displeasure to Us, you are bringing into your land a strange god. Refrain! Nay, rather increase for Us your sacrifices, render to Us yet higher reverence if you wish for Our good will.

" And, on Our side, if you desire yet another whom you may worship in your heaven, if We do not suffice for your revering, We call to Our number, to Our company, Eric, once your king, himself to be accounted among your gods."

These words, publicly proclaimed in Birka, made both for fear and for gladness among its people. Promptly they began to make sacred a temple for the honour of this Eric, even to order sacrifices and offerings before his shrine. The movement was well under way when Anskar at last arrived, and it struck him hard. Few on the island now remembered him at all, and those who still thought of him with respect could give but little comfort. His very life was in danger, they said.

The king, however, was not under the spell of fear cast by his priests; he was neutral in mind, neither for nor against Anskar. If Anskar showed him regard and attention, so declared Anskar's friends, Olaf might do what he could to protect him, to save his life. Had Anskar anything of value with him which he might offer as a token of reverence and good intention to the king? It was the people rather than their king whom the priests were arousing in hostility.

Anskar said with some heat that he was not going to bribe any king for the saving of his own life. He thought for a while, and then, as things did look very dark, he decided to ask Olaf whether they might not meet, the king and himself, outside the royal Court in private to talk over matters informally? Olaf consented. They met and talked, and the king could not resist the charm of this bishop, Christian though he was, his frank and clear discussion of his hopes, his eagerness for Olaf's co-operation. Moreover, if Anskar would not offer gifts for his own life, he had no scruple in doing so for his cause. The king accepted his offerings with childlike pleasure; we wish that Rimbert had told us what they were. But he gives us words which, so he writes, were spoken by Olaf to Anskar when he left his conference:

" Once there were priests here in Birka, Christian priests. They were driven out, not by order of the king, but by a rising of the people. For this reason I neither can nor do I dare approve this petition of yours for the renewing of Christian worship among us. The thing needful and necessary is the casting of the lots for decision, that I may learn thereby the will of our gods, and, also of my people. If the gods so direct, and my people yield consent, your desire will prosper. If not— well, I will let you know."

Casting of lots for so important a decision was regularly made in an assembly of Birka's leading men. Anskar had to keep his soul in patience until they should meet. The time passed very slowly, until at last one day, as he was saying his Mass at the altar, a feeling of awareness came upon him, of certainty that all would be well. That day the king's counsellors gathered. Olaf laid before them the question: Would they receive the worship of the Christian God? In answer they said, as he knew they would say, that the will of their own heaven must be made known to them in the casting of the lots. All then solemnly marched out to their Field of Council. The lots were cast; the report, as announced by the Chief Priest, was favourable: Christian faith might enter Swedish land. If this story is true, and it may well be, we may imagine either that the heathen priests, bitterly hostile though they were, were honest through the fear of their own religion and faithfully reported what they believed they saw, a tolerance for Christian teaching; or that the will of King Olaf, and of his chieftains who stood with him in his neutral stand, had by this time brought about a change of mind in these ministers of the old pagan faith.

The people, however, were harder to persuade; policy, if policy came into the matter, meant little to them. It was the people, King Olaf had declared, who had driven out Gauzbert, the Christian bishop, in 845. In their turn they assembled for their own meeting, not with dignity of ceremonial as their chieftains had done, but shouting, arguing, each man venting his own views. It was the calm reasoning of a senior citizen among them which brought silence and a mood of serious thought, as had happened in the case of Lebuin among the Saxons. This elder of the Swedish people now pointed out that Christians had formerly lived among them, Christian men of their own race, and that time and time again these men had declared the aid which their Christian God had given them, both on sea and on land. " Why," said he, " why should we reject any source of help and support? Even some of us, we who have travelled to Duurstede, have seen what this Christian faith can do for those who journey, as we ourselves have to journey, across seas scoured by pirates in these our days. My people, do not throw away what will be of service to us, too, if at any time our gods should turn their faces in anger away from us! With this thought in mind let us allow the servants of this Christian God to remain in peace on our isle."

The people of Birka heard, pondered, and saw the point. They gave consent. Soon subjects of King Olaf living elsewhere in Sweden followed Birka's lead, and Anskar could begin once more to plough this heathen wilderness in peace. When all was under way, and this could be said of the year 854, when workers had been found to carry on this mission, Anskar felt that he could return to his own see in Hamburg. He had been absent from this, his chief charge, for nearly two years.

8

In Hamburg, in Bremen, in Schleswig, he spent the remaining eleven years of his life, from 854 until his death in 865. At times, it is true, we grow weary of the adulation poured out in its sticky, swollen flood by those who wrote the *Lives* of these medieval saints; and Rimbert's *Life* of Anskar is no exception. Yet from his tedious pages there looks out at us a man whom we surely recognise as holy, a man utterly unselfish, devoted to his faith and to its sowing among the heathen who knew it not. In this he stands in marked contrast to his chief colleagues. Ebbo, Archbishop of Reims, did aid, did sympathise with those who worked in the north. Yet he quickly abandoned his own early mission to the Danes; the years of his life, marred by ambition, by political scheming and struggle, ran until 851 an unstable, darkened course. Gauzbert, nephew of Ebbo, consecrated bishop for the Swedish people, did work some thirteen years among them; but, as we have seen, he refused to return after his flight from their land in 845. Anskar bore these men no resentment. It was, Rimbert tells, in one of his last talks with Ebbo that he begged from him a word of encouragement for his work.

We know his prayer and fasting, as of a soul always in the Presence of God; his ministering to his people, Danish and Swedish; his care of his vast diocese, his travelling up and down, to its cities, its villages, its lonely places. He carried his people through the raids of the Northmen, still descending in these later years, though none so destructive as that of 845. He carried them through civil war and its slaughter among princes of the Danes. Often, weary in body and spirit, he turned to his little cell, built for his own use: " a quiet place," he said of it, " and a friend to grief."

At a time when religious life was slackening its taut cord of discipline, he kept faithfully the Benedictine *Rule* which he had learned as a boy in Old Corbie, difficult as this must have been at many turns of the road of his adventures. All the years of his life as bishop he kept strictly the ancient rule of tithing; one-tenth of the animals, of all the revenues which came to him, even one-tenth of all those tithes which were paid to him himself by right, one-tenth, in fact, of all his income and property from any source, he gave to the poor. Every fifth year he gave once again a second tenth of all the animals which provided for him his daily food. Each Lent he ordered that at Bremen four persons in need of help, two men and two women, should be given dinner every day. He had a special care, not only for widows and orphans, as might be expected, but for anchorites, men and women living the solitary life. Not only did he give them gifts for their support, but he took time to take the gifts in his own hands to their cells. Prisoners he redeemed with his own money, and he always carried with him in his belt a purse from which he could at once hold out coins to those who asked his charity in the streets. As bishop he blessed year by year the holy oils; day by day he anointed, not only the dying for their comfort, but the sick for their restoring to health. Many, it was said, came to receive this rite from his hands, for men believed that these hands held a gift of power.

The Psalms of the Church were his special joy. He sang them quietly to himself by day and by night, while he was making ready for Mass, while he was on his way to bed, while, in a rare hour of leisure, he turned to a bit of manual work, the weaving of nets for fishermen. He thought over them long and deeply, and day by day he worked on the writing of a brief prayer to say at the ending of each one. This prayer he called a *pigment*, the essence of the colour, the gathering of the flavour of each psalm.

His chief sorrow, as he neared the end of his days on earth, was that the martyr's crown, which long ago the Lord had seemed to promise, now seemed denied him. It was the sorrow of many medieval saints, who, like Anskar, died at home in their beds, yet long had died daily for the souls of men. Constant disappointment; work begun only to be destroyed or maimed by the assaults of Vikings, by the hatred of the heathen; loneliness; failure of support, both from the Church at home, in Frankish land, and from men who might have come north for his aid—through all these sorrows he had fought his way. His labour lived but briefly in the eyes of men after his death, for the impression of Christianity upon Scandinavia was to await the coming of kings of the tenth and eleventh centuries, of Harald Gormsson, " who made the Danes Christian "; of Olaf Tryggvason and Olaf the Saint, in Norway; of Olaf Skötkonung and Sigfrid the Saint, in Sweden.

To most persons, indeed, Anskar is now but the shadow of a name. Yet Denmark and Sweden, with those of Danish and Swedish ancestry who themselves have gone forth from their home countries, these still remember him in gratitude. Scholars in number have written of his life, and in their books he still stands as " The Apostle of the North."

CHAPTER THIRTEEN

Pilgrims to Rome and the Holy Land

THE MEANING of the word *peregrinus*, a stranger in the service of God, now changes again. From those who wandered far from their native land, they cared not whither, to wrestle with demons alone in prayer, from those who went forth to lead and to teach the heathen in the ways of Christianity, we come at this close of our study to the pilgrim who made his journey to some holy scene that he might win grace for his own soul and for the souls of his kindred or his charge.

In Europe, as the Middle Ages advanced, there were many such places, hallowed by holy living, holy dying; yet always above them towered Rome, the Eternal City, for reasons both natural and supernatural. Had not Rome from time immemorial been the Mistress of the civilised world, a State within a city, a seat of empire? Was she not to all men of culture in these early Middle Ages—British, Irish, Anglo-Saxon, Frankish—the source of learning, the city of ancient tradition and history? The Latin of Cicero's Rome was still the basis of the words spoken by the Christian priest at his altar, written by monks, by kings and nobles, in sermons and in letters, by makers of laws and charters, by compilers of chronicles and annals, by those who worked on the *Lives* of saints. It was natural that these medieval men of culture should wish to visit Rome. In imperial days of an age still pagan, had not writers of prose and poetry travelled to Rome from Gaul, from Spain, from the Orient? They had left there, too, their own impress, their foreign idiom of language, their foreign customs, above all, their religious practices—the cults of Mithras from Persia, of Isis and Osiris from Egypt—until in the first century A.D. Tacitus had written bitterly of Rome as " the cesspool of the world " and Juvenal had lamented that the Syrian river Orontes was flowing to befoul the Tiber's stream.

The centuries had passed. It was at Rome, men remembered, that the Christian faith in Europe had set foot firmly upon the road to victory over pagan cults when in 312 Constantine the First won the battle of the Milvian Bridge and the waters of the Tiber closed over his enemy, Maxentius. In 357 men had seen his son, the Emperor Constantius, approaching with awe this *asylum mundi*, this sanctuary of the world: an Emperor lost, according to the historian Ammianus, in wonder and reverence as he gazed around upon the Pantheon, the Forums, the Stadium, the columned temples of the City. At last, in the Forum of Trajan, his eye lighted upon the figure of Trajan's warhorse. " That, at least," he said, " I can imitate." At which words, we are told, the Persian prince Hormisdas, standing by his side, quickly retorted: " Can you also make as wide a stable, O Emperor, for the housing of your steed? "

It was this same Constantius who foretold the defeat of heathen worship in Rome by removing from its Senate House that Altar of Victory so dear to pagan tradition. Thereafter, more and more visitors, refugees, men of culture and of cults, of trade and business, poured into her streets, her squares, her temples, until, as the fifth century opened, Rome, now officially Christian, and Rome still pagan, Rome still imperial, super-natural and secular source of inspiration, received her pæan of praise from poets who themselves had come from afar to this centre of their life. Claudian, born, we may think in Alexandria, declared Rome the Mother of nations, embracing all in one harmony; Prudentius, born in Spain, traced to her conquests and triumphs the making ready for the advent of the Christ to earth.

2

To the early Middle Ages Christian Rome was the City of St. Peter, Prince of the Lord's Apostles. The armed march of untaught Goths conquered her secular glory, but she was still, even to these invaders, a city of awe and devotion. In the year 500 the Theodoric who had led his Goths to her conquest, heretic and barbarian though he was, came as a pilgrim to the city which he had taken by force, " with great reverence and like a Catholic," to make in her Cathedral of St. Peter his offering of respect, two great candlesticks wrought of silver. The sieges and plunderings of Goths from West and East had left a grim mark upon her buildings, but they were still a sight of marvel. Among the crowds which hailed this barbarian conqueror there stood an abbot from Africa, the well-known Fulgentius, afterwards bishop of Ruspe in Byzacena. As he looked around, " How beautiful, my friends," he said to the people pressing upon him, " how beautiful must be that Jerusalem on high, when earthly Rome shines so fair! "

Soon in their turn Christian fighters were to assault these Gothic barbarians who held the city, Christians who were duly mindful of her place in Christendom. Belisarius, general of Justinian, Emperor in the East, and defender of Rome against Gothic siege, came to offer at St. Peter's in the presence of Vigilius, Pope from 537 until 555, a golden cross inlaid with jewels, taken from spoils he had won in his conquest of the Vandals in Africa. On it he had inscribed the record of his victories.

Late in the sixth century pilgrims were crowding St. Peter's to offer their prayers for the saving of Rome from the overwhelming Lombard menace. Pope Gregory the Great welcomed them; he was, indeed, the support of Rome against the menace. He encouraged men and women to revere the holy places of

Rome, even in this time of crisis. To a great lady of Constantinople—a city which he knew well and in which he had many friends—Gregory wrote a letter of rebuke for her neglect of these shrines. " I do not understand," he said, " and you have not thought it necessary to explain to me, the delight which you find so entertaining in Constantinople that you should forget the City of Rome. If, indeed, you are afraid to come here because of Lombard swords in Italy, please rest assured that St. Peter is amply able to protect his own! "

St. Peter held the keys of Heaven. To tread the streets of his city, to pray before his tomb, to see and to hear his Vicar on earth, the holder of St. Peter's Chair, this was the hope, the desire, of all sorts and conditions of medieval men: those who needed counsel, those who mourned their dead, those beset by fear of this world or the next, those on official business, those seeking treasure, those bearing gifts, those eager for knowledge, those wrestling to no purpose, it seemed, with sin. It is told of St. Molua of Kyle, who lived in Ireland in the sixth century, that he said to his abbot, St. Maedoc of Ferns in County Wexford: " Unless I see Rome, and soon, I shall die! "

And so on throughout the early Middle Ages. The same sixth century found Gregory the Great kindling the devotion of the Anglo-Saxon to Rome. The English boys whom he saw and pitied, put up for sale as slaves in Rome's market place, stand in our earliest records of English travellers to the city. From Gregory's distress at their heathen state came the English mission which made pilgrimage to Rome the longing of English kings and queens, nobles and priests, laymen and women. In the seventh century monks set out from southern Ireland on their way thither, seeking counsel, it was said, " as sons from their Mother." They returned home to report that they had stayed in the same hostel with a Greek, a Hebrew, a Scythian, and an Egyptian, and that all had kept their Easter together at St. Peter's. In the eighth century we hear from the Venerable Bede, writing in his *Chronicle*: " At this time many of the

English race, of high rank and humble men and women, leaders and ordinary people, for love of God came constantly from Britain to Rome." In the ninth we find some of them placing in St. Gregory's chapel within the basilica of St. Peter a silver tablet in thanksgiving for the gift of their Christian faith.

3

By what route did pilgrims from England travel to Rome? The port in France to which they guided their boats across the Channel in these earlier centuries changed place twice as time went on. In the sixth century it was Boulogne. During the seventh, the eighth, and the ninth, it was Quentavic, no longer to be seen, but once a busy harbour on the river Canche, near Étaples, south of Boulogne. At the opening of the tenth century Quentavic was destroyed by a Viking raid; henceforth the port in France for pilgrims was Wissant, near Cap Gris-Nez, for this gave the shortest passage from Kent. We have a detailed account of a return journey from Rome to Wissant made at the end of the tenth century, in 990, by Sigeric, Archbishop of Canterbury. He travelled by Viterbo, Siena, Lucca, Sarzana, Piacenza, to Vercelli; then across the Alps by Aosta and the Great St. Bernard Pass into Switzerland and the mountains of the Valais, to Saint Maurice; on by Lac Léman to Lausanne; through the Jura mountains to France and northwards through Champagne to the country of the Marne; to Reims and to Laon; through Artois territory to Sombre, and so to Wissant for the Channel and his home in Kent. There was, indeed, a longer route across the Channel. Travellers from the west of England often embarked near Southampton, crossed to the mouth of the Seine, and then proceeded overland by way of Rouen and Paris.

The dangers, the trials and troubles, of the journey were many and formidable. For the English pilgrim they began at his home port, in Kent or in Hampshire. Here he usually waited for other men, in whose company he might find aid and protection; often the band of travellers was large. They embarked in open boats, sometimes without adequate rudder, frequently to encounter wild storms, now and then to fall prey to the raids of Viking ships. Professor Dorothy Whitelock has interpreted the Old English poem, *The Seafarer*, in the light of the pilgrim's perils at sea, from winds, from driving rain and hail, from cold and hunger, from weariness and lack of sleep, from solitude of barren waters:

> *I may of myself a true tale declare,*
> *Of journeys tell, how I days of toil,*
> *Times of hardship often endured,*
> *Bitter anguish of mind I suffered,*
> *Knew in the ship many places of sorrow,*
> *Dire tossing of waves, where often befell me*
> *Anxious night watch at the boat's prow*
> *When it rolls near the cliffs. Cold were my feet,*
> *Frost-bound with ice-bonds; misery there*
> *Cried grief round my heart; hunger tore*
> *The mind of a sea-weary man.*

Sometimes it was not possible to travel in the winter. Bede tells in his *History* that Theodore, lately appointed Archbishop of Canterbury, waited on his way from Rome to England all the winter of 668-669 in the house of the bishop of Paris until spring weather allowed him to continue his journey. One never knew when a boat would be available, or, if it were, when calm weather would enable it to start. Two stories illustrate these experiences, the fate of men without number. Bede's own abbot of Wearmouth-Jarrow in the north of England left his abbey, a pilgrim bound for Rome, on the fourth of June, 716. He was seventy-four years old, and his monks took him by boat across the river Wear and saw him ride off on horseback towards the mouth of the Humber, where his ship was to leave for France. The ship started on the fourth of July, put into shore three times on its way, and finally reached France on the twelfth of August. In the tenth century it was told of Abbo, monk of the monastery of Fleury-sur-Loire, that he wished to cross the Channel from France to England. He waited a whole month at his Frankish port, detained by storms. Then he decided that he had had enough. " If," he said to his ship's captain, " if by favour of St. Benedict I shall be able to set out to-morrow, set out I will; if not, I shall make for Fleury and home." Then he returned to his lodging, said his Office, made a prayer to St. Benedict and went peacefully to bed. The dawn came clear and calm, and he set out in one of a company of nine ships. Before they could reach England, we are told, a storm rose to wreck six out of the nine.

In France, once reached, there was danger not only from raiding Northmen, Danes from Scandinavia, but from bandits who roamed the country, and even from the power of State. Frankish hostility almost made an end of the life of St. Wilfrid of York about 658, on his way back from Rome; and twenty years later the same malice on the part of Frankish authority drove him, as we have seen, to travel by way of the Netherlands. Another bishop, Winfrid, who went about the same time by the usual route for pilgrims, through France, was seized instead of Wilfrid because of the confusion of their names. This Winfrid was robbed of all his money, and men in his escort lost their lives.

If the Northmen did not descend, then pilgrims might be attacked by Saracens, overrunning Europe from Spain. Cold caused intense suffering; in 959 one Elfsige died from it while crossing the Alps on his way to investiture at Rome as a newly elected Archbishop of Canterbury. The mountains, too, held their own brigands, swooping down for plunder. In northern Italy Lombard pirates were waiting; and the very soldiers who guarded the seat of Italy's government were notoriously hostile to strangers. Plague was lurking in the cities; food was expensive; fodder for horses was scarce. Worse still: not all by any means of the pilgrims themselves were saints, even in the making. Many were deep-dyed in sin, thieves, cheats, quacks, fanatics, who joined the bands of the faithful for the excitement of the experience or for the filling of their pockets. We find Charles the Great writing to Offa, king of Mercia, against those who thus dishonestly, as merchants disguised in pilgrim dress, escaped payment of customs, duties imposed upon ordinary travellers but regularly remitted by Charles for pilgrims journeying to the holy places of Rome.

So frequent, however, did these pilgrimages become, so many joined them, that the Church began to give warning even to the devout. In the eighth century we find an abbess, Eangyth, writing on this matter to St. Boniface. She is very unhappy, overwhelmed by the burden of her monastic charge, by the problems of her convent's property, by taxes, by worries concerning her own kinsfolk. Could she not, she asks Boniface, go for her comforting to Rome? So many of her friends have gone there. There, too, she would find release from this dreadful weight of the sins of her long life. It is true, she admits, that many authorities in England are looking coldly upon these continual pilgrimages. A professed religious, they are declaring, should fulfil his vows in stability, in the place of his monastic profession, not in running to and fro on this earth. Boniface writes back that he can neither boldly encourage nor utterly forbid her. If, indeed, she *cannot* find peace of prayer in her cloister, she may do well to seek it in Rome. But she had better wait, he warns her, until the Saracens have abated somewhat their assaults upon Italy.

Far stronger were the words of this same Boniface written in 747 from his German station to Cuthbert, Archbishop of Canterbury: " All the truest and best informed servants of God here believe that your rulers of Church and State in England would do well to stop your married women, and your nuns, from going so often to and from Rome. Many of them meet their ruin; few remain unharmed. There are very few cities of the Lombards in Italy, of the Franks in France, in which some courtesan or prostitute of English race is not found. It is a scandal, my dear brother, a disgrace to your whole Church." Also in the same eighth century Theodulf, bishop of Orléans and poet of the Court of Charles the Great, wrote in his verse that no pilgrimage in itself made one a saint: " Not a man's feet, but his way of life, lead him to Heaven." Perhaps Theodulf was thinking of St. Augustine's comment on the words of the Lord in the seventh chapter of St. John's Gospel: " The Lord cries to me: ' *If any man thirst, let him come to me.*' If we thirst, let us come; yet not by our feet, but by our heart; not by going from one place to another, but of our love. He who begins to love does indeed change his stand. But it is one thing to move with the body, another to move with the heart." And from the ninth century there comes to us a bit of Irish satire on the same subject:

> *To go to Rome*
> *Gives much trouble, little good;*
> *The King thou seekest there thou wilt not find,*
> *Unless thou bring Him with thee.*

4

Nevertheless, there were comforts and consolations for the pilgrims bound for Rome. Before they started on their long road, they went to their shriving by the Church, then lay prostrate before the altar while psalms and prayers were offered for their intent, that the Lord would lead them in the path which He should choose, would shield them from the arrow which flieth by day and the terror that walketh in darkness, would accept their sacrifice and bring it to fulfilment. Then all stood for the blessing of scrip and staff, of the medal of St. Peter and St. Paul, which the priest placed around their necks, in their hands, on their breasts, as he said the appointed prayer:

Receive this support of thy journey and thy toil on the pilgrim's road; that thou mayest overcome all the power of the enemy and come safely to those dwellings of the saints whither thou dost desire to arrive; that, thine obedience rendered, thou mayest in gladness return home again to us.

The Mass of the Pilgrims was now celebrated; and at its close, fortified and ready, all went forth to meet whatever should happen on their way. In their packs they carried letters of introduction to kings and nobles, bishops, abbots and abbesses, according to their rank as travellers; in nearly every dwelling, whether Court, castle, or cloister, were found hosts quick and glad to offer welcome, that in return peace might rest upon their own doors. There were hostels, too, along the road of travel, definitely provided by the alms of the devout for pilgrims who lacked funds and money; some of these had been built by fellow-countrymen for the Irish and the English in their companies. Near the harbour of Quentavic in the eighth century the English Alcuin ruled as abbot a little house of Saint Josse, or Judoc, where monks had been placed for the express service of English travellers to Rome.

So on they went, and at last, after weeks or months, there came the moment when they first caught sight of Rome in the distance, Rome of the Seven Hills. Then they broke into songs of joy, such as that written in those famous lines of, probably, the late tenth century:

> *O Roma nobilis, orbis et domina . . .*
> *Salutem dicimus, tibi per omnia*
> *Te benedicimus; salve per secula! . . .*

> *O Rome of glory, mistress of the world,*
> *Hail to thee; and blessing for ever;*

> *O Peter, mighty bearer of the keys of Heaven,*
> *Hear evermore those who cry unto thee . . .*

'O Paul, receive our prayers . . .
That the wisdom which filled thee
May fill us through thy truth!

Thus, long before, the children of Israel had chanted, looking back upon pilgrimage to Jerusalem:

I have lifted up my eyes to the hills
Whence shall come my help. . . .
Our feet stood in thy courts, O Jerusalem,
Jerusalem which is built as a city
Fitly compacted in itself.
For thither the tribes went up,
The tribes of the Lord, the testimony of Israel,
To confess the Name of the Lord . . .

Pray ye for the peace of Jerusalem;
Peace be in thy strength
And abundance in thy towers.

5

In Rome the English of the eighth century could go directly to their own quarter, near St. Peter's and the river Tiber: the *Schola Saxonum*. It was no school, in the modern sense. It had originally been a military station, formed that the English, too, might have their own share in the defence of the Holy City from invaders. As time went on, rooms for the lodging of pilgrims were added, and a church of Our Lady, and also a quiet place for the burial of the English who died, and many did die during their stay, of the plague, or of exhaustion, or from old age.

Now all, of whatever nation, went on their various missions, the errands for which they had endured those many hardships and perils. Young men had come to offer themselves and their

lives, as did Wilfrid in 654, kneeling before the altar in the
oratory of St. Andrew. Priests came to ask the Pope's blessing
on their missionary work, as did Willibrord about 692 before
his beginning in Frisia, and Boniface in 718, starting out for
German lands. Bishops came for consecration, Archbishops for
the receiving of the pallium. Kings came in answer to appeals
for aid from the Holy See in time of assault, as did Pippin the
Short and Charles the Great. Statesmen sent their delegates
to ask counsel, as in 751, when envoys from the Franks came
to ask whether Pippin the Short, king in all but the name,
might hold in actual title the Frankish throne.

Kings came in their own person to worship at the seat of
holy Peter. Charles the Great came time after time. He came
in 774, while he was besieging Pavia, headquarters of the
Lombard king. It was Holy Saturday. A mile outside the
City he descended from his horse to walk humbly on foot
within its walls, escorted by priests, magistrates, soldiers, and
by children waving branches of palm and olive. At last he
reached the steps of St. Peter's, everyone of which he kissed in
veneration as he went up to take the hand of Pope Hadrian,
waiting to receive him at the great doors. He came again in
781. Nearly twenty years later, on Christmas Day, 800, he
entered those doors to hear Mass and to be crowned Emperor
of the Romans by Pope Leo the Third. Thither, too,
came to give and to receive honour his grandsons, Lothar
and Charles the Bald, and his great-grandson, Louis the
Second.

To Rome came Ethelwulf, king of Wessex, England's West
Country, with his little son Alfred, across land full of the terror
of the Northmen, to pray in St. Peter's for his own English
people, threatened by these same invaders. But the Viking
raids went on. *Visum est Deo*, men said; it was the will of
Heaven, angry at earth's sin.

Some came pleading to be heard in Papal conclave as they
cried out against injustice at home, as did Wilfrid of York, in
679 and 703. Some sought protection from evil for their

monasteries, as Aldhelm of Malmesbury, about 693. Suppliants brought offenders for trial at Rome as a last resource when all their own efforts had failed. We have seen Boniface sending there his charges against the heretics Aldebert and Clement. By order of Charles the Great, Angilbert brought Felix of Urgel for the punishment of his long disloyalty to the creed of the Church.

Many brought gifts or alms. The English abbot of Wearmouth-Jarrow carried in his hands during his long journey of 716 a priceless Codex of the Bible. He did not, indeed, deliver it at St. Peter's, for he died upon the way. Offa, king of Mercia, in the eighth century promised to Rome a gift of money every year; in the ninth, Alfred of Wessex sent there " the alms of the West Saxons and of King Alfred," as the *Anglo-Saxon Chronicle* records. These gifts were the heraldings of Peter's Pence.

But far more travellers, and these an endless number, came to the Holy City to win for their churches at home treasures in return for their offerings, that these churches might be hallowed by the memory, by the presence, as it were, of saints of long ago, through which they might gain increase of beauty and honour. With vast pride they bore home relics, pictures, books, vessels of costly design and material, vestments richly woven and adorned. The founder of Bede's monastery, Benedict Biscop, in the seventh century made six journeys to Rome, to bring back those pictures which the boy Bede studied so seriously in Wearmouth's church of St. Peter.

Lastly, men came to spend their last days, to die in peace near the tomb and under the protection of Peter who was keeper of the gates of Heaven. For this end king after king laid down his crown. In Northumbria in the seventh century its ruler, Oswy, begged his bishop, Wilfrid, to bring him safely to that peace, and died, in 671, on the eve of starting. In 688 a king of Wessex, knowing that death was near and troubled in conscience, hastened to the same refuge. His record was dark. He had seized control of Wessex, had ravaged Sussex and killed its ruler, had marked his years of power by capture of the Isle of Wight, by murder of its princes and by thrusting out his hands, too, over Surrey and over Kent. He was a heathen; but he had been generous to men who preached Christ, and now he listened to their words of warning and left the Wessex he had won. At Rome he received baptism, a new name of Peter in place of his heathen one, Caedwalla, and died some days afterwards, still wearing the white of the newly reborn. So, too, in Rome died his successor, the great Ine of Wessex; so, too, in the eighth century, Cenred, king of Mercia, and a prince of Essex, Offa, went together from their lands on the same journey, that in monastic habit they might live their last days and find peace in their departing. In the ninth century Cyngen, ruler of Powys in Wales, found under the shadow of St. Peter's relief from Mercian invasion of his country; and Burhred, another king of Mercia, brother-in-law of Alfred the Great, beaten by the assaults of the pirate Danes, fled to Rome that he might leave his tired body in that quiet church of Our Lady, protector of the pilgrims from his land.

6

" It would take long," declared St. Jerome at the ending of the fourth century, " to tell how many bishops, how many martyrs, how many men learned in the faith of the Church, have come to Jerusalem since the Lord ascended from earth to Heaven. They believed that religion, that knowledge, that virtue, would be lacking to them, had they not adored the Christ where the Gospel first flashed forth from the Cross. A faithful Christian must needs worship where the feet of the Lord have stood; must see, as though still fresh, the traces of the Nativity, the Cross and Passion."

Such was in truth the feeling in regard to pilgrimages to the Holy Land in these early Middle Ages. Pilgrims went in their multitude, as they did to Rome, disregarding the distance and the danger; and out of the multitude some have left for us written descriptions of their experiences.

The earliest of these descriptions was made in 333 by a man who did not give his name and is known merely as " The Pilgrim from Bordeaux." Here he provides for the use of pilgrims of future days a list of the countries through which he journeyed, the smaller stopping places, the cities on his road. In modern naming he begins with Toulouse, Carcassonne, Narbonne, Nîmes, Arles, Avignon, Orange, Valence. Then we follow him through the Cottian Alps into Italy; to Turin, Pavia, Milan, Verona, Padua; to the head of the Adriatic; across the Julian Alps and Yugoslavia to Belgrade; south to Bulgaria and Sofia; on to Turkey and Istanbul; south to Ankara, then to Tarsus and to Antioch; then southwards along the coast to Beirut; and so finally to Jerusalem. The journey followed the course of the main roads and highways of the time.

In the Holy Land this " Pilgrim " stopped to look curiously and reverently at points of special interest. At Mount Sinai he saw a spring and was told that " if a woman bathes in its waters, she becomes pregnant with child "; soon afterwards he passed " the plain where David killed Goliath "; and, at Bethel, the scene " of Jacob's sleep and his wrestling with the angel." In Jerusalem he saw " a very high tower," the place of the Temptation of the Lord; and " Solomon's Palace, with the room in which he sat and described Wisdom "; and " the perforated stone to which the Jews come every year to anoint it, and with mourning and wailing to rend their garments, and so depart."

The most famous traveller to Palestine in the fourth century was St. Jerome, who left Rome in 385 that he might win peace on less tumultuous ground. " Much of my life," he wrote before he left Italy, " I have spent in a heavy sea, and my ship even now is shaken by storms, broken by dashing against rocks. Now, then, the first moment I can, I will enter some haven of quiet in the country. There my food shall be bread, and vegetables grown under my own hands, and milk, that delight of rustic dwellers—food commonplace enough, but innocent. Sleep will not keep me from prayer, nor a full stomach from my reading. In summer, the shade of a tree; in autumn, cool air and rest on fallen leaves; in winter, fuel not bought by money. Let Rome keep her uproar and tumult; let her arena rage, her circus riot, her theatres revel in luxury, her women hold their parliaments. It is good for me to cleave to God."

To Jerome all was either black and foul, or white and shining; moderation was not his love. He could write, and did, with still greater force concerning the devout men and women of prayer and self-denial, even at this time living in Rome.

Of course, he went here and there in Palestine, to look upon sacred sights. But we like best to think of him in his chosen home at Bethlehem, directing the monks of his monastery, the nuns of his convent; writing his many commentaries on the Bible, his many letters; aiding refugees, the sick, the poor, all who came in trouble to his cloister's gate; burdened by loneliness, as his friends one by one died, by blindness, by poverty even more than monastic, until in 420 he himself found peace through death.

7

There are stories left for us to read of women who during this fourth century left their houses and families in Rome to seek further inspiration in the Holy Land. Jerome knew and encouraged them. Upon his steps as he turned towards Bethlehem followed the wealthy and aristocratic Lady Paula, whom he had taught in that threefold way so dear to him and his pupils, of prayer, fasting, and study, while he was still in Rome. After her death in 404 he wrote to her daughter, Eustochium, his praise of her mother's decision in leaving her kith and kin. " She went to the port of sailing escorted by her brother and her children. And now the sails filled out in the breeze, and the sailors rowed the ship seawards. Her little son, Toxotius, held out his hands to her; her daughter, Rufina, said not a word, only her tears begged her mother to stay yet a while, until her marriage day should come. But Paula's eyes were dry. She looked towards heaven, conquering her love for her family by her love for God. She would know herself no more as mother, in order that she might prove herself the handmaid of Christ. She turned away her eyes from the sight which gave her agony, her children standing upon the shore."

With the same ardour she knelt and worshipped in every sacred spot on her way to Jerusalem. There she lived in a little cell and " made the round of all places with such zeal that, had she not been hastening to others, she would never have left the first ones she saw." At last she, too, with Eustochium, settled at Bethlehem, in a nunnery.

Just as enthusiastic were two women of the same name, Melania, grandmother and granddaughter, known as the Elder and the Younger, and the Younger was held a saint. The elder Melania, like Paula, belonged to a family which had served Rome in high office of State and which was extremely well endowed. Within one and the same year, when she was but little more than twenty, she had lost by death her husband and two of her sons. Jerome, who in earlier days admired her much (although later on, when she became very friendly with his opponent, Rufinus, his admiration turned to bitterness and he called her " as black as her name "), wrote to Paula with much enthusiasm about Melania's courage in bereavement: " May the Lord, Paula, grant it to you and to me to share her lot when He comes at that Last Day! Not a tear at her loss! She stood unmoved, and throwing herself at the feet of Christ, she smiled and said, ' More easily shall I serve thee, Lord, now that thou hast freed me from so great responsibility.' " She left her only remaining child, a little boy, to the care of one of Rome's ministers of government, turned over to him all her possessions in the city, and departed about 372 for Egypt to visit its hermits of the desert. From Egypt she went on to Jerusalem and founded a convent of nuns, administered by herself, on the Mount of Olives. Her son sent her money for its maintenance, as well as for her constant generosity to bishops, priests, monks and pilgrims.

More than twenty years passed, and she decided once again to visit Italy. She came ashore at Naples, and her kinsman Paulinus, then living as a recluse near Naples, at Nola, of which he was to become bishop some twelve years later, went to meet her. All members of her family still living were there, with her friends—senators and magistrates, women of wealthy and aristocratic circles—alighting from their coaches of state, their horses decked with silver trappings, their carriages gilded without and cushioned within, all crowded along the Appian Way in a blaze of brilliance; and all doing homage, Paulinus writes, to a woman wrapped in old black rags, mounted on a half-starved nag which was worse than any donkey.

At last once more, in 408, she left Italy and started on fresh travel, to Sicily, to Africa, and finally to Jerusalem, where she died shortly after her reunion with her nuns on the Mount of Olives.

Her granddaughter, Melania the Younger, was married, when she was about fourteen, to a youth called Pinian, whose chief mission in life, it seems, as they both grew to mature years, was to serve his wife's restless energy in matters devout. This energy lost her, soon after her marriage, a new-born son; a little daughter also died; and after these tragedies she was allowed to live the austere life for which she yearned. In a passion of self-denial she parted with vast sums of money for the aid of the poor and sick, for pilgrims and priests and monks, as her grandmother had done. She left Rome with her husband in 408, just before Alaric the Visigoth laid siege to the city; she landed in North Africa, founded there two monasteries, and paid deep reverence to Augustine; she visited Jerusalem; she wandered in Egypt after the example of her grandmother, that she might visit its solitary monks and learn from them. Finally she settled at Jerusalem, and, again like Melania the Elder, gathered there a community of religious, with Pinian's constant support for her aid.

A long time she lived in this community; for years, also, after her husband had died, she remained enclosed in a little cell on the Mount of Olives. With joy she welcomed visits from Bethlehem of the younger Paula, granddaughter of Paula, the great friend of Jerome. Once she travelled to Constantinople to try to convert her uncle, a man of important office in Rome, then on a mission of State to the East. Not only did she succeed, but she also took active part in Constantinople's unending theological disputes, made friends with the Empress Eudoxia, and encouraged her to come as pilgrim to the Holy Land. The Empress did come, and was received with high respect by her enthusiastic friend. Melania the Younger died in 439, surrounded by her nuns in Jerusalem.

More interesting, so far as the description of a pilgrimage goes, is the story of another woman, Etheria, very probably the abbess of a convent in Spain, who started out about 393 to spend more than three years journeying with undaunted courage in Europe and Asia Minor. For her nuns she wrote an account of her adventures in visiting the scenes told of in the Bible, in visiting, also, the Christian monasteries and churches built for the honour of these sacred places. Here is a plain and pleasant narrative of wanderings, unmarked by ferment of fervour. Among many other experiences she traced in her travel the story of Moses; she saw what was held to be the site of the burning bush; she looked with awe upon Mount Sinai; upon " the stream which gushed out from the rock to give water to the children of Israel "; and upon Mount Nebo and its wonderful view over Palestine. She saw, too, she tells her nuns, her " lady sisters," the place where Lot's wife became a pillar of salt, though she declares very honestly that the pillar cannot now be seen; she saw the place where Jacob met Rachel, and Mount Horeb, and the river Jordan, and Job's tomb, with much more, she writes, than can be told in her pages. She states frankly, " I am quite curious about things "; and certainly, according to her story, she asked endless questions of the monks who were her guides. Much of her narrative describes the Liturgy of Jerusalem, as it was celebrated in the churches of the Resurrection, of Golgotha, of the Mount of Olives and others; the customs observed at various seasons of the ecclesiastical year; the ritual of processions; the practice of fasting then followed in the East.

This is her description of her ascent of Mount Sinai:

" It was late on the Sabbath when we came to the mountain and its monasteries; and the monks who dwell at its base received us very courteously and showed us all kindness. There is a church there with a priest; and there we spent the night. Early on Sunday we began the ascent, with the priest and monks. There are several mountains, and they are unspeakably difficult to climb; for you cannot go up slowly and round and round the steep sides, like a snail; instead, you have to go straight at them, as if up the wall of a house. You have to go up and go down several mountains that surround Sinai before you get to it itself, standing in their midst. But it was the Lord's will, and so, helped on by the prayers of the holy men who went with us, I really did not mind the labour, which, all the same, was really immense. It is not possible to go up on a saddle; I had to go on foot. In the middle of all this toiling I kept on thinking: ' Well, here I am, doing what I longed to do, and what the Lord told me to do! ' We reached the summit of this Sinai, this holy Mount of God, at the fourth hour of the day, this mountain where the Law was given, which was wrapped in smoke on the day when the majesty of the Lord descended upon it."

She had made the ascent fasting. In the church at the summit she and her companions heard Mass and received Communion. Then they were shown all around " until our desire was satisfied."

8

We pass on to the seventh century, which gives us the story of the pilgrimage of one Arculf. He was a bishop of Gaul, who about 670 travelled far and wide in the Holy Land and on his way back was driven by storm upon the west coast of Britain. He found his way to the Scottish island monastery of Iona, told his adventures to his host, Adamnan, Iona's ninth abbot in succession from Columba, and, when Adamnan was assured that he was telling the truth as he saw it, was invited to make a long visit to the abbey. For the next nine months guest and abbot, whenever Adamnan was free from his monastic duty, talked incessantly and had a wonderful time. They examined all Arculf's statements, asked each other questions and did their best to find the answers, compared what Arculf declared he had seen with the statements of Holy Scripture. Finally Abbot Adamnan, as the one more versed in literary form, wrote out in Latin the description of Arculf's wanderings, an account which we can still read in the Vienna Corpus.

Arculf had much to say about Jerusalem. The City had been captured by the Persians in 614 and by the Arabs in 638; at the time of his visit it was still under Moslem control. A number of its churches had been damaged or destroyed, and here and there Arculf was looking upon restorations. We still have plans which he drew for Adamnan on tablets covered with wax. Among the treasures of the city, he said, he saw the Chalice of the Last Supper. It was protected by a wide-meshed grille, and through one of the holes in this screen he was able to touch the Cup with his hand and his lips. He spoke, too, of seeing the linen laid around the Lord's head in His tomb, and of this he told a tale, declared, he assured Adamnan, by all at Jerusalem to be true: that this holy cloth had been disputed for possession between Christians and Saracens and had actually risen of its own accord like a bird in the air to descend into the hands of the faithful. Another holy linen seen by him was said to have been woven by the Mother of the Lord. It was partly red in colour, partly green, and bore the portraits of Christ and of the Twelve Apostles.

Every year on the fifteenth of September, Arculf said, a great Fair was held in Jerusalem, to which buyers and sellers from many countries flocked in multitude. For some days before, the city was full of lodgers, with their trains of camels and horses, donkeys and oxen, and at the end it was foul and filthy beyond words. Wonderful to relate, during the night that followed, when the Fair had closed, every year without fail the heavens opened and a deluge of rain poured down to cleanse all the streets and squares. Moreover, of God's gracious design, Jerusalem was built upon a slope, and so the rain did not collect in pools, but ran down to sweep away the mess and finally to disappear. "How dear to Heaven," Arculf concludes, " must Jerusalem be! "

The Mount of Olives he saw bright with green fields and flowers. In the Church of the Ascension on this Mount, he said, the marks of the feet of Christ could clearly be traced. The church was round, and its centre had no roof. Why? asked Adamnan, who was interrupting the narrative with questions at every point. Partly, answered Arculf, in order that pilgrims, like the Apostles, might gaze directly up towards Heaven; partly for a more cogent reason. Every year on the Feast of the Ascension, at noon, just after High Mass, a mighty wind came rushing through the church, so strong that all who were there threw themselves on the ground. No roof could possibly stand against this mighty wind. He himself had felt its force. The church, he said, had eight windows; and from them a blaze of radiance streamed out every night towards Jerusalem.

In Bethlehem Arculf visited the Cave of the Nativity, overlaid with marble; and, so he told, he saw the tombs of David, of St. Jerome, and of three shepherds who beheld the vision of angels on Christmas night. In the vale of Mamre he rejoiced in gazing upon the rock tombs of Abraham, Isaac, and Jacob, marked by memorials carved in white stone to represent a church. Adam's grave, too, was pointed out to him, but at a distance from the others. Unlike theirs, it was made only of earth. When Adamnan, of course, asked why, Arculf rather scornfully replied: " Did not the Lord say to Adam, *Dust thou art and unto dust thou shalt return?* " Sarah, Rebecca, and Leah also had their memorials, resting close at hand; but, as Arculf carefully noted, these were smaller and cheaper than those of the Patriarchs. Of Abraham's tree in the plains of Mamre he was shown only a diminished stump, protected under shelter of a church and not too well protected, since so many pilgrims had cut away pieces to carry home.

From thence he travelled on: to Jericho, where, so at least he said to Adamnan, the walls of Rahab's house were still standing; to Nazareth, which he had to leave before his enthusiasm was satisfied, because his guide grew so impatient; to the river Jordan, the Dead Sea, and the Sea of Galilee; to the spring in the desert from which, men believed, John the Baptist drank; to Damascus, where the unbelieving Saracens had built a mosque; to Alexandria, a city so great and thrilling that it took him one whole October day to pass through it from end to end; and finally to Constantinople, where he visited the Church of the Holy Rood, to which, as the story went, the precious relics of the True Cross had been taken from Jerusalem.

9

We have seen pilgrims to the Holy Land from France, from Italy, and from Spain. We will now look at one from England. The *Lives* of British saints have told us of men from Wales, from Cornwall, journeying to Palestine; St. David, St. Teilo, St. Petroc. It would be rash to say that their statements are true. Yet some ten years or so before the end of even the fourth century, St. Jerome had written from Bethlehem: " Every leading man of Gaul is hastening here. The Briton, sundered from our world, if he has made progress in religion, leaves his western sun and seeks a place known only to him by fame and the narrative of the Scriptures. Why should I speak of Armenians, Persians, the peoples of India and of Ethiopia, of Egypt, so near us, fertile in monks, of Pontus and Cappadocia, of Coele-Syria and Mesopotamia, and all the swarms of the East? Hither to the holy places they run, as the Lord said: *Wheresoever the body is, thither will the eagles be gathered together*." In the mid-fifth century, Theodoret, bishop of Cyrus in Syria, also wrote of British pilgrims in Palestine.

Our English pilgrim, Willibald, belonged to the eighth century; the story of his travels in Palestine is of special interest. It was written, about 775, by a nun. Her name was Hugeburc, and her monastery was at Heidenheim in Bavaria, near Eichstätt, seat of a bishopric held by Willibald after his journeyings. Hugeburc was herself English by birth, and her fellow-countryman Willibald told her his story in Germany when he was very old. Then she wrote it out in the best Latin she knew. Of course, as a woman, and a nun writing about a bishop, she was very diffident of her powers. She had reason to be, too, for her Latin is not easily read by those trained in Cicero. With rambling apology for her sex and her consequent lack of wisdom, and with much rhetoric of flowery words, fortified by prayer to God and to man, she told

how Willibald decided to travel from England to Rome;
how from there he went on to Palestine, hungry for wider
knowledge.

His journey took him to Naples; then to Sicily, where, so he
told Hugeburc, the natives place a relic of St. Agatha with
excellent result across the path of Mount Etna's lava in
eruption. From Sicily he went to Greece, to Asia Minor and
to Ephesus, where he visited the place of the Seven Sleepers
and the shrine of St. John; then on through Syria, where he
suffered horribly from hunger. In Syria the Saracens threw
him and his seven fellow-pilgrims into prison, certain that they
were spies; and in prison they stayed until a kindly Spaniard
won their freedom from the Saracen ruler. Soon we find them
at Damascus, offering prayer in the church—two miles outside
the city, Willibald said—on the very spot where St. Paul
heard the voice of the Lord. In Nazareth they learned that
Saracens were trying to destroy its church; and in Cana of
Galilee they drank wine drawn, they were told, and they were
not slow to believe it, from the one firkin which remained from
the six of the Lord's miracle at the marriage feast. In the
marshes of Jordan they saw the long-horned cattle burying
themselves in the mud to find relief from summer heat.
Willibald, too, had reason for complaint. Sickness interrupted
his travel; once he was blind for two months through some
infection. Altogether this pilgrimage of his took six years of
his life, from 723 until 729.

Of course he, too, visited Jerusalem and its churches. Just
one story we will have of his adventures there, and that entirely
secular. He bought some balsam, no doubt as a gift for friends
in England, and placed it in the rounded shell of a pumpkin,
carefully dried. It was delightfully fragrant, and he took great
pleasure in it. Then he heard that balsam was strictly contraband for travellers, that customs officers would be on the
watch at Tyre, threatening instant death to Christians found
smuggling forbidden export. Willibald could not bear to throw
away his gift. So, through the middle of the pumpkin he ran

a tiny tube and filled it with petroleum, which smelled hideously to heaven. Only the open space at the end of the tube could be seen, and its edges he most carefully hid. When the customs officers barked, " Have you anything to declare? " he held out the pumpkin in his own hands for their inspection. Petroleum was not contraband, and one whiff was enough. Then Willibald departed, withdrew the tube, and all was well. Of course, the nun Hugeburc, when she tells of the incident, refrains from comment.

10

Now and again, in the midst of this passion for pilgrimage to the Holy Land, as to Rome, we hear a note of warning. It is perhaps most outspoken in a letter, sent to a friend about 380 by Gregory, bishop of Nyssa in Cappadocia, a country in Asia Minor south of the Black Sea. Its words drew upon him the wrath of the West, where men were afraid that pilgrims might be deterred from their souls' delight and benefit. " If more of Divine grace were abiding in the places of Jerusalem than elsewhere," Gregory wrote, " the sin of those who live there would not be so constant and customary. Of a truth, there is no sort of impurity which is not practised among its dwellers: malice, adultery, theft, idolatry, poisoning, envy, and murder; and all these sins so frequent, so incessant, that nowhere else are found hands so prompt to kill. There, indeed, for the sake of empty gain men rush like wild beasts even upon those of their own land. I myself have seen those things with my own eyes. Listen, then, to my words. Before I even saw Jerusalem, I knew that Christ was Very God. My stay there neither took from nor added to my faith. I knew that God was born of a Virgin before I saw Bethlehem's stable. I believed in the Lord's Resurrection before I looked upon the church built in its memory, and I held the Ascension true when I had never laid eyes upon the Mount of Olives. This little profit alone did I get from my journey: I learned that our places at home are far more holy than those abroad. So, you who fear the Lord, praise Him, wheresoever you are. Change of place does not bring God nearer; everywhere God will come to you if there be found within you a home where He may walk and dwell."

Some fifteen years later, St. Jerome, who had fled from Rome to live in Bethlehem, who confessed that he was held fast in the East by his " abiding cleavage to its holy places," who so joyfully welcomed pilgrims to the same comfort of inspiration, wrote to Paulinus, the recluse of Nola in Italy, in something of the same mind: " Not to have been at Jerusalem, but to have lived a good life at Jerusalem, is worthy of praise. That city is not to be sought which killed the prophets and poured out the blood of Christ, but the city set upon a hill, mother of the saints. In saying this I do not mean to charge myself with inconsistency, to think that for nothing I have followed Abraham into exile from my kin and country. No! I write thus, only because I dare not limit the almighty power of God by narrow bounds. I cannot shut within a little space of earth Him whom the heavens cannot contain. Those who adore God do so, not of necessity in Jerusalem or on Mount Gerizim, but in spirit and in truth. God is a Spirit, and the Spirit moves where it wills. The courts of Heaven may be reached equally well from Jerusalem or from Britain, because the kingdom of God is within us. If the scenes of the Cross and the Resurrection were not in a crowded city, in which are found all things that are found in any city—magistrates, soldiers, harlots, strolling players, clowns and parasites—if only a multitude of monks dwelt in it, Jerusalem would truly be a home for monks. Now, as things are, it would be the height of folly for a man to renounce the world, give up his own country, leave his own cities, become a monk, and live abroad among more people than he would be among at home. People hasten to Jerusalem from all over the world. The city is full of people of every race; so densely massed is its crowd that a man in search of solitude would be utterly crushed in its streets beneath the burden he was trying to escape."

Yet still there pressed on towards those crowded streets, foul with crime and filth, where danger lurked and weariness lay in wait, those men and women from every nation under heaven, hermits and missionaries, monks and nuns, layfolk of high and low estate, all down the centuries, with the same eagerness, joy, and disdain of hardship with which they had pressed on towards the Holy City of Rome.

ABBREVIATIONS

C S E L: *Corpus scriptorum ecclesiasticorum latinorum,* Vienna

D A C L: *Dictionnaire d'Archéologie chrétienne et de Liturgie,* Paris

D H G E: *Dictionnaire d'Histoire et de Géographie ecclésiastiques,* Paris

M G H: *Monumenta Germaniae Historica*

N A: *Neues Archiv der Gesellschaft für ältere deutsche Geschichtskunde,* Hanover

S R G S: *Scriptores rerum Germanicarum in usum Scholarum (Monumenta Germaniae Historica)*

S R M: *Scriptores rerum Merovingicarum (Monumenta Germaniae Historica)*

S S: *Scriptores,* ed. Pertz *(Monumenta Germaniae Historica)*

BRIEF LIST OF BOOKS

GENERAL

Bright, William: *Chapters of Early English History*, ed. 3, 1897
Butler's Lives of the Saints: edited, revised, and supplemented by Herbert Thurston, S.J. and Donald Attwater, I-IV, 1956
Chadwick, Nora K.: ed. *Studies in Early British History*, 1954
Crawford, S.J.: *Anglo-Saxon Influence on Western Christendom, 600-800*, 1933
Deanesly, Margaret: *A History of Early Medieval Europe, 476-911*, 1956
Duckett, Eleanor S.: *The Gateway to the Middle Ages*, 1938
Hauck, Albert: *Kirchengeschichte Deutschlands*, I-II, 1904-1912
Horstmann, Carl: ed. *Nova Legenda Anglie*, I-II, 1901
Hunter Blair, Peter: *An Introduction to Anglo-Saxon England*, 1956
Laistner, M. L. W.: *Thought and Letters in Western Europe, A.D. 500-900*, ed. 2, 1957
Painter, Sidney: *A History of the Middle Ages, 284-1500*, 1953
Plummer, Charles: ed. *Baedae Opera Historica*, I-II, 1896
Stenton, Sir Frank: *Anglo-Saxon England*, ed. 2, 1957
Strayer, Joseph R.: *Western Europe in the Middle Ages*, 1955
Wallace-Hadrill, J. M.: *The Barbarian West, 400-1000*, 1952
Whitelock, Dorothy: ed. *English Historical Documents*, I (*c. 500-1042*), 1955

CHAPTER ONE

Jackson, Kenneth Hurlstone: *A Celtic Miscellany: translations from the Celtic literatures*, 1951
Loomis, Charles Grant: *White Magic: an introduction to the folklore of Christian legends*, 1948
Meyer, Kuno: trans. *Selections from ancient Irish poetry*, ed. 2, 1913
Vita Sancti Severini, ed. P. Knöll: *C S E L* IX, 2, 1886

CHAPTER TWO

Bieler, Ludwig: " The Mission of Palladius ": *Traditio* VI, 1948, 1 ff.
————: *The Life and Legend of St. Patrick*, 1949
————: ed. *Libri Epistolarum S. Patricii*, 1952
————: trans. and annotated: *The Works of St. Patrick*, 1953
Bury, J. B.: *The Life of St. Patrick and his Place in History*, 1905
Grosjean, Paul, S. J.: " Recent Research on the Life of St. Patrick ": *Thought* V, 1930, 22 ff.

Grosjean, Paul, S. J.: *Analecta Bollandiana:* LIV, 1936, 196 ff.; LIX, 1941, 217 ff.; LXIII, 1945, 65 ff.

Levison, Wilhelm: " Bischof Germanus von Auxerre ": *NA* XXIX, 1903, 95 ff.

MacNeill, Eoin: *St. Patrick, Apostle of Ireland*, 1934

Mulchrone, Kathleen: ed. *Bethu Phatraic: The Tripartite Life of Patrick,* 1939

René, Louis: " Le séjour de Saint Patrice à Auxerre," *Mélanges d'Histoire du Moyen Age dédiés à la mémoire de Louis Halphen*, 1951, 445 ff.

Stokes, Whitley: ed. *The Tripartite Life of St. Patrick*, Rolls Series LXXXIX, i-ii, 1887

Ulster, Annals of, ed. with trans., William M. Hennessy, I (A.D. 431-1056), 1887

White, Newport J. D.: *St. Patrick: His Writings and Life*, 1920

CHAPTER THREE

Acta Sanctorum Boll.: May III, 584 ff. (St. Carantoc); June I, 399 ff. (St. Petroc)

Anderson, Alan Orr: " Ninian and the Southern Picts ": *Scottish Historical Review* XXVII, 1948, 25 ff.

Bowen, Emrys: *The Settlements of the Celtic Saints in Wales*, ed. 2, 1956

Chadwick, Hector Munro: *Early Scotland: the Picts, the Scots and the Welsh of southern Scotland* (ed. with introduction by Nora K. Chadwick), 1949

Chadwick, Nora K.: " St. Ninian: A Preliminary Study of Sources ": *Transactions of the Dumfriesshire and Galloway Natural History and Antiquarian Society* XXVII, 1950

Cuissard, Ch.: ed. *Vie de Saint Paul de Léon en Bretagne* (Wrmonoc): *Revue Celtique* V, 1883, 413 ff.

De Smedt, C., S.J.: ed. *Vita S. Winwaloei, auctore Wurdestino: Analecta Bollandiana* VII, 1888, 167 ff.

Doble, Gilbert H.: " Welsh Saints " Series: *St. Dubricius*, 1943; *St. Illtut*, 1944

————: " Cornish Saints " Series: *St. Docco and St. Kew*, 1927; *St. Brioc*, 1928; *St. Carantoc*, 1932; *St. Mawgan*, 1936; *St. Budoc*, 1937; *St. Cadoc*, 1937; *St. Mawes*, 1938; *St. Petroc*, 1938; *St. Winwaloe*, 1940; *St. Paul of Léon*, 1941

Duine, F.: *Mémento des Sources hagiographiques de l'Histoire de Bretagne*, 1918

Fawtier, Robert: ed. *Vie de Saint Samson: Bibl. de l'École des Hautes Études,* No. 197, 1912

Gildas Sapiens: *De Excidio et Conquestu Britanniae:* ed. T. Mommsen, *M G H: Auct. Antiq.* XIII, i, 1894

Grosjean, Paul, S.J. : *De Codice Hagiographico Gothano: Analecta Bollandiana* LVIII, 1940, 90 ff.

Grosjean, Paul, S. J.: ed. *Vie de Saint Cadoc de Llancarfan* (Codex Gothanus): *ibid.*, LX, 1942, 35 ff.

Largillière, René: *Les saints et l'organisation chrétienne primitive dans l'Armorique bretonne*, 1925

Levison, Wilhelm: " An Eighth-century Poem on St. Ninian ": *Antiquity* XIV, 1940, 280 ff.

Lloyd, J. E.: *A History of Wales*, I-II, ed. 2, 1939

Loth, J.: " La Vie la plus ancienne de Saint Samson, abbé-évêque de Dol ": *Revue Celtique* XXXV, 1914, 269 ff.; XXXIX, 1922, 301 ff.; XL, 1923, 1 ff.

Plaine, F. Beda, O.S.B.: ed. *Vita S. Brioci: Analecta Bollandiana* II, 1883, 161 ff.

Rees, W. J.: trans. *Lives of the Cambro-British Saints*, 1853

Taylor, Thomas: *The Life of St. Samson of Dol*, 1925

Wade-Evans, A. W.: trans. *Life of Saint David*, 1923

————: trans. Nennius, *History of the Britons*, 1938

————: ed. and trans. *Vitae Sanctorum Britanniae et Genealogiae*, 1944 (*Vitae SS. Cadoci, Carantoci, David, Iltuti*, etc.)

Williams, A. H.: *An Introduction to the History of Wales*, I-II, 1941-1948

CHAPTER FOUR

Acta Sanctorum Boll.: May II, 579 ff. (St. Comgall)

De Smedt, C., S.J. and De Backer, J., S.J.: ed. *Acta Sanctorum Hiberniae ex codice Salmanticensi*, 1888

Gougaud, Louis, Dom: *Christianity in Celtic Lands*, trans. M. Joynt, 1932

————: " Clonmacnois ": *D A C L* III, ii, 2012 ff.

Grosjean, Paul, S.J.: ed. *Vita S. Brendani Clonfertensis e codice Dubliniensi: Analecta Bollandiana* XLVIII, 1930, 99 ff.

Hughes, Kathleen: " The Historical Value of the Lives of St. Finnian of Clonard ": *English Historical Review* LXIX, 1954, 353 ff.

Kenney, J. F.: *The Sources for the Early History of Ireland*, I, 1929

Macalister, R. A. S.: *The Latin and Irish Lives of St. Ciaran, Abbot of Clonmacnoise*, 1921

Plummer, Charles: " Some New Light on the Brendan Legend ": *Zeitschrift für Celtische Philologie* V, 1905, 124 ff.

————: ed. *Vitae Sanctorum Hiberniae*, I-II, 1910

————: ed. and trans. *Bethada Náem nÉrenn: Lives of Irish Saints*, I-II, 1922

Ryan, John, S.J.: *Irish Monasticism*, 1931

CHAPTER FIVE

Anderson, Alan Orr: *Early Sources of Scottish History*, I-II, 1922

Duke, John: *The Columban Church*, 1932; reprinted 1957

Forbes, A. P.: ed. *Lives of St. Ninian and St. Kentigern: Historians of Scotland* V, 1874

Fowler, J. T.: ed. Adamnan, *Life of St. Columba,* 1920

Gougaud, Louis, Dom: *Scottish Gaelic Studies,* II, 1927, 106 ff.

Grosjean, Paul, S.J.: ed. *The Life of St. Columba from the Edinburgh MS.:* *Scottish Gaelic Studies,* II, 1928, 111 ff.

————: *Analecta Bollandiana* XLVI, 1928, 197 ff.; LIV, 1936, 408 ff.

Jackson, Kenneth Hurlstone: " The Sources for the Life of St. Kentigern ": *Studies in the Early British Church,* ed. Nora K. Chadwick, 1958

Reeves, William: ed. Adamnan, *Life of St. Columba: Historians of Scotland,* VI, 1874

Simpson, W. D.: *The Historical St. Columba,* ed. 2, 1927

————: *The Celtic Church in Scotland,* 1935

CHAPTER SIX

Bede the Venerable, St.: *Historia Ecclesiastica Gentis Anglorum:* ed. Charles Plummer, vols. I-II, 1896, Book II, chs. 5, 9 ff., 20; III, 1 ff., 5 ff., 9 ff., 14 ff.; IV, 27 ff.; trans. Everyman's Library

Colgrave, Bertram: *Two Lives of Saint Cuthbert,* 1940

Colgrave, Hilda: *Saint Cuthbert,* 1947

The Relics of Saint Cuthbert: Studies by various scholars, ed. C. F. Battiscombe, 1956

CHAPTER SEVEN

Fuhrmann, J. P.: *Irish Medieval Monasteries on the Continent,* 1927

Gougaud, Louis, Dom: *Gaelic Pioneers of Christianity,* 1923

————: *Les Saints irlandais hors d'Irlande,* 1936

Grosjean, Paul, S.J.: *Analecta Bollandiana* LXIV, 1946, 200 ff. (On St. Columban and the Paschal controversy)

Hay, M. V.: " Columbanus and Rome ": *Revue Celtique* XXXVIII, 1920-1921, 315 ff.

Joynt, Maud: trans. *The Life of St. Gall,* 1927

Kendig, Perry F.: trans. *The Poems of Saint Columban,* 1949

Levison, Wilhelm: " Die Iren und die fränkische Kirche ": *Historische Zeitschrift* CIX, 1912, 1 ff.

McNeill, John T., and Gamer, Helena M.: *Medieval Handbooks of Penance,* 1938

Martin, E.: *Saint Columban,* 1905

M G H: Epistolae III: *Columbani abbatis Luxoviensis et Bobbiensis Epistulae:* ed. W. Gundlach, 154 ff.

M G H: S R M II: *Chronicorum quae dicuntur Fredegarii Scholastici libri IV cum Continuationibus,* ed. B. Krusch, 1 ff.

————: *ibid.: Liber Historiae Francorum,* ed. B. Krusch, 215 ff.

M G H: S R M IV: *Vitae Columbani abbatis discipulorumque eius libri duo auctore Iona:* ed. B. Krusch, 1 ff.; *Vita Galli, ibid.* 299 ff.

Seebass, O.: ed. *Ordo S. Columbani abbatis De vita et actione monachorum:* *Zeitschrift für Kirchengeschichte* XIV, 1894, 76 ff.

Seebass, O.: ed. *Regula monachorum S. Columbani abbatis: ibid.* XV, 1895, 366 ff.

———: ed. *Regula coenobialis fratrum S. Columbani abbatis: ibid.* XVII, 1897, 220 ff.

———: ed. *Poenitentiale Columbani: ibid.* XIV, 1894, 430 ff.

Timerding, Heinrich: *Die christliche Frühzeit Deutschlands,* I-II, 1929

Walker, G. S. M.: *Sancti Columbani Opera: Scriptores Latini Hiberniae,* vol. II, 1957

CHAPTER EIGHT

Acta Sanctorum Boll.: January II, 35 ff. (St. Fursey); August VI, 598 ff. (St. Fiacre); October XIII, 370 ff. (St. Foillan)

Bede, *Historia Ecclesiastica:* Lib. III, c. 19 (On St. Fursey)

Berlière, U., Dom: " La plus ancienne Vie de S. Foillan ": *Revue Bénédictine* IX, 1892, 137 ff.

Grützmacher, G.: " Die Viten des heiligen Furseus ": *Zeitschrift f. Kirchengeschichte* XIX, 1898, 190 ff.

M G H: S R M II: *Vita Sanctae Balthildis,* ed. B. Krusch, 475 ff.

M G H: S R M IV: *Vita Richarii confessoris Centulensis auctore Alcuino,* ed. B. Krusch, 381 ff.

——— *ibid.: Vita virtutesque Fursei abbatis Latiniacensis, et de Fuilano additamentum Nivialense,* ed. B. Krusch, 423 ff.

——— *ibid.: Vita Sigiramni abbatis Longoretensis,* ed. B. Krusch, 603 ff.

——— *ibid.: Vita Eligii episcopi Noviomagensis,* ed. B. Krusch, 634 ff.

M G H: S R M V: *Vita Audoini (Ouen) episcopi Rotomagensis,* ed. W. Levison, 536 ff.

——— *ibid.: Vita Faronis episcopi Meldensis,* ed. B. Krusch, 171 ff.

M G H: S R M VII: *Vita Richarii sacerdotis Centulensis primigenia,* ed. B. Krusch, 438 ff.

——— *ibid.: Chronologica regum Francorum stirpis Merowingicae:* scripsit B. Krusch, 468 ff.

Traube, Ludwig: *Perrona Scottorum: Vorlesungen und Abhandlungen* III, 1920, 95 ff.

Wattenboch-Levison: *Deutschlands Geschichtsquellen im Mittelalter,* Heft I, 1952

CHAPTER NINE

Acta Sanctorum Boll.: November III, ed. A. Poncelet, 414 ff. (St. Willibrord)

Amand, Saint: *D H G E* ii, 942 ff. (E. Lesne)

Chapman, John, Dom: *Saint Benedict and the Sixth Century,* 1929

Essen, L. Van der: *Etude critique et littéraire sur les Vitae des Saints mérovingiens de l'ancienne Belgique,* 1907

Grieve, Alexander: *Willibrord, Missionary in the Netherlands,* 1923

Levison, Wilhelm: " Willibrordiana ": *NA* XXXIII, 1908, 525 ff.

Levison, Wilhelm: " À propos du calendrier de S. Willibrord ": *Revue Bénédictine* L, 1938, 37 ff.

————: " St. Willibrord and his place in history ": *Durham University Journal, New Series*, I, 1940, 23 ff.

M G H: S R M II: *Vita Sanctae Geretrudis*, ed. B. Krusch, 447 ff.

M G H: S R M V: *Vita Amandi episcopi*, ed. B. Krusch, 395 ff.; *Testamentum Amandi*, 483 ff.

M G H: S R M VII: *Vita Willibrordi archiepiscopi Traiectensis auctore Alcuino*, ed. W. Levison, 81 ff.

Moreau, de, É: *Saint Amand*, 1927

————: *Histoire de l'Église en Belgique*, I, ed. 2, 1945

————: " La Vita Amandi Prima et les Fondations monastiques de S. Amand ": *Analecta Bollandiana* LXVII, 1949, 447 ff.

Verbist, G. H.: *Saint Willibrord, Apôtre des Pays-Bas*, 1939

Wattenboch-Levison: *Deutschlands Geschichtsquellen im Mittelalter*, Heft II, bearbeitet von Wilhelm Levison und Heinz Löwe, 1953

Wilson, H. A.: ed. *The Calendar of St. Willibrord:* Henry Bradshaw Society, LV, 1918

CHAPTER TEN

Acta Sanctorum Boll.: October VII, ii, 1050 ff. (St. Lull)

Bonifatius, Sankt: *Gedenkgabe zum zwolfhundertsten Todestag. Herausgegeben von der Stadt Fulda in Verbindung mit den Diozesen Fulda und Mainz*, 1954

Duckett, Eleanor S.: *Anglo-Saxon Saints and Scholars*, 1947

Eigil, *Vita Sancti Sturmi: S S* II, 365 ff.

Emerton, Ephraim: trans. *The Letters of Saint Boniface*, 1940

Greenaway, George W.: *Saint Boniface*, 1955

Hahn, Heinrich: *Bonifaz und Lul*, 1883

Levison, Wilhelm: ed. *Vitae S. Bonifacii*, 1905

————: *England and the Continent in the Eighth Century*, 1946

M G H: Epistulae III: *S. Bonifatii et Lulli Epistulae*, ed. W. Gundlach, 154 ff.

M G H: S R G S: Vita Lulli Archiepiscopi Mogontiacensis, auctore Lamperto: Lamperti monachi Hersfeldensis Opera, ed. O. Holder-Egger, 1894, 307 ff. See also *S S* XV, i, 132 ff.

M G H: S S XV, i: *Vita Leobae abbatissae Biscofesheimensis auctore Rudolfo Fuldensi*, ed. G. Waitz, 118 ff.

Schieffer, Theodor: *Winfrid-Bonifatius und die christliche Grundlegung Europas*, 1954

Talbot, C. H.: *The Anglo-Saxon Missionaries in Germany*, 1954

Tangl, M.: ed. *Die Briefe des heiligen Bonifatius und Lullus*, 1916

Wallace-Hadrill, J. M.: Review of Professor Schieffer's book: *English Historical Review* LXIX, 1954, 619 ff.

CHAPTER ELEVEN

Diekamp, W.: ed. *Die Vitae S. Liudgeri: Geschichtsquellen des Bisthums Münster* IV, 1881, 1 ff. See also *S S* II, 403 ff.

Hofmeister, A.: " Die Jahresversammlung der alten Sachsen zu Marklo": *Historische Zeitschrift* CXVIII, 1917, 189 ff.

M G H : S S XV, 1 : *Vita Gregorii abbatis Trajectensis auctore Liudgero*, ed. O. Holder-Egger, 63 ff.

M G H: S S XXX, ii: *Vita Lebuini antiqua*, ed. A. Hofmeister, 789 ff.

Tangl, M.: *N A* XL, 1916, 768 ff. (On Gregory of Utrecht)

CHAPTER TWELVE

Acta Sanctorum Boll.: November III, 835 ff. ed. A. Poncelet (St. Willehad). Also in *S S* II, 378 ff.

M G H: S R G S: Vita Anskarii auctore Rimberto, ed. G. Waitz, 1884; trans. C. H. Robinson, 1921

Moreau, de, É.: *Saint Anschaire*, 1930

Oppenheim, P.: *Der heilige Ansgar*, 1931

CHAPTER THIRTEEN

Glover, T. R.: *Life and Letters in the Fourth Century*, 1901, c. VI, " Women Pilgrims."

Gougaud, Louis, Dom: " Sur les Routes de Rome et sur le Rhin avec les ' peregrini ' insulaires ": *Revue d'Histoire ecclésiastique* XXIX i, 1933, 253 ff.

Hieronymi, Sancti Eusebii: *Epistulae*, ed. Hilberg: *C S E L* LIV, LV, LVI, 1910-1918

————: *Lettres* (Latin text and French trans.), ed. Jérôme Labourt, Budé Series, vols. I ff., 1949

Itinera Hierosolymitana, saec. IV-VIII, ed. Geyer: *C S E L* XXXIX, 1898. Narratives of " The Pilgrim of Bordeaux," 1 ff.; of Etheria, 34 ff.; of Adamnan, 219 ff.

McClure, M. L. and Feltoe, C. L.: *The Pilgrimage of Etheria*, 1919

M G H: S S XV, 1: *Vita Willibaldi episcopi Eichstetensis auctore Heidenheimensi*, ed. O. Holder-Egger, 80 ff.

Parks, George B.: *The English Traveler to Italy*, 1954

Pèlerinages aux Lieux Saints: D A C L XIV, i, 1939, 65 ff. (H. Leclercq)

Wright, Thomas: *Early Travels in Palestine*, 1848 (trans. narrative of Adamnan, 1 ff.; of Willibald, 13 ff.)

In the Norton Library

CRITICISM AND THE HISTORY OF IDEAS